Nebraska
Symposium on
Motivation
1980

Nebraska Symposium on Motivation, 1980, is Volume 28 in the series on
CURRENT THEORY AND
RESEARCH IN MOTIVATION

University of Nebraska Press
Lincoln/London 1981

Nebraska Symposium on Motivation 1980

Cognitive Processes

Herbert E. Howe, Jr. — *Series Editor*

John H. Flowers — *Volume Editor*

Michael I. Posner — *Professor of Psychology*
University of Oregon

Mary K. Rothbart — *Associate Professor of Psychology*
University of Oregon

David LaBerge — *Professor of Psychology*
University of Minnesota

Raymond Nickerson — *Senior Vice-President*
Bolt Beranek and Newman, Inc.

John R. Anderson — *Professor of Psychology*
Carnegie-Mellon University

Edward E. Smith — *Professor of Psychology*
Stanford University

James J. Jenkins — *Professor of Psychology*
University of Minnesota

"The Library of Congress has cataloged this serial publication as follows:"
Nebraska Symposium on Motivation.
 Nebraska Symposium on Motivation. [Papers] v. [1]—1953—
 Lincoln, University of Nebraska Press.
  v. illus, diagrs. 22 cm. annual.
 Vol. 1 issued by the symposium under its earlier name: Current Theory and
Research in Motivation.
 Symposia sponsored by the Dept. of Psychology of the University of Nebraska.
 1. Motivation (Psychology)

BF683.N4   159.4082   53–11655

 Library of Congress

Preface

For the last decade, the Nebraska Symposium on Motivation has focused each year on a different area of psychology. The theme for the twenty-eighth volume is cognitive processes. Great appreciation is due Professor John Flowers, volume editor, whose energy and skill in organizing and following through with the symposium were exceptional. Thanks also to the six contributors whose presentations were enthusiastically received by the unusually large audiences that attended both sessions of the symposium.

This year's edition of the Nebraska Symposium on Motivation is dedicated to the memory of Harry K. Wolfe, one of America's early psychologists. A student of Wilhelm Wundt, Professor Wolfe established the first undergraduate laboratory in psychology in America at the University of Nebraska. As he was the pioneer psychologist in Nebraska, it is especially appropriate that funds donated to the University of Nebraska Foundation in his memory by his late student, Dr. Cora L. Friedline, are used to support the Nebraska Symposium. The editors thank the University of Nebraska Foundation for its support.

HERBERT E. HOWE, JR.
Series Editor

Contents

ix John H. Flowers — *Introduction*

1 Michael I. Posner and Mary K. Rothbart — *The Development of Attentional Mechanisms*

53 David LaBerge — *Unitization and Automaticity in Perception*

73 Raymond Nickerson — *Motivated Retrieval from Archival Memory*

121 John R. Anderson — *Concepts, Propositons, and Schemata: What Are the Cognitive Units?*

163 Edward E. Smith — *Organization of Factual Knowledge*

211 James J. Jenkins — *Can We Have a Fruitful Cognitive Psychology?*

239 — *Subject Index*

245 — *Author Index*

Introduction

F OR each of the past several years, the Nebraska Symposium on Motivation has focused on a single topic per area of research from within the field of psychology. The area of focus for the 1979–80 symposium is human cognition, which, over the past two decades, has developed into an extremely broad discipline. Some contemporary psychologists actually view the study of cognitive processes as an interdisciplinary area of study extending beyond the traditional domain of psychology itself. The term *cognitive science* has recently emerged to describe this broader view of human cognition.

Given the extreme breadth of the topical area, and our interest in providing a forum for the exchange of ideas among speakers, faculty, and students, we decided to invite, for each of the two sessions, groups of speakers who shared some degree of research interests and objectives, but who were also likely to provide some interesting contrasts in their approach to the study of cognitive processes. Speakers for the fall session (John R. Anderson, Edward E. Smith, and James J. Jenkins) were chosen on the basis of their previous research activities within the "structural" aspects of cognition (e.g., knowledge structures and units, conceptual and categorization processes, semantic memory models, etc.). For the spring term, we invited three speakers (Michael I. Posner, David LaBerge, and Raymond S. Nickerson) whose previous contributions have emphasized slightly different areas of human cognition, primarily topics related to the attentional, perceptual, and performance aspects of cognition.

Despite differences in the specific subject matter addressed in the various papers, which ranges from attentional development (Posner and Rothbart) to factual comprehension (Smith), each of the papers reflects, to some degree, a response to perceived shortcomings in the scientific progress made by cognitive psychologists over the past several years. As its title suggests, Dr. Jenkins's paper, "Can We Have a Fruitful Cognitive Psychology?," constitutes a very direct criticism of both our current state of knowledge about cognitive psychology and, in particular, the criteria by which we evaluate research progress within the field. While the remaining papers do not offer a general critique as their primary goal, they nevertheless show concern either with current inadequacies in typical research objectives of experimental psychologists or with insufficiencies of experimental methodologies.

In their paper entitled "The Development of Attentional Mechanisms," Drs. Posner and Rothbart address two related criticisms of cognitive psychologists: their failure to provide general knowledge of how the mind works that has ecological validity outside of the laboratory setting, and the failure of cognitive psychologists to relate theories to psychobiology of the organism (evolution and development). The authors argue that one can gain significant insights into the relationship between different neurological structures and attentional control by studying the human infant as it develops the capacity of selective attention necessary for adult functioning. Furthermore, such an approach makes it possible to assess the relative contribution of innate orientation mechanisms and acquired skills to the development of attention. In contrast to early assumptions about overt attention in infants, Drs. Posner and Rothbart argue that visual fixations are not an index of an infant's visual preferences, but that overt orienting systems must be brought under the control of central attentional mechanisms (through learning and maturation) during the first month of life.

In their paper, Drs. Posner and Rothbart argue that despite recent criticisms of laboratory methods employed by cognitive psychologists, techniques which are designed to trace information flow offer a basis for "bridging psychological and physiological analyses," particularly in the area of attention. Posner and Rothbart thus strongly defend the utility of experimental tasks which do not necessarily resemble "what subjects do in the real world," but which "tap assumed psychological processes in their simplest form." The use of "model systems" developed through the systematic application of such laboratory procedures, will, in turn, provide the basis for understanding the performance of complex real-world tasks.

Dr. LaBerge's paper, entitled "Unitization and Automaticity in Perception," is concerned with the development of a high level of perceptual processing efficiency in tasks for which extremely intense and sustained training is undertaken. Reading is perhaps the most widely investigated example of such a task. Specifically, Dr. LaBerge's paper discusses the process of forming holistic cognitive units from smaller components (e.g., processing word units as opposed to individual letters) and ways in which such unitization processes may be assessed in the laboratory. In additional, Dr. LaBerge's paper is concerned with automaticity, which is another characteristic of skilled performance that has received a considerable research effort over the past several years. Automaticity refers to processing without conscious attention, such that the capacity and time limitations imposed by "conscious" tasks are eliminated. One of the consequences of automatic processing is the inability to ignore stimuli when they are irrelevant to task performance. Therefore, one may measure the degree of automaticity by measuring increased performance impairment across the time course of skill acquisition. Dr. LaBerge provides us with examples of data using Stroop-like interference tasks and speculates about the possibility of using these paradigms as converging operations to study the acquisition of automaticity of reading skill development and other tasks.

Dr. Nickerson's paper, "Motivated Retrieval from Archival Memory," focuses, as the title suggests, upon the nature of information representation in memory and the processes of retrieving it. By use of the term *motivated retrieval,* Dr. Nickerson is referring to information recall which requires an active, effortful, and consciously directed search process such as that which typically occurs when one has to recall details of events or learned facts. Such effortful, motivated recall may be contrasted with the more spontaneous passive and automatic recall occurring, for example, in retrieval of word meanings during conversation. With the application of a variety of converging approaches to the study of motivated retrieval, some interesting properties of memory emerge. These properties bear upon the very broad issues of content, selectivity, and representation of information in memory in addition to the recall process itself. One very clear objective of Dr. Nickerson's paper is to raise issues and questions for future research into the structure of memory.

Dr. Nickerson presents examples of four different approaches to studying motivated retrieval. These include looking at memory for common objects, studying the ability of subjects to estimate unknown quantities, the use of introspective observations of one's own effortful retrieval processes and pathways, and finally, the study of list-generation processes. It is this latter approach involving tasks in which subjects must try to produce lists of items from memory conforming to a set of experimenter-imposed constraints (e.g., all words which rhyme with *pair*, all words which have *c* in the third-letter position, or names of baseball players), to which Dr. Nickerson devotes most of the body of his paper. By looking at commonalities across item categories for temporal patterns in which the items are recalled, and evaluating these temporal patterns of recall through using a mathematical model, Dr. Nickerson provides an excellent example of how normative modeling processes can help the investigator ask some interesting and appropriate questions. In the present case, these questions involve the nature of the constraints upon memory search processes and why they are constrained on some dimensions but apparently not upon others, and what determines which dimensions will be effective constraints and which ones will not. Dr. Nickerson completes his paper with an actual list of major findings (which summarizes knowledge obtained about motivated retrieval) plus a list of questions raised by this research which can be pursued in future research endeavors.

Dr. Anderson's paper, "Concepts, Propositions, and Schemata: What Are the Cognitive Units?," is concerned with the nature of the information pieces or packages which constitute mental data. While Dr. LaBerge's presentation dealt with this issue at the perceptual level, Dr. Anderson's essay focuses upon the role of unitization in information manipulation within active memory, including both information coming from the environment (as in prose comprehension) and information retrieved from long-term memory. By examining data from a wide variety of contemporary experiments, including both recall-accuracy measures and reaction-time measures for performance, Dr. Anderson considers whether a concept, a proposition (composed of several concepts), or a schema (composed of a set of related propositions) should be viewed as a basic cognitive unit, satisfying the criteria of all-or-none encoding and all-or-none retrieval. Dr. Anderson suggests that all three of these structures may be considered to be cognitive units, depending upon the properties of the individual task, and that furthermore, it may not be useful to regard propositions and schemata as separate "species" of units but rather as "two manifestations of the same species." Dr. Anderson demonstrates the role of unitization processes in comprehension and recall of material through showing several examples of how the use of a prior-knowledge structure (e.g., an analogy or schema) affects the ability to recall story passages. This paper thus sets forth a highly general theory of cognitive processing in which cognitive units are hierarchically arranged and, depending upon the demands of the particular task, the term *unit* may be appropriately applied to a wide range of levels from individual concepts to large story texts.

Dr. Smith's contribution, "Organization of Factual Knowledge," is very closely related to Anderson's paper, and draws heavily upon previous findings and theoretical models of knowledge structures developed by Anderson and his colleagues. Like Anderson, Dr. Smith is concerned with limitations of previous network models of semantic memory and their ability to explain the integration of new knowledge and the organization and elaboration of new input facts into existing structures. Dr. Smith stresses that elaboration of input material is one of the most crucial processes in comprehension of prose. Through a critical review of recent research in prose comprehension, Dr. Smith develops a description of knowledge representation which he refers to as the higher unit hypothesis. According to this position, there exists a single unit or node for a set of related propositions, but within this node all propositions and subsequent concepts are explicitly represented. Dr. Smith makes a strong argument for studying memory for integrable facts. Previous experimentation in sentence memory, in Dr. Smith's view, has tended to underemphasize the relationships between memory and comprehension, since most studies used materials possessing low levels of integrable relatedness.

As previously mentioned, Dr. Jenkins's paper entitled, "Can We Have a Fruitful Cognitive Psychology?," provides a rather poignant criticism of the current state of cognitive psychology. Dr. Jenkins suggests that despite the tremendous boom in research activity among cognitive psychologists, "an unbiased observer studying the history of psychology from some distant point in time would have more reason to see progress and cumulative knowledge in the theories of learning in that period than in the activities of cognitive psychologists over the last two decades."

Dr. Jenkins, nevertheless, suggests that signs of progress exist, as evidenced both by a spreading awareness of the problems within cognitive psychology and by the development of several lines of research which he believes constitute a response to the problems of limited generality and noncumulativeness. To illustrate examples of approaches to cognitive psychology which he feels offered promise to our understanding of cognitive processes, Dr. Jenkins gives an overview of research in visual event perception (providing specific examples from his own laboratory), and research on expertise currently pursued by Paul Johnson and his colleagues at the University of Minnesota. These research examples each provide some very intriguing analogies with the views expressed by Dr. Smith and Dr. Anderson with respect to the importance of previous knowledge on comprehension, and the conclusion that cognitive "units" come in a variety of forms and sizes (a viewpoint which Jenkins labels "representational populism").

Dr. Jenkins, nevertheless, suggests that signs of progress exist, as evidenced both by a spreading awareness of the problems within cognitive psychology and by the development of several line of research which he believes constitute a response to the problems of limited generality and noncumulativeness. To illustrate examples of approaches to cognitive psychology which he feels offered promise to our understanding of cognitive processes, Dr. Jenkins gives an overview of research in visual event perception (providing specific examples from his own laboratory), and research on expertise currently pursued by Paul Johnson and his colleagues at the University of Minnesota. These research examples each provide some very intriguing analogies with the views expressed by Dr. Smith and Dr. Anderson with respect to the importance of previous knowledge on comprehension, and the conclusion that cognitive "units" come in a variety of forms and sizes (a viewpoint which Jenkins labels "representational populism").

It should be pointed out that Jenkins's presentation was the last of the fall session, and directly followed the presentations of Anderson and Smith. Because the paper includes a general statement about the field of cognitive psychology as a whole, in addition to including content directly relevant to Smith's and Anderson's presentations, the papers from the fall and spring sessions were interchanged in the published volume. It also appeared to the editors that the ordering of topics from attention through perceptual processing into memory and then knowledge structures at a more general level seemed a reasonable one.

Like other volumes in this series, the 1979–80 Nebraska Symposium on Motivation raises a number of general issues about the current state of knowledge and scientific progress within psychology, and also sets forth several specific research problems for future investigation. In addition to providing summaries of research activity within several important areas of human cognition, it is hoped that these papers will encourage and stimulate further investigations on the part of other researchers in the field.

JOHN H. FLOWERS
Volume Editor

REFERENCE

Newell, A. You can't play 20 questions with nature and win. In W. G. Chase (Ed.), *Visual information processing*. New York: Academic press, 1973.

The Development of Attentional Mechanisms[1]

Michael I. Posner and Mary K. Rothbart
University of Oregon

*M*IND may be studied in multiple ways: through introspection, through the study of performance, and through the study of neural processes. An approach to the study of mind currently productive at all of these levels has been an information-processing analysis, allowing exploration of separate processing systems and the time course of their activation. In spite of its successes, however, the information-processing approach has at times provided a limited perspective. The reliance of information-processing approaches on computer metaphors, for example, has sometimes blinded practitioners to the unique questions arising from the biological heritage of the human brain.

In his recent book, Ulric Neisser (1976) suggests that information processing has produced "ingenious and scientifically respectable methods," but faults it as having "not yet committed itself to any conception of human nature that would apply beyond the confines of the laboratory" (p. 6). Neisser's prescription for cognitive psychology is to explore tasks more closely resembling the real world. Thus he argues for the importance of ecological validity, for the study of performance extended over time, and for the examination of the integration of cross-modal information. In addition, Neisser argues for the importance of a developmental and evolutionary perspective. To this end, he adopts a view

1. A version of this paper was presented to the Nebraska Symposium, March 1980. The research of the authors and the writing of the paper were supported in part by NSF Grant BNS–176–18907–A03 and by NIMH Grant SR01MH26674–04. The paper was written while the first-named author held a John Simon Guggenheim fellowship. The authors are grateful for very helpful comments from Marc Bornstein, Doug Derryberry, Harold Hawkins, Steven Keele, Diana Pien, and are especially grateful to Gordon Shulman, whose literature review of infant visual attention did much to initiate and inform this inquiry.

modified from Gibson's approach to perception. This view places emphasis, not upon mechanisms of mental processing, but rather upon characteristics of the environment that might have worked through evolution to produce the human mental apparatus.

Although we are sympathetic to the limitations Neisser has identified, we would not wish to emphasize too strongly evolutionary and developmental analysis as a substitute for laboratory work. One approach to cognition does not replace the other, any more than evolutionary theory might be expected to replace neurobiological experimentation in furthering our understanding of biological brain mechanisms. One expects neurobiology to be illuminated and informed by an understanding of evolution, but there has been no substitute for the detailed analysis of the internal structure of neurons and synapses. Although cognitive psychology should be informed by an appreciation of both the evolutionary history and the developmental sequence of the human mind, there is no substitute for a detailed empirical analysis of the internal mechanisms underlying cognition. In fact, the methods available to cognitive psychology, particularly those designed to trace the time course of information flow in the nervous system, provide a basis for bridging biological and psychological analyses. This is particularly true for perhaps the most fundamental area linking analysis of brain to analysis of mind—attention.

We believe the understanding of mechanisms that is developed through laboratory research in attention can illuminate difficult problems in development. Accordingly, a major goal of this paper will be an analysis of attentional mechanisms in the first year of life in light of the ideas we believe have emerged from studies of adult attention. We realize the potential experimental situations in which attention can be studied are so vast that it is impossible to survey so large a field. We have therefore adopted a "model systems" approach to the study of the relationship between attention in the newborn and in the adult. The model systems approach involves the development of tasks allowing us to tap assumed psychological processes in their simplest and most analytic form. Such an approach does not require that the task studied resembles what subjects do in the real world, but that the processes studied via the task illuminate fundamental aspects of internal mechanisms. It is expected that the understanding of internal processes we develop through the study of model systems will give us new analytic tools to apply to the understanding of complex performances achieved by people in the real world. The study of letter and word matching, for example, has been used as a model system for understanding basic operations in achieving a phonetic description of a visually presented stimulus. In turn, the insights gained from the study of letter and word matching provided us with tools and concepts for an analysis of a complex skill like reading (LaBerge & Samuels, 1974; Posner, 1978).

For the present analysis, we have selected model systems placing minimum emphasis upon linguistic analysis and other learned behaviors that might prevent comparisons between the nonverbal infant and the verbal adult. In the next section, we outline theoretical ideas developed for describing mechanisms of attention in adults (Posner, 1978, 1980). In the following sections, we compare data obtained with infants and with adults on aspects of model systems involving attention. The third section deals with external control of orienting to visual stimuli. We attempt to compare the relation of external and central control as it may develop over the life-span of an organism. In section four, we examine purely internal mechanisms which eventually achieve control over orienting; here we consider what might be inferred about the ontogeny of consciousness.

Our final substantive section deals with the perspective of individual differences. In this regard Papousek (1979) argues:

> Infant psychology is ultimately important for its examination of individual differences. Individual infants differ not only along quantitative dimensions but above all in their qualitative behavioral strategies. Human observers are able to detect much more subtle behavioral changes in the human infant than in any other animal. This may be valid for emotional and communicative behavior as it is for observable signs of thinking. Obviously we all use external signs as feedback elements in communication with others. Therefore, such signs cannot escape our attention whenever we see them in the infant. Every parent is able to list patterns of emotional behavior that significantly exceed that set used to describe emotion in rats, usually the number of boluses or the amount of self licking. Moreover, parents will gladly offer interpretations of emotional behavior in babies, and, surprisingly enough, such interpretations will have much to do with thought processes. (p. 253)

While in the earlier sections our emphasis is on taking models developed in adult work and applying their perspective to the infant, in this section the reverse strategy is employed. The analysis of adult dimensions of individual differences seems seriously troubled by the very flexibility and complexity with which adults engage their environment. The simplification that potentially occurs in dealing with infant temperament may provide a perspective on possible enduring dimensions of personality and thus give new direction to work with adults.

I. MECHANISMS OF ATTENTION

For the purposes of this paper, we take our view of the mechanisms of attention from the work described by Posner (1978). This view outlines a series of internal mechanisms associated with attention. Although there is no claim that all mechanisms of attention have been identified, nor that the mechanisms identified are necessarily mutually exclusive, a tripartite division of mechanisms seems justified by both internal logic and the data. These involve (a) an intensive mechanism associated with alteration in the organism's state, (b) parallel internal pathways activated by external input or by thought, and associated with selection, and (c) a mechanism of limited capacity associated with awareness. The elementary mental operations of alerting, pathway activation, and orienting and detecting are associated with operations of various of these mechanisms.

Any external stimulus can be thought of as having several distinct effects upon the nervous system. The stimulus produces a general change in state, called alerting, that may affect the general level of receptivity of organism. A stimulus at the same time activates specific pathways biasing the organism toward particular events. It may also produce a change in the orientation of sensory and central systems (orienting). Finally, it may occupy focal attention (detecting). In this way the internal consequences of any stimulus for the information processing of the organism become quite complex. A major consequence of changes of state and pathway activation in the adult is to help guide access of stimuli to a central attentional mechanism highly correlated with our awareness of the stimulus. The idea that changes in pathways and alerting may precede conscious attention is an important aspect of our framework, since it separates automatic effects from strategic ones.

Alerting

Although changes in an organism's state of alertness are most easily observed in association with the diurnal cycle, more rapid changes in alertness also occur in connection with the presentation of specific stimulus events. For example, the waning of receptivity to external stimuli occurring early and late in the day also occurs when a subject engages in an extended repetitive activity on a single low-demand task (Posner, 1978). On the other hand, an increase in alertness occurs with the presentation of sufficient· stimulus change, particularly when a stimulus signifies interesting consequences, as is true of a warning signal. The Orienting Reaction (Sokolov, 1963) occurring in response to such stimulation reflects a rapid change in bodily state, including heart rate deceleration and negative shifts in EEG that index increased receptivity to the stimulus itself or to signals following the warning. These phasic changes in alertness have been studied in detail in connection with a number of human performance domains (Posner, 1978). It is likely that several physiological mechanisms, both biochemical and electrical, relate to both intrinsic rhythms and the phasic alerting induced by warnings. The reticular activating system, both at the midbrain and thalamic levels, has often been seen as the major mechanism related to alerting, and there have been proposals that such mechanisms involve norepinephrine pathways arising in the locus coeruleus (Foote, Aston-Jones, & Bloom, 1980).

Pathway Activation

The pathway activation aspect of attention is more consistent with the information-processing metaphor, and has been more thoroughly examined, than alertness. In pathway activation, there is evidence of two major ways in which an organism may be biased toward becoming aware of a particular stimulus. The first requires presentation of a priming stimulus that biases the nervous system in favor of subsequent events using some or all of the same pathways activated by the prime. The second involves the primary effects of simply thinking about an event or concept. Priming works at many levels of generality. For example, the presentation of visual stimuli tends to improve the selectivity of other stimuli which share that modality. The presentation of a visual word primes the representation of that word in both the visual modality and the auditory modality. A word will also prime words sharing the same meaning, even though they may be physically and phonetically quite distinct. Priming effects subside over time with the major effect occurring during the first seconds after presentation of the priming item. However, there are reports in the literature of priming effects occurring for some minutes or even an hour (Underwood, 1965; Warren & Warren, 1976).

The importance of priming as a means of facilitating awareness of an item is greatly enlarged because it can arise from purely internal activity. If a persons thinks about the name of a word and then turns attention to something else, there will be facilitation in the processing of any item sharing that name for some period of time after the original thought (McLean & Shulman, 1978). Similar results occur for visual representations (e.g., pictures) or other purely mental activity (Cooper, 1976). Indeed, an important discovery of the last several years is that the internal representation of an item in the memory system occurs by a pathway activation process mimicking its presentation externally (Neely, 1977). Although a thought does not activate all of the codes, particularly the more concrete uses activated by an external stimulus (e.g., thinking about the name of a word does not usually activate its physical code), the way in which activation guides subsequent attention seems to be identical.

Orienting and Detecting

A third attentional mechanism subserves the operations of orienting and detecting. Overt orienting is defined as the alignment of the organism's sensory receptors to a stimulus; covert orienting, as the alignment of the central processing system to the stimulus. Detecting involves access of a stimulus to the subjective impression we call awareness. Orienting and detecting may be viewed as separable features of a single internal mechanism.

Much work on orienting (Sokolov, 1963) has assumed that alignment of attention to a source of input is identical to detection of a stimulus event. The orienting reflex, for example, does not distinguish between the processes occurring prior to detection (awareness of the stimulus event) and those occurring subsequently. The relatively slow nature of the autonomic changes usually measured preclude such a division. Although orienting of attention is measured by changes in the efficiency of detecting, the two mental operations must be quite distinct. For overt orienting, this is obvious because the eyes may move to a potential source of signals before any stimulus is actually presented. Since one can move attention to a potential source of signals before any input has occurred, covert orienting can also occur without detection.

The ability to dissociate orienting and detecting mechanisms is congruent with observations on brain-injured individuals. In the case of occipital lesions (field cuts), there is a relative sparing of the ability to do overt orienting, along with an inability to detect (be aware of) stimuli in the blind field (Gassel & Williams, 1963; Perenin & Jeannerod, 1978; Weiskrantz, Warrington, Sanders, & Marshall, 1974). On the other hand, damage in the right parietal region often produces a severe deficit in orienting, with a less severe loss in the ability to detect a stimulus once orienting is accomplished (Heilman & Watson, 1977). When only one event is presented, subjects may show good acuity in the neglected field, but when competing events are presented, there is a deficit in orienting toward the side opposite the lesion.

In additional work studying the separability of orienting and detecting (Posner, 1978, 1980), it has been shown that critical events involving covert attention can be time-locked to the occurrence of internal and external stimulation. Not all aspects of internal activation of even higher level semantic concepts produce awareness. Rather, only a certain subset of these operations involves mechanisms subserving awareness. For example, semantic nodes seem to be contacted without awareness, in a parallel fashion. On the other hand, both overt responses and the storage in long-term memory of activated ideas are more dependent on the availability of limited-capacity central attentional mechanisms. For reasons that are really not at all understood, the activation of this central mechanism seems to be accompanied with reports of subjective experience of the type available to introspective accounts.

The existence of a highly parallel semantic network and a relatively serial mechanism responsible for conscious awareness may seem at first puzzling. Indeed many investigators have wondered about the biological reality of coupling two such different mechanisms (Broadbent, 1971). Although there is no complete answer to this difficulty, a major solution may be found in the necessity to coordinate the external behavior of an organism so that antagonistic responses do not occur. The flexibility allowing the human organism to respond in different ways to the same stimulus event depending upon context seems to require some mechanism providing inhibitory control over the activation of inappropriate response tendencies. A basic principle of nervous system processing seems to be that activation at one level is inhibited by higher centers. In this light it might not be too surprising that at the highest level of processing would be a system of limited capacity, making certain that only a small range of the potentially activated responses to a stimulus are evinced in behavior.

An effort to develop a life-span approach to mechanisms of attention requires a method of study (model system) that can be used with infants and yet plays an important role in cognition. For this paper we have chosen to focus our study on spatial attention. Spatial behavior emerges early in evolution and can be studied in the head and eye movements of newborns. There are clear higher order cognitive capacities concerned with our ability to orient in space, and such abilities differ in interesting ways among individuals. Most of our discussion will be of vision, although we do deal to some extent with the role of other modalities.

Biology of Spatial Attention

The visual system may be usefully viewed in terms of two different subsystems, both intimately involved in the apprehension of space. The retinal-collicular system is designed to allow the high-acuity fovea to be brought rapidly and efficiently to areas of importance. In lower animals this system is the primary visual pathway for the apprehension of objects in space, but in higher organisms it apparently is designed to control eye movements, while the retinal-geniculate striate system subserves object recognition.

The organization of eye movement systems must be viewed in light of the binocular character of vision in the higher vertebrates. Because of the limited size of foveal vision, it is a critical problem to be able to use peripheral stimulation to provide better foveal access. This problem may be solved efficiently by powerful links between the peripheral visual field of each eye and midbrain structures subserving eye movements of the opposite side, such as are known to exist in the cat. Thus temporal visual stimuli to the left eye operate via the right midbrain to move the conjugate eye movement system, so that both foveae become aligned with the visual stimulation (Arbib, 1972; Posner & Cohen, 1980). Powerful inhibitory connections between the two sides allow each eye to control the conjugate saccadic movements of both eyes. Thus evolution has designed a system in which each eye can operate more or less independently on its own temporal field input to drive the whole system.

In the absence of external input, eye movement systems of all higher organisms show a spontaneous movement pattern allowing them to sample information from the external environment. For example, Mates (1973) has found that the relatively independent eyes of the chameleon show, even in the dark, a time distribution of interresponse time similar to the sampling patterns of adult humans. This oculomotor activity is probably not a characteristic of deliberate attentive scanning of the environment, but represents a kind of patterned spontaneous activity similar to the output of many motor systems.

Even this cursory glance at the evolutionary background of the visual system suggests the crucial but complex role of oculomotor control in spatially governed behavior. The oculomotor system appears to have control mechanisms from many parts of the nervous system, including the frontal eye fields, parietal lobe, and occipital lobe, as well as retinal-to-midbrain structures. There is parallel activation, for example, of forebrain and collicular systems in the control of saccadic eye movements (Schiller, True, & Conway, 1979). Moreover, the oculomotor system is responsive to more than visual input. For example, in many mammalian organisms (e.g., the cat), the midbrain structures responsible for controlling eye movements receive direct collaterals from auditory and some somesthetic systems, as well as from visual systems. Similarly, control mechanisms at the level of the parietal lobe also receive somesthetic as well as visual input. Although the movement of the eyes can be intimately related to higher levels of cognitive processing, it need not be. Indeed, the similar patterning of spontaneous eye movements in chameleon and human suggests that in many cases the eye movement system is driven by mechanisms that do not require postulation of higher level attentive processes.

Students of the visual system often separate the oculomotor system from the so-called primary visual system designed to mediate higher levels of identification and perception. This primary visual system relies on retinal-geniculate-occipital pathways and includes access to mechanisms of color orientation and depth, as well as form. This primary visual system also provides important information about the spatial organization of the visual world. Nearly point-to-point projection from foveal input to several spatially distributed maps in the cortex has been demonstrated in a number of experimental investigations (see Cowey, 1979, for a review). The primary visual system provides not only information about the general orientation of the organism in space (e.g., with respect to body posture), but also detailed information about where one object lies with respect to other objects in the same plane and in depth.

It is now understood that at birth, mammals show a highly organized system for feature analysis of visual stimuli at the level of the striate cortex (Hubel, 1977). Although the term *feature* may itself be controversial, there is little question that initial stages of information about orientation and contour are organized at birth in the striate cortex. In the anesthetized or newly born organism, a good deal of analysis of form is available. Much of the output of this analysis would also be available to eye movement systems via occipital-to-collicular pathways. The primary and secondary visual systems, though relying heavily on independent pathways, have much information in common that can be passed between them.

Components of Spatial Attention

Much of the work described above has been done on anesthetized infrahuman organisms. Recently the focus of a variety of literatures has begun to change to the internal control mechanisms that might mediate spatial selectivity in the alert organism. In part, this change reflects the ability to record single-cell activity from alert monkeys trained to shift attention either with or without movements of the eye (Goldberg & Wurtz, 1972; Mountcastle, 1978).

Similarly, a number of investigations of adult human performance (Posner, 1980) have explored the detailed relationships between covert orienting of attentional mechanisms and overt shifts of the head and eyes. Movements of covert attention are indexed by changes of the efficiency of detecting stimuli occurring at various positions in visual space. Efficiency may be gauged with a variety of chronometric techniques (Posner, 1978), such as reaction time, probability of reporting near threshold signals, evoked potentials, or the poststimulus latency histograms of single cells. A surprising result of these studies is the relative independence of the mechanism responsible for overt orienting from those responsible for movements of covert attention.

For example, it is possible to shift covert attention around the visual field with the eyes fixed (Bushnel, Robinson, & Goldberg, 1978; Posner, 1978). In human subjects this is easily accomplished by presenting a cue that indicates where in space a detection stimulus is most likely to occur. Subjects are more efficient at detecting luminance changes at expected than at unexpected positions (Posner, 1978). Moreover, an unexpected luminance change occurring peripherally while the subject attends to the foveal area incurs about the same cost in efficiency as it would when the subject attends to the periphery and the stimulus occurs foveally. Thus when acuity is unimportant, the fovea plays no special role in attention, but attention cannot compensate for reduced acuity due to differences in the wiring of foveal and peripheral tissue. The relative independence of costs in luminance detection from the fine structure of the retina suggests that the mechanisms of attention are not themselves dependent upon the detailed characteristics of the sensory system.

A second sense of independence is that covert movements of attention are relatively independent of the saccadic eye movement system (Posner, 1980). Not only can subjects move attention without moving their eyes, but under circumstances where eye movements do not depend upon the presentation of peripheral stimuli, attention can be left fixed as the eyes are moved across the visual field (Remington, 1980). Indeed, we have been able to show that attention can move in the opposite direction of the eye movement in certain circumstances (Posner, 1980). On the other hand, the attentional system and the eye movement system are often functionally interrelated. For example, we (Posner, 1980) have shown that when a peripheral stimulus occurs to which the subjects must move their eyes, attention moves to the target area prior to the beginning of the eye movement by about a hundred milliseconds. This result found in reaction time and threshold detection in humans has also been reported in alert monkeys by the selective enhancement of superior collicular neurons whose receptive field is in the neighborhood of the target prior to the eye movement (Goldberg & Wurtz, 1972; Wurtz & Mohler, 1976). Thus there is a strong functional interrelationship between eye movements and movements of attention, but not one that seems dependent on the same underlying physiological mechanism.

A third sense of independence between covert attentional mechanisms and the visual system has been recently reported by Shulman (1979). We (Posner & Cohen, 1980) had previously shown that eye movements to monocularly presented stimuli are biased in the direction of the temporal visual field. This finding is congruent with the neural and anatomical relationships between eye movement systems and peripheral stimuli we have outlined above. Shulman asked if the same bias toward the temporal visual field from monocularly presented stimuli would occur for covert attentional mechanisms. He tested this by presentation of simultaneous stimuli to the temporal and nasal visual field of a single eye. Under these conditions when subjects were asked to move their eyes, the eye movements were powerfully biased in the temporal direction. However, when subjects were required to move attention, there was no similar bias in the direction of the temporal visual field. Thus if the temporal-nasal bias is an indicant of pathways linking peripherally presented stimuli to eye movement control, these same pathways do not appear to be involved in the control of covert spatial orienting.

In summary, three different tests seem to indicate a strong sense of independence between the mechanisms subserving covert visual attention and those subserving specific characteristics of the visual system. We think this to be important because it has often been assumed that the location of the eyes is a good indicant of the direction or orienting of covert attention. To some extent, this assumption is justified under the conditions of study of normal adult cognition. In demanding tasks, particularly ones which have acuity demands, subjects do indeed move their eyes to align the fovea with the portion of the visual field on which they are concentrating. The strength of this functional tendency is illustrated by Kahneman (1973), who finds that in verbal reports concerning stimuli no longer present in the visual field, there is a strong tendency for subjects to align their eyes at the place where the stimulus being described had been presented. Nonetheless, the problem of identifying covert attention with the line of sight becomes much greater when dealing with an organism, like the infant, not capable of telling us directly about its attention. If the mechanisms underlying covert attention were closely dependent on the overt orienting visual system, one would feel this identification to be fully justified. However, the clear evidence of independence of these mechanisms suggests that at the very least converging evidence would be necessary.

Summary

In this section, we have outlined a general framework for the study of attention and have developed a model system concerning orienting to stimulus events occurring at various positions in space. The study of this model system from a physiological and psychological viewpoint leads to the conclusion that covert orienting is the property of a central mechanism, and that there is a great deal of independence between the covert mechanism and the eye movement system. The relative independence of mechanisms of conscious attention from the structure of the visual system is important for an understanding of the analysis of mind in the first few months of life. Although it has proven very convenient to monitor head and eye movements in the infant, results obtained with adults lead us to be wary of the conclusion that eye movements and fixations mark the necessary operation of covert attentional mechanisms.

II. EXTERNAL CONTROL OF ORIENTING

Fixation as Preference

In a 1973 compendium of infant research (Stone, Smith, & Murphy, 1973), the editors remark upon the prior conviction of developmental psychologists and lay people that the infant has few cognitive capacities. They quote from an authoritative popular summary, as of 1964, the claim that "consciousness, as we think of it, probably does not exist in the newborn, but the sense of pain does, and the baby is also sensitive to touch and pressure . . . the responses to all these sensations, however, are of purely reflex character and are mediated . . . below the level of the cerebral cortex." (p. 4).

The flood of research in infancy over the last 20 years has generally erased this conviction and replaced it by a strong general feeling that is well portrayed by the title of the book *The Competent Infant*. An extremely important role in this metamorphosis of opinion has been played by the demonstration that infants portray a preference for one visual pattern over another almost from birth (Fantz, 1965). These preferences are evident in the eye movement and fixation patterns infants show when presented with visual stimuli. As such, they rest heavily upon an assumption of the close relationship between conscious preference as found in the judgments of adults and the line of sight of the infant.

There is, of course, much evidence that adult humans look at and examine those stimuli in which they're interested or to which they are currently paying attention (Russo & Rosen, 1975). It is relatively natural to suppose that the reason for this close identification is that visual attention and the position of the eyes rest upon a single neurological system present in some primitive form at birth. Eye position would then provide direct insight into the attentional pattern of all organisms. We have seen in the last section, however, that this assumption is probably incorrect. Although the position of the eyes and attention in adults are coordinate under most circumstances, it is not because they rest upon common neurological structures. Rather, the experiments described above argue that in cases where covert attention and positions of the eyes are coordinated (e.g., in orienting toward peripheral stimuli), this coordination rests upon a learned functional relationship, not upon identity of neurological system. Our results thus raise serious problems with a close identification between the line of sight of newborns and their cognitive preferences.

If eye position does not indicate in the newborn a cognitive preference in the same way it does for an adult, what factors could govern the fixation and control of eye movements in the first months of life? One proposal (Bronson, 1974) comes from our understanding of the relatively slow myelination of the cortex in comparison to the midbrain structures. Bronson proposes that the newborn is essentially a midbrain organism whose eye movements are controlled directly by retinal-to-collicular pathways. There is much to recommend this view. Particularly in the first two months of life, the eye movements of the newborn are heavily governed by simple factors of stimulus motion, intensity, and contour density that might very well be mediated by midbrain structures. On the other hand, the idea of a strictly midbrain mechanism has been criticized by Haith and Campos (1977) as resting on relatively weak physiological evidence. Such a dichotomy of midbrain versus cortical control is probably not a very adequate one in light of the evidence obtained by Hubel (1977) of the beautiful organization of the striate cortex in the newborn monkey. In addition, Haith and Campos argue that the newborn is influenced by the presence of a central stimulus in detecting a peripheral one, suggesting that foveal vision is available and thus that vision is not entirely mediated by midbrain structure. As Haith and Campos also observe, too strong an emphasis on midbrain versus cortical control is probably not useful; it may be more fruitful to recognize that all neurosystems in early infancy are immature and to accept the task of describing how these immature systems are orchestrated.

In understanding such orchestration, it is important to examine the relative control over the eye movement system of midbrain and cortical centers in the infant, and methods may now be at hand for doing this. Although every eye movement is probably controlled from a variety of centers, and thus it is not reasonable to suppose that any movement is itself the clear result of any particular pathway, Posner and Cohen (1979) have pointed to a sign of the retinal-collicular pathway that is quite prominent in monocular eye movements in the adult. This sign is the tendency to turn toward the temporal direction when equivalent stimuli are presented simultaneously on the nasal and temporal side of fixation. Moreover, work in our laboratory (Posner, Cohen, & Shulman, 1979) has shown that with binocular stimulation the direction of eye movements can be predicted from the temporal field of the dominant eye (Coren & Kaplan, 1973). As long ago as 1968, Salapatek reported that with monocular stimulation of the left eye of newborns, there was a very strong tendency to turn the eye to a stimulus presented to the temporal side in comparison with a stimulus presented to the nasal side. In his study this strong left-going bias was not studied in the opposite eye, so one could not discriminate between a temporal bias and, for example, dominant right hemisphere control. However, a study by Mendelson and Haith (1976) shows clear evidence of a temporal bias by each eye (see their Figure 16). Lewis, Maurer, and Milewski (1979) also reported that with a single stimulus presented monocularly, newborns showed a powerful bias in the direction of the temporal visual field. This strong bias dropped out over the first two months of life. Although no complete report of this last study is yet available, it does fit quite strongly with the bias found in the adult. One might wonder how it is that the adult bias can be found if the bias in newborns tends to be eliminated by two months

(Lewis, Maurer, & Milewski, 1979). While the details of the reconciliation might rest on knowing more about the conditions of the infant experiment, the infant study apparently used unilateral stimulation to one visual field, while the adult data involved bilateral simultaneous stimuli to both fields. If unilateral stimulation is presented to the adult, there is little or no bias. The eyes move in the direction of the stimulus, and there is only a tiny (8 msec) residual difference in reaction time (Posner, Cohen, & Shulman, 1979). With bilateral stimulation, there is an enormous bias favoring the temporal field.

The difference between the effectiveness of unilateral and bilateral stimulation in teasing apart subtle neuropsychological differences has been documented in a number of literatures involving normal and brain-injured adults. For example, Boles (1979) has shown that differences in hemispheric function are much more strongly indicated when subjects are presented with simultaneous bilateral rather than single unilateral stimuli. The left hemisphere appears to be better in detecting word stimuli by about 3–5% with unilateral stimulus presentation, but by the use of simultaneous input to the opposite visual field, this hemispheric assymetry is increased to about 20%. In parietal lobe injury, there frequently is little or no evidence of damage when unilateral stimuli are presented, but there is evidence of "extinction" of the stimulus contralateral to the lesion with bilateral presentations (Heilman & Watson, 1977).

The picture emerging is that newborns show particularly strong signs of the retinal-to-collicular pathway, even with unilateral stimuli. The influence of the nasal visual field appears to be weak, and this changes dramatically over the first two months of life. In adults, the influence of the retinal-collicular pathway can be demonstrated, although the temporal advantage is evinced only when there is genuine competition between stimuli. These data are in conformity with the general outline of Bronson's view; however, they would not require a crude dichotomy between midbrain and cortical control, but instead argue for a steady increase in more central control over the eye movement system. Insofar as the eye movement system is dominated heavily by retinal-collicular pathways, one would certainly expect little influence of variables requiring the primary visual system.

Our view then does not posit the relationship between covert attention, preference, and eye movement position usually suggested. We believe covert attention arises as an entirely different neural system than that used for driving the eyes. It may be the task of development itself to coordinate the neural system(s) responsible for covert attention and the pattern of eye movement. Preference need not be reflected in eye position during the first month or two of life. Instead, the growth of mechanisms responsible for conscious preference should become increasingly coordinated with the eye movement pattern. One might object to this basic idea that attention and eye movement patterns need to be coordinated in the early part of life, by pointing to the presence of endogenous rhythms not driven by external input in the newborn (Haith, 1978). This argument is somewhat vitiated by the presence of similar eye movement rhythms throughout the animal kingdom, as low on the phylogenetic scale as the chameleon. As we have pointed out earlier, it is a property of all neurosystems to show spontaneous activity, and thus the movement of the eyes in the dark as reported by Haith does not provide sufficient evidence to suppose that they are driven by search or scanning patterns corresponding to the deliberate search of adults. Rather, they may represent the outflow of the spontaneous activity of neural control systems, which only later become coordinated with cognitive intentions to produce search patterns typical of the adult.

A second set of data showing that newborn fixation may not indicate a cognitive preference corresponding to adult preference comes from more anecdotal reports of the phenomenon called "obligatory attention." While use of the term *preference* in connection with adult fixation patterns suggests a positive or at least an interestedly neutral attitude on the part of a subject, descriptions of infant behavior during extended fixation suggest that such an attitude may not always be evident.

It has been frequently reported that the young infant shows highly extended fixations to external stimuli. Friedman (1972) reports mean initial fixation times of newborns to checkerboard stimuli of 55 seconds when the stimuli are presented for 60-second trials. Stechler and Latz (1966) report that two out of the three infants they studied intensively showed extreme periods of fixation when the duration of trials was not limited, with one child looking at a partially disorganized face stimulus for 35 minutes on the 10th day of life, and a second child looking at a bull's-eye pattern uninterruptedly for 52 minutes. Stechler and Latz also report that these long periods of looking are terminated by strong distress, and they have labeled the phenomenon as "obligatory attention."

Tennes, Emde, Kisley, and Metcalf (1972) report infants' reaction to bull's-eye and striped stimuli. They report obligatory attention between 4–5 and 8 weeks of age with an initial reduction of activity (of 10–30 seconds) followed by increased activity and fussiness, terminating in hard crying and the infant's turning away from the stimulus and/or closing the eyes. They report that during prolonged fixations, "The infant may glance away for one or two seconds, but returns his gaze spontaneously, as if compelled to look at the target or as if 'stimulus bound' " (p. 16).

Finally, Cohen (1976) reports on the reactions of 14-week-old infants to pictures of adult male faces: "It may well be that the reason they have longer fixation times is that they have difficulty releasing their attention from the visual stimulus. We get the subjective impression when observing some of these infants that they look intently for a while, then become increasingly agitated with their eyes still glued to the pattern, and finally avert their gaze in an inconsistent manner. It is almost as if they wanted to turn away earlier but couldn't" (p. 235).

Certainly, sustained orienting in young infants, at least as elicited with some visual stimuli, shows little of the behavioral concomitants of "preference" usually associated with sustained orienting in adults.

The powerful controlling influence of externally presented stimuli over infant eye movements via exogenous pathways, and the difficulty the newborn has in breaking contact with visual stimuli, could form the same general picture. The problem of the infant seems to be to bring various peripheral mechanisms, such as the hand, the head, and the eye under endogenous control via the exercise of as yet incomplete central mechanisms. This view of infants' developing gradual voluntary control of their own behaving systems is not new. Bruner (1968) has described the course of achievement of control over sucking and looking in much the same way.

What seems to have been poorly understood in the literature is that the oculomotor system also must be brought under volitional control of already existing attentional mechanisms. Movement of the eyes does not always directly reflect attention. Rather, the infant goes through a period in which attention must come to exercise control of eye movements in the same way it will later exercise control of head and hand movement.

We do not believe our evidence should be used to refute advances of the last 20 years or to return to a blind acceptance of a noncognitive or reflexive view of infancy. Rather, increased experimental understanding of the component processes of attention may allow us better use of the infant as a model for the study of the development and coordination of separate neural systems. We believe it is improper either to argue that the infant is conscious or unconscious. It is important rather to look at the orchestration of the subcomponents that make up consciousness in the adult in hopes of understanding its developmental substrate.

We (Posner & Cohen, 1980) have tried to work out the functional organization of eye, hand, and attention in adults. The experience of the infant seems ideal for furthering our understanding in simplest form of how these functional links develop.

Cross-Modal Stimulation

Few issues in the experimental psychology of perception are more difficult and poorly understood than how cross-modality information is coordinated. So much of our present knowledge is dependent upon understanding the organization of specific sensory systems that the problem of the organization of our perceptual world across the modalities of touch, sight, and sound seems vitually insurmountable. There is much current research on cross-modal stimulation in infancy; we argue that the development of cross-modal integration in the infant may be illuminated by adult findings.

Work in adult information processing (Posner, Nissen, & Klein, 1976) suggests that the simplest level of coordination between sensory modalities depends upon the temporal correspondence of the signals. If an adult is asked to perform a visual-processing task, the occurrence of an irrelevant auditory signal either shortly before or shortly after the occurrence of a visual signal will produce marked improvement in the speed of processing (intersensory facilitation). We now know (Nickerson, 1973; Posner, Nissen, & Klein, 1976) that improvement in visual performance occasioned by a simultaneous auditory event does not represent a very profound sense of coordination between the two modalities. Rather, the rapid processing of auditory events, together with their ability to effect changes in alertness, produces an improvement in speed and a reduction in accuracy that is the sign of a change in the availability of central processing mechanisms to the expected visual event. The argument from the adult data has been that one cannot avoid the change in alertness automatically induced by the auditory signal. An increase of alertness brings to the visual modality a more rapid attentional response. There is no similar improvement in auditory reaction time when a visual stimulus is presented either coincident with, or even somewhat before, the presentation of the auditory stimulus (Posner, Nissen, & Klein, 1976).

This powerful control of auditory stimuli over alerting contrasts with the relative prominence of vision for control of awareness. In many literatures, it has been shown that visual stimuli tend to dominate auditory and tactile stimuli for entry into conscious awareness (Klein, 1977; Posner, Nissen, & Klein, 1976). This bias toward vision has been shown in a particularly striking way in simple bimodal information-processing tasks (Colavita, 1974; Colavita & Weisberg, 1978; Egeth & Sager, 1978; Klein, 1977). In these tasks, subjects are asked to respond with one key if a stimulus is auditory, and another if a stimulus is visual. They are led to believe that only a single stimulus will occur on any given trial. On a minority of trials, stimuli from both modalities are presented simultaneously. In this case, it has been shown repeatedly that subjects will tend to respond to the visual stimulus, and they may be completely unaware of the auditory event. Similar findings also occur for visual-tactile pairs (Jordan, 1972; Klein, 1977).

One is tempted to link the powerful automatic alerting effects of auditory and tactile stimuli (see also Posner, 1978, chap. 7) to the prominence of visual stimuli over the conscious awareness of subjects. Such a correlation could have two directions of causation. It is possible that vision originally has a deficient alerting capability and that this makes it necessary for subjects to learn to direct their attention to vision. Thus vision dominates the conscious attention of the subject because the subject learns to connect the attentional system to vision. It is also possible that causation goes in the other direction. An attentional bias toward vision would make it unnecessary for vision to retain the strong connections to alerting mechanisms that other modalities have.

It is in the hope of determining the direction of causation that the infant case is of interest. If, as we have argued (Posner, 1978), it is possible to link alerting effects with control of conscious awareness, one ought to find the relevant learning taking place in the early months of life. Indeed there are important ideas about the role of vision and audition in the human newborn that may provide the needed links. First, the cortical visual system matures earlier in the newborn than the cortical projections of the auditory system (see Trevarthen, 1979). Second, there is evidence of an alerting effect for auditory stimuli in the newborn. Newborns show some modification of visual scanning patterns when auditory stimuli are presented (Mendelson & Haith, 1976), but these modifications seem to be a result of differences in the alertness of the organism in the presence of auditory stimuli. Thus significantly greater eye opening and more active scanning patterns occur during auditory stimulation than without it. There is also a small but significant tendency for the direction of the auditory stimulus to influence the scan patterns. However, the directional influence of auditory stimuli over scanning appears to be very much less in the newborn and young infant than the directional control of visual stimuli (Mendelson & Haith, 1976). The presence at birth of a well-developed oculomotor system allows the infant in the early months to develop a close coordination between the presentation of visual stimuli and orienting of covert mechanisms of spatial attention. Thus it may not be surprising that vision tends to dominate the spatial environment not only during the early months of life but even during adulthood, where auditory and tactile stimuli are frequently displaced toward the location of what appears to be the relevant visual information (Morais & Bertelson, 1973). Even auditory localization seems to depend a good deal upon the visual function, since it deteriorates greatly when vision is not allowed or when vision is interrupted in some way. In short, the infant data suggest that attention could develop a special affinity for the visual sense in the early months of life.

Summary

We have related three aspects of attention and sensory systems in the newborn to those of adults. Each forges potential links between the early experience of the newborn and adult performance. First, the newborn, like the adult, shows a very strong bias in the eye movement system toward the temporal visual field of the monocular eye. The size of this bias cannot be accounted for either in the newborn or in the adult by any general advantage of visual information from the temporal field on perception. Rather it is specific to the control of exogenous stimuli over the eye movements of the organism. While this phenomenon is present in the infant when only a single visual stimulus is presented, in the adult it seems to require bilateral conflict before the bias can be observed.

Secondly, the infant seems to show difficulty in disengaging visual stimuli, even when an analysis of its emotional state suggests it is important to do so. We argue that this difficulty in disengagement indicates the necessity of the baby to gain control of the eye movement system via central attentional routines. Although the newborn does show powerful autonomous scanning patterns even in the dark, these do not seem to be easily under the access of voluntary control until the child learns to bring a functional relationship between the eye movement system and attention.

Finally, there are influences of other modalities upon the visual scanning of the newborn. These influences seem related to alerting or arousal effects. One hypothesis is that as infants bring the oculomotor system under voluntary control, they also allocate attention to the visual system. In the adult, this is reflected in the tendency to commit attention to vision in the absence of competing stimulation.

III. THE DEVELOPMENT OF INTERNAL CONTROL MECHANISMS

In a recent review of the literature on infant development, Emde and Robinson (1978) identify the period of time of about 2 months as being critically important in the development of the child's internal control over sensory stimulation. They argue:

> Before two months, classical avoidance conditioning is very difficult and the effects of operant conditioning short lived. After two months this is not the case. Similarly, it is difficult if not impossible to establish habituation before two months whereas after that time, experimental habituation has been established in auditory and visual modalities in a number of carefully controlled studies. Certainly learning through active adaptation and through reciprocal interaction takes place before two months. But after that time, its modes and mechanisms evidence a shift in organization. In terms of perception, more studies need to be done after the newborn period. However, substantial evidence already exists for a shift to perceptual organization during the second month. (p. 75)

Other aspects of the 2-month shift identified by Emde and his associates (Emde, Gaensbauer, & Harmon, 1976) include a marked decrease in quiet sleep and in activation of transitory reflexes. There is also a decrease in fussiness and an increase in smiling to visual stimuli during the 2–3-month period. Emde et al. (1976) also note changes in visual scanning patterns with greater fixation of internal features.

In this section, we seek not so much to document the two-month shift as being a critical one in the infant's life, but rather to examine increasing internal control by the infant in light of information about the nature of adult memory and the relationship between memory and components of attention.

Habituation

Habituation is defined as the waning of a response to a stimulus with repeated presentation (Thompson & Spencer, 1966). Much of what we know about the cognitive capacities of the infant rests upon the study of habituation in one or another form. However, there has been a great deal of confusion in the infant literature because waning of response may depend upon a number of different neural systems, any of which may habituate. Moreover, the definition of habituation as waning of response does not take into account skills that might be required to meet the criterion of habituation imposed by a given paradigm.

Habituation has been demonstrated reliably as far down in the animal kingdom as the giant sea slug aplysia (Kandel, 1976). The simple form of habituation found in aplysia involves a reduction of the effect of a stimulus on ongoing natural behavior. It might be expected that this type of habituation would be evidenced in newborns, and such habituation has been demonstrated for olfactory stimuli (Engen, Lipsitt, & Kaye, 1963; Engen & Lipsitt, 1965). There is little evidence, however, that such habituation involves the central mechanism of attention, since it can be shown even when infants are asleep.

A somewhat more complex paradigm for studying habituation involves presenting a stimulus repeatedly and observing the organism's "interest" in the stimulus by the degree to which it fixates the stimulus event. There has been evidence that newborns can habituate in this situation (Friedman, 1972), but that habituation is rather slow and sometimes not very stable. We have discussed this paradigm above in dealing with oculomotor orienting and visual capture. The argument that central attention is being habituated in this paradigm rests upon the assumption that the position of the eyes directly represents the direction of attention.

A third habituation paradigm is the one Fantz (1965) used to demonstrate visual preference in young infants. In this case, two stimuli are presented at once. One gauges the waning of interest in one stimulus (the repeated one) by looking at the increase in time of fixating the more novel stimulus. This habituation does not seem to occur before two months of age. It requires the infant to have sufficient control of the eye movement system to direct eye movements at one of the two stimuli.

The operational definition of habituation as the waning of response tends to obscure both the variety of skills that may be studied by the habituation procedure and the mechanisms that may be involved. Investigators in the infant literature have often identified any habituation in a visual scanning paradigm as necessarily a habituation of "attention." Since habituation can be demonstrated in aplysia or in the spinal cat, it is obviously not very useful to attribute any waning of response to attention.

In the adult literature there have been some efforts to separate the nature of the internal processes undergoing habituation. It is well established that exposure to an intense visual stimulus can raise the threshold and thus reduce the responsiveness to a similar stimulus falling upon the same retinal position (Blakemore & Campbell, 1969). This form of habituation appears to affect mainly sensory pathways, since it does not extend to new retinal positions (Sekuler, 1974). Similarly, repetition of the same phoneme will often affect its perception (Eimas & Corbit, 1973), but this effect is more likely to occur in acoustic, not phonetic, pathways (Sawusch & Jusczyk, in press). Efforts to establish habituation of higher levels of input pathways have not been very successful, although it seems likely that some form of habituation of these systems is possible (see Posner, 1978, for a review). The whole area of habituation of input pathways is under very intensive study.

There is very good evidence that continued repetition of a stimulus reduces the alertness of the organism (Mackworth, 1969). Alertness shifts may represent a change in state affecting all input stimuli—as though the subject has gone to sleep. It is also possible to suppose that continued repetition of a stimulus habituates the specific alerting pathways for that specific event, without changing the overall alertness of the subject (Mackworth, 1969).

Finally, there is evidence of a rather habituation-like process involved in the storage of repeated items. A stimulus presented twice in succession is not stored as well as one whose presentation is spaced. This spacing effect has been demonstrated with a variety of materials (Hintzman, 1976) and in infants as well as adults (Cornel, 1979).

The adult literature provides abundant evidence that the study of habituation is complex and involves a number of internal mechanisms, each of which may undergo habituation at very different rates and under differing input conditions. The complexity of the question of what habituates indicates that careful experimental studies will be necessary to tease apart these components in children.

One effort to do this has been in studies designed to separate habituation of general state from specific pathways (Kraut, 1978). The studies distinguish between a pathway activation effect specific to a given stimulus and general alerting that would effect all stimuli. The idea is that repeated presentation of a stimulus habituates its alerting capability, but does not habituate activation of specific internal codes representing the stimulus. It has been shown with children that repeated presentation of a stimulus such as a colored light, buzzer, or geometrical form increases its reaction time in comparison with the same stimulus when novel. Kraut (1978) used 6-year-old children as subjects. In his choice reaction time task they responded with one key to a red circle and another to a blue circle. Before the reaction time test, children were familiarized by repeated presentation of one stimulus or the other. The novel stimulus produced faster reaction times than did the familiarized stimulus. Kraut reasoned that this effect might be due to habituation of the alerting response to the familiarized stimulus. He attempted to separate the alerting response from pathway activation by using either the familiarized stimulus or a novel one as a warning stimulus in a reaction time task requiring response to an imperative event. He found responding to the imperative slower when the familiarized stimulus was used as a warning signal than when a novel stimulus was used. When a strong neutral warning signal was used in a choice reaction time task between a familiarized and a novel stimulus, the familiarized stimulus was actually responded to more rapidly than the novel stimulus. He argues that the alerting component of attention is susceptible to rapid habituation by the familiarization procedure, but that the pathway activation component is not.

These findings provide a clarification of how habituation may work in the newborn. The dominant view currently stems from the orienting reflex and does not distinguish between different internal mechanisms responsible for habituation. Often habituation is confused with the learning involved in recognition or attaching meaning to the stimuli. If we distinguish pathways producing stimulus recognition from alerting pathways, habituation in the infant can be viewed as a reduction in the flow of information from the recognition pathway into the alerting system. Input is still processed along the recognition pathway, but its failure to activate the alerting system reduces the availability of the central processor and hence of nonhabitual responses. The lowered level of alerting produced by repeated stimuli often leads to sleep. This is not to deny the possibility of habituation in the recognition pathway as well, but evidence of this form of habituation in the adult has been rather weak (see Posner, 1978, chap. 4, for a review).

Work on the ontogeny of habituation should examine various components of attention if a coherent view of the achievements of the newborn is to be developed. The importance of the habituation procedure in understanding higher level cognitive processes in babies (e.g., in the study of speech perception, visual constancies, and other perceptual phenomena) suggests the importance of a detailed account of processes involved in habituation. Insofar as process accounts are possible based on current data, there seems to be continuity between habituation components of attention in adults and in children.

Generic Memory

In understanding the ontogeny of internal control, it is important to note the increasing role of internal memory systems in the interpretation of stimuli. In examining the infant, we adopted as a model system spatial attention, which demands relatively little learning to interpret stimulus events. The study of internal control involves the development of recognition systems that allow the infant to interpret the world. In the first section of the paper, we outlined the concept of pathway activation. In the last several years, our ability to understand the evolution, development, and organization of internal storage systems has been greatly expanded. We do not wish to argue that the particular structures we will talk about exhaust the structures of generic memory, but they do provide important links between our understanding of concepts and categories in development.

The idea that categories may be represented by prototypical instances stored from past experience (Posner & Keele, 1968; Rosch & Lloyd, 1979) has had spectacular development in the last several years. It is now known that organisms as primitive as the pigeon (Cerella, 1979) do very well at forming generic categories, allowing them to recognize instances (e.g., of leaves or trees) that they never before experienced. The encoding of experience in terms of prototypical representations apparently extends throughout the animal kingdom and helps us understand the continuity of generic memory between children and adults. While schooling allows children and adults to develop dimensional analyses of categories, there is abundant evidence that the basic organization of categories in the mind of the adult is often in terms of prototypical instances. This categorization makes it easy to recognize instances that fit well with the prototype, but much more difficult to deal with those distant from it. It accounts for the relative ease of learning categories concerning objects where instances of the same category are perceptually similar in comparison to the difficulty or impossibility of more abstract learning where instances of the category have no basic similarity.

As Strauss (1979) recently put it:

> Children at a young age are aware of many conceptual categories that exist in the world. For example, even a preverbal 11- or 12-month old infant responds in a behaviorally appropriate manner to categories such as food, toys, and people. But how does a young child initially learn this information about categories? Since knowledge of few categories is specifically and formally taught, a child must somehow abstract this knowledge from experience with the exemplars of the categories. Yet, despite the importance of this basic cognitive developmental process, not much is known about how young children and infants acquire this knowledge. (p. 618)

Strauss (1979) used habituation in 10-month-old infants to demonstrate their particular sensitivity to the prototype or average value of a set of faces shown during learning. Their sensitivity was so great that the prototype was responded to as more familiar than even a so-called modal face whose features had been shown three times more often during the learning process. Sensitivity of children and adults to prototypes provides something of a solution to the ancient problem of how the mind represents universals. At least some types of universals are represented, not as abstract categories, but as concrete prototypes that in turn stand for the category.

The discovery that infants represent their world in terms of prototypes provides a challenging possibility for tests of a hypothesis developed by Haith (1978) on the relationship between current stimulation and attention. Haith argues that newborn visual scanning obeys the principle of maximizing neural firing. The idea is that the infant's eyes are drawn to that part of the visual field showing the maximum contour density and thus producing in the nervous system the strongest electrical responses. This interpretation, Haith argues, accommodates a wide variety of findings, such as scanning of newborns in darkness and patternless fields, fixation in crossing of contours, early preference for contour density and high contrast stimuli, and later development of accommodation and binocular fixation. Bornstein (1981) has used the same idea to account for not only infants' scanning of checkerboard patterns but also their color preference. Prototypical colors are maximally effective in producing electrical activity and are also preferred by the infant.

An intriguing hypothesis based on Haith's idea is to suppose that as complex internal pathways having to do with the meaning or significance of stimuli are developed, the child's attention will be attracted to those external events that activate internal codes most strongly. Bornstein (1981) has suggested that this will be the prototype of categories, since prototypical stimuli are most successful in activating the class. An older idea (Oldfield, 1954) is that stimuli discrepant from prototypes and thus somewhat surprising will be optimal for producing orienting of attention. These ideas may not be mutually exclusive, since optimal activation may differ with amount of repetition or degree of expectancy. The general idea that the level of pathway activation influences orienting of attention has the advantage of supposing that other things being equal, the principles Haith (1978) proposes to govern the direction of attention to sensory events also guide its relationship to the semantic memory system. The vagueness of these theoretical ideas makes them difficult to evaluate, but a strategy of studying orienting of attention to semantic structure in infants and adults might provide a basis for choice.

One example of this strategy involves the role of emotion in the orienting of attention. For adults, words stored within a single cognitive structure tend to pool their affective content, making affective information more readily available when that category is accessed (Posner & Snyder, 1975). For example, the number of words presented on a list slows the time to accept or reject a word as having been on the list; but if all the words are positive in affect, it becomes increasingly efficient to reject a negative word as a candidate. As list size grows, the affect is pooled and can be used to reject instances that don't fit the pooled impression. There is some evidence that such affective information can become available even when the cognitive content is not (Wilson & Zajonc, 1980). If this kind of cognitive organization is a feature of memory, it should be possible to explore whether attention is drawn to structures linked to positive affect and repelled by those where affect is negative. Such an outcome might serve to explain the unconscious emotion effects that have so absorbed investigators of childhood memories who take a psychoanalytic perspective.

Aspects of Self-Recognition

Of the categories acquired in childhood, one of the most important is the concept of the self. The idea that one somehow abstracts from ongoing behavior an enduring self is a basis for much psychological theory. Developmental psychology has been enriched by ideas about how the child comes to understand and thereby regulate its own perception, learning, and memory (metacognition). Metacognition clearly presupposes a developing concept of the self, but studies of metacognition have not generally been based on any evolutionary or developmental thinking about the self. Such thinking is beginning to develop from experiments dealing with the behavior of primates and other organisms in front of mirrors. Gallup (1979) has reported an important operational definition of self-awareness based on the ability of the organism to recognize itself in a mirror. Rather surprisingly, Gallup shows that this skill does not separate the human from infrahuman organisms, but rather seems to separate one group of primates, the monkeys, from another group, the great apes. Extensive experimentation with monkeys and apes in front of mirrors has suggested that with the exception of humans and great apes, other primates fail to exhibit self-recognition, even after extended exposure. These experiments suggest that a particular development in brain evolution produces the basis of metacognition, namely the recognition of the self as a unique entity that can be presented perceptually. Gallup's findings have been extended to the study of children (Lewis & Brooks-Gunn, 1979), with the result that children begin to respond to the self in a mirror as if confronted with another infant before 6 months of age, but do not show signs of self-recognition until much later, perhaps as late as 18–24 months of age.

The ability to deal with an organism seen in a mirror as a perceptual object to whom it is appropriate to initiate social behavior is a capacity which man and monkey share with many other organisms. Recognition of the self, however, appears to be restricted to the great apes and humans. Infants prior to 6 months of age are developing perceptual skills of awareness of the world around them, as we have discussed in the last section. During this period, they show social behavior toward mirrored objects. Evidence from the special self-recognition tests of grooming and cleaning Gallup has developed suggests that a self-recognition involves another level in the organism's development of attention, a level involving awareness of being aware (i.e., recognition of the self as a distinct entity who can represent the environment). This higher form of attention, which Bartlett (1932) referred to as turning around on one's own schema, is presumably a necessary condition for the development of theories of the mind, including one's own mind, that underlie metacognition.

Summary

Over the early months of life, the infant changes from an organism heavily driven by biological programs and exogenous stimulation to one with increasing internal control over its own peripheral mechanisms, such as eye movements, hand movements, and body movements. Although studies of habituation have been a tool for the analysis of that increased internal control, habituation itself may be seen as a developing process dependent upon the particular skills to be habituated. Studies of habituation need to be sensitive to the different internal mechanisms that may be reduced in efficiency with repeated exposure.

The study of the development of internal control in the infant must reflect changes in memory. The last several years have shown the importance of mental structures based on prototypes extracted from visual experience. If in fact prototypes serve a unique role in the nervous system, then the electrical activity generated by the activation of such prototypes may serve as the basis for linking the attention-attracting aspects of external and internal events in infancy to those found in the adult.

Of all the categories learned by the infant, perhaps the most crucial and the most difficult to understand is the category of the self. Recent results on the evolution of mind in monkeys and apes suggest that the ability to recognize the self evolves in phylogeny somewhere between the older monkeys and the newer apes. The ability for self-recognition develops slowly in the child, arising in the period from 18–24 months and forming the basis for children to develop theories of their minds and those of others. Thus metacognition would seem to depend upon the development of attentional mechanisms capable of self-awareness.

V. INDIVIDUAL DIFFERENCES AND DEVELOPMENT

The present section reverses the direction of our previous approach. Current work on adult individual differences in attentional processes is discussed in light of ideas arising from the study of individual differences in infants. As in previous sections, this section will be illustrative rather than comprehensive.

Approaches to Individual Differences

Until recently, individual differences in cognition have rarely been studied within an information-processing framework. The major historical approach to individual differences in cognition has been the psychometric tradition of intelligence and mental abilities testing. Developed originally to predict an individual's performance in school environments (Tyler, 1976), the study of intelligence has primarily followed a methodology involving comparisons among individuals on mental tests and on such criterion measures as school performance. The study of intelligence in the psychometric tradition has not been widely influenced by process theory. Theoretically inclined investigators have chiefly used factor analyses of item or test scores in an attempt to determine what might be the basic components or primary factors of intelligence.

Recently, there has been excitement about the possibility that students of information processing might provide a process theory for the study of individual differences that traditional psychometric research has lacked (Hunt, Frost, & Lunneborg, 1973; Tyler, 1978, chap. 12). It was hoped that by developing measures strongly grounded in cognitive theory and methodology, we might be able to come to a greater understanding of basic dimensions of variability in cognitive processes.

Although considerable work is being done in this area (Resnick, 1976), much of the new research continues to bear strong ties to the psychometric tradition. For example, Hunt and his associates (Hunt, 1978; Hunt, Frost, & Lunneborg, 1973; Hunt, Lunneborg, and Lewis, 1975) have related measures of information-processing parameters to scores of subjects on verbal and quantitative ability tests. They have found, for example, that the speed of retrieval of phonetic codes of letters and words relates to individual differences in verbal skill. Sternberg (1979) has decomposed intellectual tasks into subtasks and further into information-processing components and metacomponents. Componential scores are then related to overall scores through multiple regression techniques. The tasks he analyzes are chiefly taken from tests of reasoning (analogies, classifications, completions, and syllogisms).

In both Hunt and associates' and Sternberg's approaches, there is continued emphasis on interindividual comparisons based on ordering of subjects, even though the ultimate goal of the work is an understanding of individual differences in psychological processes. After extensively reviewing recent work on individual differences in information processing, Carroll (1978) has concluded that "we have made little progress, thus far, in identifying psychological processes, at least through individual differences research. In most of the individual differences research I have surveyed, it seems that wherever one tries to find a process, one really finds a trait" (p. 103).

Some researchers have attempted to approach processes more directly by deriving them from theories of attention. Keele and his associates (Keele, Neill, & de Lemos, 1978) have attempted to infer a common process of flexibility of attention from intercorrelations of flexibility measures derived from several different information-processing tasks. Flexibility is defined as the ease with which an individual switches from one expectation to another, and is measured in terms of reaction time costs and benefits on a priming task, a rare event task, an alternation task, and a dichotic listening task. It relates closely to the idea of orienting of covert attention outlined above. Correlations among scores were high enough to suggest that a process of covert orienting is involved in the tasks studied.

In contrast to positive results with measures attempting to assess a single attentional mechanism, studies seeking a single process in more complex skills have been less successful. For example, Hawkins, Rodriguez, and Reicher (1979) have explored the possibility that time sharing of tasks requiring attentional capacity might be a unitary dimension. In our framework, time-sharing ability corresponds to the operation of no single attentional mechanism. Rather, it depends on alertness, flexibility of orienting, covert attention capacity, and pathway processes. One might expect this function to lack unity. In an attempt to determine whether a unitary dimension was involved in time sharing of tasks, Hawkins et al. tested subjects in dual-task situations, varying input modality, output modality, and task difficulty. They found correlations among measures of time-sharing efficiency when tasks shared similar processing demands, but no correlations when the processing demands were relatively dissimilar. They concluded that time sharing tends to be relatively task-specific rather than being a single capacity.

A third major tradition studying individual differences in cognition is the area of cognitive styles. This tradition has evolved from the psychoanalytic (Gardner, Holzman, Klein, Linton, & Spence, 1959) and developmental (Witkin, Dyk, Faterson, Goodenough, & Karp, 1962) traditions. Cognitive controls studied by psychoanalytic investigators include *leveling-sharpening*, defined as differences in assimilation of stimuli to memory, with levelers not distinguishing between similar but nonidentical stimuli, and sharpeners heightening such distinctions; *scanning*, defined as width of attention deployment; and *constricted versus flexible control*, defined as capacity to shift from one to another mode of control. In Witkin and Goodenough's (1977) reworking of the field dependence-independence dimension, another attentional dimension is identified: the individual's reliance chiefly on internal (field-independent) versus external (field-dependent) stimuli in dealing with the environment, and the individual's mobility in switching orientation from one set of cues to the other.

Neither information-processing researchers nor students of cognitive styles have attempted to link their theoretical concepts or findings to underlying biological mechanisms. An alternative approach to the study of individual differences in adult cognition has attempted to derive research variables directly from hypothesized individual differences in the nervous system. Pavlov (1955) argued that individual variability might be expected in strength of excitatory processes, in the balance between excitation and inhibition (equilibrium), and in mobility versus inertness of the nervous system. Pavlov (1955), Teplov (1964), Nebylitsyn (1972), and other Soviet investigators have carried out extensive research on measures designed to assess each of these hypothesized nervous system characteristics. Most of the research to date has been carried out on the "strength" dimension, defined as the capacity of the nervous system to continue to respond to frequent or prolonged excitation. This theory has the problem discussed previously in connection with habituation techniques, namely, that it does not specify the level of analysis at which inhibition occurs.

Theories of introversion-extroversion as developed by H. J. Eysenck (1967) and Gray (1972) also refer to internal processes. Eysenck has proposed that given standard stimulating conditions, introverts will be more highly aroused than extroverts. This higher level of cortical excitation will result in relatively inhibited behavior in the introvert because of cortical control over more impulsive lower brain centers. There has been some attempt to link H. J. Eysenck's theory with information-processing concepts (Broadbent, 1971; M. Eysenck, 1977; Revelle, Humphreys, Simon, & Gilliland, 1980). For example, extroverts tend to begin faster on motor performance tasks, while introverts catch up over time and show fewer effects of fatigue (Wilson, Tunstall & Eysenck, 1971). However, the approach has not succeeded in providing detailed accounts of the organization of mental processes involved.

The attractive part of the psychobiological approach to individual differences appears to us to rest on its promising of information about the relative organization of internal mechanisms within an individual, rather than being merely a means to compare people on some attribute (e.g., intelligence) or some internal process (e.g., speed of orienting). If intraindividual differences in the structure of mechanisms can be combined with a detailed information-processing framework, we might be able to develop a more satisfying approach to the problem of individual behavior.

As a concrete example of this approach, consider the use of our framework to explain changes in information processing over the life-span (Posner, 1978, pp. 146–149). In tasks involving rapid response to simple linguistic stimuli, children and old people both tend to be relatively slow compared to normal adults. However, children tend to show high error rates coupled with slow performance, while the elderly tend to be slow, but more accurate than young adults. One analysis of this constellation of data supposes that the pathways analyzing input information are not yet well formed in young children. Young children are unable to rely on efficient pathways for distinguishing among stimulus events and formulating responses. On the other hand, elderly people have efficient analysis of input information, but may demonstrate slowing of covert orienting to activated pathways. Orienting to the activated pathway is slow, but, since it occurs after much automatic analysis is complete, tends to be accurate. Another example (Kraut, 1978; Schnur, Lubow, & Ben-Shalom, 1979) involves the relative sensitivity of children and adults to the alerting effects of input. Prefamiliarization with a stimulus reduces its effectiveness as an alerting cue for 6-year-old children, but increases the efficiency of the specific pathway for decoding that item (Kraut, 1978). For adults, prefamiliarization has small, if any, effects on performance (Schnur et al., 1979) presumably because the adult remains at a relatively high level of alertness throughout the testing session.

One difficulty in the application of our attentional framework to the problem of individual differences in adults is that adults' highly developed strategies for dealing with particular problems frequently obscure the underlying mechnisms. Moreover, the adult personality must represent a complex interaction between basic mental processes and the efforts a person makes to adapt to those processes through a lifetime of learning. Papousek (1979) has argued persuasively that this problem may be addressed by the use of young infants, who have a simpler learned response set. Escalona (1968) emphasized the primacy of infant temperament research in the title of her book *The Roots of Individuality*. Studying the protosystems that will form the base for later individual differences in cognitive function allows us to consider an organism in the process of developing its first strategies rather than one having had years of experience with them. It allows us to consider an organism relatively uninstructed about the proper expression or repression of emotion in reaction to stimulation. This is not to discount the possibility that neuromaturational changes will be related to major changes in behavior during the early years; it does suggest that we can learn about the sources of individuality by studying the earliest concomitants of attention and following the course of their development as strategies for dealing with stimulation are added.

Most work on individual differences in infancy has been done within the area of temperament. Temperament is defined as constitutional differences in reactivity and self-regulation. "Constitutional" refers to the relatively enduring biological makeup of the individual influenced over time by the interaction of heredity, experience, and maturation. Temperament is closely associated with the biology of the organism, and can be appropriately applied to other species (Diamond, 1974), as well as to the study of very young human beings.

Infant temperament has been studied in several ways. One approach, inspired by the early interview work of Thomas, Chess, and their associates (Thomas, Chess, Birch, Hertzig, & Korn, 1963; Thomas, Chess, & Birch, 1968) involves use of caretakers as informants about their infant's reactions and stimulus-seeking or stimulus-avoiding behaviors (Bates, Bennett, & Lounsbury, 1979; Carey, 1970; Carey & McDevitt, 1978; Pederson, Anderson, & Cain, 1976; Rothbart, Furby, Kelly, & Hamilton, 1977). Since the infant's caretakers observe it closely over an extended period of time, far longer than we are able to observe in laboratory or home observation, they can be excellent informants to the extent that response biases and distortions of memory may be overcome. One way of attempting to overcome these biases is to ask parents about the occurrence of specific concrete events within a specified recent time period. In doing so, we can take advantage of adults as recorders of frequency information (Hasher & Zacks, 1979) and as integrators of information concerning the infant. It is not necessary that the observer be able to compare an infant's behavior with that of other infants, for example, agreeing with the statement "The infant is very active." These comparisons may be made by the investigator from the relative-frequency information offered by the caretaker.

Caretaker scales show low to moderate levels of agreement between mothers and fathers or babysitters and considerable stability for some scales (Rothbart, 1980; Rothbart & Derryberry, in press-b); more global caretaker scales show low but significant correlations between home observations and caretaker ratings (Bates et al., 1979).

A second source of information about infant temperament involves the use of home observation of infant reactions and self-regulatory behaviors. Observational codes are developed for the infant's temperament-related behaviors and relevant environmental events, and these codes are recorded sequentially over a limited observation period. During this observation period, caretaker and infant may follow their usual daily routine, or specific kinds of interaction may be requested by the observer (e.g., mother-infant play, a diaper change). Temperament measures involve frequency or duration of infant reactions over a given period of time or their percentage of occurrence within a given stimulus situation (e.g., reactions to possible fear-inducing stimuli). Home observations are limited by the expense of placing observers in the home for extended periods, by the caretakers' and infants' response to the presence of the observer, and by the fact that observers are limited in the number of codes they can accurately record within a short period of time. To date, home observation has been used chiefly as a source of validation information in connection with caretaker report (Bates et. al., 1979; Rothbart, 1980), rather than as an independent source of information about temperament.

Finally, in an attempt to standardize stimuli presented to infants, recognizing that infants may be receiving widely varying patterns of stimulation in the home, laboratory observations have been made of infant reactions to a set of stimulus presentations (Birns, Barten, & Bridger, 1969; Escalona, 1968).

As part of a larger project on infant temperament (Rothbart & Derryberry, in press-b), we have had the opportunity to observe the behavior of 3–12-month-old infants in a standard laboratory environment. Although the data have not been fully analyzed, several observations seem to relate to differences among infants, even as young as 3 months of age, in their response to stimulation.

According to our framework for the analysis of attention, a stimulus event gives rise to a complex of internal events we have called alerting, orienting, detecting, and pathway activation. We believe that the patterning of these events provides basic characteristics of responsivity to the environment. From the earliest moments of life, differences in tonic alertness are apparent (Brazelton, 1973). The effectiveness of stimuli in causing orienting and in producing phasic changes in alertness and motor, vocal, and emotional reactions forms the basis for the earliest distinctions among infants. Some infants seem almost immediately able to sustain orienting into an ongoing act producing extended interaction with the environmental objects. Others are dominated by the tendency of reorienting to each new event in the external and internal world. Still others show low thresholds for defensive responses, resulting in termination of contact with the stimulus objects.

In our laboratory observations, presentation of a stimulus such as a three-dimensional object or a colored-light and sound display to 3-month-old infants results at the outset in a response including arrest of body movements, heart rate deceleration, and orientation of the sense organs toward the source of stimulation.

If attention to the stimulus is sustained over time, we observe in some infants changes in motor activity and emotional and vocal expressions. Frequently body movement is increased, followed by changes in facial expression and occurrence of vocalization. There is individual variability in the precise channels involved in this reaction. Some infants show extended overt orienting, with intent facial expressions but little body movement. Others show extensive motor reactions, sometimes accompanied with vocalization. Some other infants show a reaction to the same object or colored-light and sound display that begins with overt orienting and terminates in distress. Although initial heart rate deceleration and orienting to the stimulus occur, with repeated or sustained presentations the infant's facial expressions become more and more negative as the heart rate function levels off or begins to accelerate; the infant looks away from the stimulus from time to time and may suck on hand or fingers for self-soothing. Such a sequence may terminate in the infant's crying, with eyes closed and loud wailing, resulting in apparent withdrawal of the infant's attention from the external environment.

In our laboratory observations, we have noted that an orienting reaction may soothe the infant who has become distressed. As the infant's accelerating heart rate takes on a decelerating pattern in response to a new stimulus presentation, we see the infant's facial expression and body tension relaxing. Caretakers probably take advantage of this effect by presenting a distressed child with a distracting stimulus (e.g., an object or the caretaker's own voice or face). Older infants may similarly disengage their attention from a highly amusing stimulus and refocus on a less arousing or more comforting object (Tennes et al., 1972).

We would hypothesize that the individual differences observed in infants' sustained attentional reactions are related to differences in nervous system sensitivity and to the response channels most automatically activated in a given infant. Infants who show distress more rapidly are either infants who are more generally sensitive or whose sympathetic distress reactions are more easily activated. Individual variability in the temporal dimension of the infant's reaction is also important: some infants seem to build rapidly to a high peak of motor and vocal excitement and recover quickly, while others become excited more slowly, peak at lower levels, and recover more slowly. As we have mentioned, infants also differ in the channels through which they express reactivity: some chiefly vocal, others motoric as well as vocal, and some chiefly through motor tension.

What we have described relates almost entirely to individual patterns of control of exogenous stimuli in infants. Clearly the temporal organization and vigor of the orienting, alerting, and detection systems provide considerable scope for patterns of temperament even at the earliest ages. However, these reactions are accompanied by development of routines for handling stimuli and methods of self-regulation.

Self-regulatory variables studied in infants include both approach-withdrawal and attentional processes. We argue that once having achieved sufficient internal control of orienting, an older infant uses it as a strategy to shift away from an arousing stimulus. This reorienting may initiate a recovery process that results in the child's ability to reengage the distressing stimulus. Attentional processes thus provide young infants with a major means of self-regulation. Even before the infant can physically approach or avoid an object through directed reaching or crawling, the older infant can orient toward or away from stimulus objects in such a way that reactivity is initiated (in the visual modality by looking toward), enhanced (by looking intently), maintained (through extended orienting), reduced (through gaze aversions), or terminated (by looking away) (Rothbart & Derryberry, in press-a).

Temporal aspects of the infant's reactivity should interact with the development of self-regulation. Infants who become excited or distressed slowly may have more time to practice self-regulatory behaviors than infants whose distress builds very rapidly. Infants who shift overt orientation more radily may also learn self-regulatory techniques more easily with possibly more frequent experiences of being soothed by having attention redirected.

We have described a series of reactions in the infant corresponding to alerting and overt orienting. Detecting is difficult to assess in the infant, since we cannot verbally instruct the infant to perform arbitrary responses to the presence of a given stimulus, and infants cannot verbally report to us about what they are experiencing. Pathway activation, however, becomes increasingly important in affecting the infant's responsivity and self-regulation.

After the first two months infants' patterns of response become increasingly dominated by what they have learned about certain stimuli. As internal coding systems for dealing with familiar objects are developed, these pathways become related to infant temperament.

In the course of development, we can expect that different individuals will become differentially reactive to a given event, not only on the basis of their previously demonstrated reactivity but also on the basis of what they know and expect. Highly familiar stimuli will lead to less orienting than will more novel stimuli (Cohen, 1976). Stimuli associated with negative consequences may lead to withdrawal (Bronson, 1978), while stimuli associated with positive consequences may lead to excited approach. In addition, learned strategies for the use of attention in problem solving and task completion will result in different patterns of attention given a particular task (Brown & Deloache, 1978). Additional developmental changes might be expected in which behaviors will require effortful processing and, therefore, "limited capacity" attention.

One way of demonstrating a "limited capacity" effect is noting the extent to which one response interferes with the performance of another response. Bruner (1968) describes the time course of the infant's achievement of control over sucking and looking as follows:

> One can summarize the relation between sucking and looking by noting that it goes through three phases in its growth. The first is suppression of one by the other—and mostly it is looking that suppresses sucking. The second phase is simple succession of sucking and looking organization by alternation. The third phase is place holding in which the two acts go on, with one in reduced form that is sufficient for easy resumption while the other goes on in full operation (p. 21–22)

Bruner gives similar descriptions of the development of visually guided reaching.

Even these few considerations of attentional development should point up some of the complexities involved in treatment of individual differences in attentional processes among adults. Differences among individuals in experiences, knowledge base, and deployment of strategies, as well as in motivation to perform a task, will influence results on a given task. While it may be possible to find some stability across age in attentional characteristics, insights into the basic structure of individual differences in attention do not seem possible from such an approach.

What directions might then be taken by researchers working with adults? First, efforts should be made to identify basic attentional processes that will generalize across different task domains. These processes are likely to be closely related to biological mechanisms. To some extent, such attentional mechanisms have been the focus of previous investigation; for example, there is evidence that speed of orienting to internal and external events is correlated over a wide variety of tasks (Keele et al., 1978). In studies of pathway activation, there have been repeated findings that time to access phonetic codes correlates over very different task situations (e.g., the correlation of verbal abilities scores with performance on visual letter matching and understanding artificial speech). It has also been shown that the ability to form visual images correlates with perceptual thresholds (Paivio & Ernest, 1971) and that detection of signals in noise in different modalities is correlated across subjects (Rao, 1978). These findings contrast with frequent failures to find such correlations with components that are less likely to reflect underlying mechanisms.

Studies using correlation across individuals alone will not provide an adequate framework for understanding attentional differences, however. In order to understand the processes underlying individual differences, it will be necessary to study different patterns of interrelationship of attentional mechanisms within a given individual. An exmple of this approach is in the study of reading (Baron & Strawson, 1976). In activating semantic pathways, normal individuals can obtain the meaning of words from either a phonetic or visual code. A few individuals, however, rely almost entirely on either the phonetic or the visual code. One of these groups shows dominance of visual over phonetic analysis, performing well in identifying spelling errors but poorly at using phonetic information to judge whether a nonsense string of letters sounds like a word. These readers have great difficulty reading mixed-case words, but have no problem reading words that do not follow the phonetic rules of English. They may be fast or slow overall, but they show a distinctive balance between two internal pathways for achieving meaning.

In a similar way some brain injuries may be seen as upsetting the balance between opposed internal mechanisms. Kinsbourne (1975) argues that inattention to one side of space produced by lesions in one hemisphere is due to imbalance in the mechanisms that control directional orienting, so that both covert attention and eye movements are biased to the side of the lesion. He argues that even in normal subjects activation of one hemisphere can unbalance orienting, producing a bias toward the side of space opposite the activated hemisphere. A change in the balance of internal mechanisms has been proposed to describe cognitive deficits in normal aging (Hines & Posner, 1976). In this case it has been argued that automatic pathway-activation processes are slowed to a smaller degree than the mechanisms subserving orienting and detecting, producing the stereotyped mental caution (slow but accurate) often found in the elderly.

It seems likely that smaller and more subtle differences in the relative efficiency of internal mechanisms form enduring aspects of normal personlity. An efficient orienting system could produce rapid switching between external and internal events. High levels of alertness associated with a strong ability to focus the central systems on a single topic may give us a personality dominated by intense preoccupation and concentration. The literature abounds with dichotomies and taxonomies of individual types. It would be easy but not productive to take time to translate them into the language of internal attentional systems.

We believe the best approach to formulating likely taxonomies lies in the first year of life, when the mechanisms of attention are developing. The use of a systematic information-processing framework for identifying individual differences in attentional mechanisms in infants should allow the testing of proposed taxonomies in normal adults. In this way, insights from infancy research may provide a means for predicting basic cognitive styles in adults. Such an approach has the promise of linking the mechanisms of attention in infancy with the subtle performances a lifetime of learning produces in normal adults. Even if adult personality does not ultimately lend itself to categorization, the study of how individuals develop strategies adapted to their own attentional mechanisms may provide the basis for a more cognitive approach to idiographic biographical analysis.

Summary

Studies of individual differences performed within an information processing framework have stressed interindividual comparisons of subjects on complex cognitive characteristics such as verbal ability.

We suggest that adult individual-differences research might profit by examining variables found to characterize individual differences in infant attention. These variables have chiefly been studied by temperament researchers focusing upon individual constitutional differences in reactivity and self-regulation.

Researchers of individual differences in adults should attempt to (a) identify basic attentional mechanisms that will generalize across task domains, and (b) assess the interrelations between mechanisms. Patterns of interrelations of internal mechanisms may show stability over time.

VI. SUMMARY AND CONCLUSIONS

This paper was begun with the hope of finding links between the study of early child development and our current understanding of attentional mechanisms in the adult. We had very little idea of the specific directions needed to meet our goal when we began our inquiry.

We have arrived at the conviction that current work in adult attention has important implications for infant research. The data on spatial attention in normal adults and alert animals indicate that there are specific isolable mechanisms underlying attentional processes. Two of these separate mechanisms are the systems for control of eye movements and for the movement of attention. This separation of the mechanisms of eye movements and of covert visual attention in adults makes it reasonable to view the infant as having an eye movement system heavily under exogenous control, and with less voluntary control over direction of gaze than is implied by research equating direction of gaze with attention to or preference for a given stimulus. In this view, the infant may be seen as learning to coordinate the eye movement and attention systems over the early months of life.

A second example in which adult findings have implications for infant research is in the study of habituation. While research on infant habituation has been successful in exploring aspects of the infant mind, the operational definition of habituation as waning of behavior is not precise enough to further our understanding of the early development of internal mechanisms. Examination of the adult literature on habituation of internal pathways, alertness, memory storage, and orienting will be necessary if infant researchers are to separate the mechanisms underlying attention for careful study. Some studies in older children have already indicated that repetition of a stimulus reduces its alerting capability without reducing activation of recognition systems. This result suggests methods for using habituation to separate attentional mechanisms in the infant.

We believe that the period of infancy provides the potential for identifying enduring biological properties of human beings. Studies of infant temperament indicate that patterns of individual behavior emerge during the first months of life. Although we suspect that these patterns remain important throughout the life-span of the individual, correlational studies of adult behavior in complex situations seem poorly designed to uncover them. Instead, we must assess the relationship among internal mechanisms in the infant and then explore the extent of stability of these patterns during the first years of life. Adult studies also need to identify patterns of internal mechanisms and must develop tasks in which these patterns produce differentiable behaviors. It is detailed comparisons of differences among individuals in patterns of internal mechanisms that are most likely to allow for a life-span theory of individual differences in attention.

Our most general conclusion is that goals in both developmental and adult research may best be realized only if research in information processing is linked to biological mechanisms of attention.

For many years, reserchers in cognitive psychology have seen the establishment of links between information processing and physiological mechanisms as an eventual but remote goal. Recent advances in cognitive theory and the development of methods for studying physiological cognitive processes in humans have made realization of that goal more likely. The study of human development offers a special opportunity for furthering our understanding in this area.

REFERENCES

Arbib, M. A. *The metaphorical brain*. Wiley, N.Y.: 1972.

Baron, J., & Strawson, C. Use of orthographic and word specific knowledge in reading words aloud. *Journal of Experimental Psychology: Human Perception and Performance*, 1976, *2*, 386–393.

Bartlett, F. C. *Remembering*. Cambridge, England: The University Press, 1932.

Bates, J. E., Bennett, C. A., & Lounsbury, M. L. Measurement of infant difficultness. *Child Development*, 1979, *50*, 794–803.

Berlyne, D. E. Arousal and reinforcement. In D. Levine (Ed.), *Nebraska Symposium on Motivation 1967*. Lincoln: University of Nebraska Press, 1967.

Birns, B., Barten, S., & Bridger, W. Individual differences in temperamental characteristics of infants. *Transactions of the New York Academy of Sciences*, 1969, *31*, 1071–1082.

Blakemore, C., & Campbell, F. W. On the existence of neurons in the human visual system sensitive to the orientation and size of retinal images. *Journal of Physiology*, 1969, *203*, 237–267.

Boles, D. *The bilateral effect: Mechanisms for the advantage of bilateral over unilateral stimulus presentation in the production of visual field asymmetry.* Unpublished doctoral dissertation, University of Oregon, 1979.

Bornstein, M. H. Perceptual organization near the beginning of life. In W. A. Collins (Ed.), *Minnesota Symposia on Child Psychology* (Vol. 14). Hillsdale, N.J.: Lawrence Erlbaum Associates, Inc., 1981.

Brazelton, T. B. *Neonatal behavioral assessment scale*. Philadelphia: Lipincott, 1973.

Broadbent, D. E. *Decision and stress*. London: Academic Press, 1971.

Bronson, G. The postnatal growth of visual capacity. *Child Development*, 1974, *45*, 873–890.

Bronson, G. Aversive reactions to strangers: A dual process interpretation. *Child Development*, 1978, *49*, 495–499.

Brown, A. L., & Deloache, J. S. Skills, plans, and self-regulation. In R. S. Siegler (Ed.), *Children's thinking: What develops?*. Hillsdale, N.J.: Lawrence Erlbaum Associates, 1978.

Bruner, J. S. *Processes of cognitive growth: Infancy*. Waltham, Mass.: Clark University Press, 1968.

Bushnel, M. C., Robinson, D. L., & Goldberg, M. E. Dissociation of movement and attention: Neuronal correlates in posterior parietal cortex. *Neuroscience Abstracts*, 1978, 621.

Carey, W. B. A simplified method for measuring infant temperament. *Journal of Pediatrics*, 1970, *77*, 188–194.

Carey, W. B., & McDevitt, S. C. Revision of the infant temperament questionnaire. *Pediatrics*, 1978, *61*, 735–739.

Carroll, J. B. How shall we study individual differences in cognitive abilities? Methodological and theoretical perspectives. *Intelligence*, 1978, *2*, 87–115.

Cerella, John. Visual classes and natural categories in the pigeon. *Journal of Experimental Psychology: Human Perception and Performance*, 1979, *5*, 68–77.

Cohen, L. B. Habituation of infant visual attention. In T. J. Tighe & R. N. Leaton (Eds.), *Habituation*. Hillsdale, N.J.: Lawrence Erlbaum Associates, 1976.

Colavita, F. B. Human sensory dominance. *Perception and Psychophysics*, 1974, *16*, 409–412.

Colavita, F. B., & Weisberg, D. A further investigation of visual dominance. *Perception and Psychophysics*, 1978, *24*, 345–352.

Cooper, L. A. Demonstration of a mental analog of an external rotation. *Peception and Psychophysics*, 1976, *19*, 296–302.

Coren, S., & Kaplan, C. P. Patterns of ocular dominance. *American Journal of Optometry*, 1973, *50*, 283–292.

Cornel, E. H. *Distributed study facilitates infants' delayed recognition memory*. Manuscript submitted for publication, 1979.

Cowey, A. Cortical maps and visual perception. *Quarterly Journal of Experimental Psychology*, 1979, *31*, 1–17.

Diamond, S. *The roots of psychology*. New York: Basic Books, 1974.

Egeth, H. E., & Sager, L. C. On the locus of visual dominance. *Perception and Psychophysics*, 22, 1978, 77–86.

Eimas, P. D., & Corbit, J. D. Selective adaptation of linguistic feature detectors. *Cognitive Psychology*, 1973, *4*, 99–109.

Emde, R. N., Gaensbauer, T. J., & Harmon, R. J. Emotional expression in infancy. *Psychological Issues, Monograph 37*, 1976.

Emde, R. N., & Robinson, J. The first two months; recent research in developmental psychobiology and the changing view of the newborn. In J. Noshpitz & J. Call (Eds.), *American Handbook of Child Psychiatry*. New York: Basic Books, 1978.

Engen, T., & Lipsitt, L. P. Decrement and recovery of responses to olfactory stimuli in the human neonate. *Journal of Comparative and Physiological Psychology*, 1965, *59*, 313–316.

Engen, T., Lipsitt, L. P., & Kaye, H. Olfactory responses and adaptation in the human neonate. *Journal of Comparative and Physiological Psychology*, 1963, *56*, 73–77.

Escalona, S. K. *The roots of individuality: Normal patterns of development in infancy*. Chicago: Aldine, 1968.

Eysenck, H. J. *The biological basis of personality*. Springfield, Ill.: Thomas, 1967.

Eysenck, M. *Human memory: Theory, research and individual differences*. Oxford: Pergamon, 1977.

Fantz, R. L. Visual perception from birth as shown by pattern selectivity. *Annals of the New York Academy of Science*, 1965, *118*, 793–814.

Foote, S. L., Aston-Jones, G., & Bloom, F. E. Locus coeruleus neurons in the awake rat and monkey respond to sensory stimuli and to arousal. *Proceedings of the National Academy of Sciences*, 1980.

Friedman, S. Habituation and recovery of visual response in the alert human newborn. *Journal of Experimental Child Psychology*, 1972, *13*, 339–349.

Gallup, G. G. Self awareness in primates. *American Scientist*, 1979, *67*, 417–421.

Gardner, R., Holzman, P. S., Klein, G. S., Linton, H., & Spence, D. P. Cognitive control. *Psychological Issues*, 1959, *1*(4).

Gassel, M. M., & Williams, D. Visual function in patients with homonymous hemianopia. Part II: Oculomotor mechanisms. *Brain*, 1963, *86*, 1–36.

Goldberg, M. E., & Wurtz, R. H. The activity of superior colliculus in behaving monkey II effect of attention on neuronal responses. *Journal of Neurophysiology*, 1972, *35*, 560–575.

Gray, J. A. The psychophysiological nature of introversion-extroversion: A modification of Eysenck's theory. In V. D. Nebylitsyn & J. A. Gray (Eds.), *Biological bases of individual behavior*. New York: Academic Press, 1972.

Haith, M. M. Visual competence in early infancy. In R. Held, H. Leibowitz, & H. L. Teuber (Eds.), *Handbook of sensory physiology* (Vol. 8). Berlin: Springer Verlag, 1978.

Haith, M. M., & Campos, J. J. Human infancy. *Annual Review of Psychology*, 1977, *28*, 251–293.

Hasher, L., & Zacks, R. T. Automatic and effortful processes in memory. *Journal of Experimental Psychology: General*, 1979, *108*, 356–388.

Hawkins, H. L., Rodriguez, E., & Reicher, G. M. *Is time-sharing a general ability?* Center for Cognitive and Perceptual Research Technical Report No. 3, University of Oregon, 1979.

Heilman, K. M., & Watson, R. T. Mechanisms underlying the unilateral neglect syndrome. In E. A. Weinstein & R. P. Friedland (Eds.), *Hemi-inattention and hemisphere specialization*. New York: Raven Press, 1977.

Hines, T., & Posner, M. I. *Slow but sure: A chronometric analysis of the process of aging.* Paper presented at the meeting of the American Psychological Association, Washington, D.C., September 1976.

Hintzman, D. L. Repetition and memory. In G. H. Bower (Ed.), *The psychology of learning and motivation* (Vol. 10). New York: Academic Press, 1976.

Hubel, D. H. Architecture of the monkey striate cortex. In *Neurosciences Research Program Bulletin*, 1977, *15*, 327–335.

Hubel, D. H., & Wiessel, T. N. Receptive fields and functional architecture of the monkey's striate cortex. *Journal of Physiology*, 1968, *195*, 215–243.

Hunt, E. Mechanics of verbal ability. *Psychological Review*, 1978, *85*, 109–130.

Hunt, E., Frost, N., & Lunneborg, C. Individual differences in cognition:

A new approach to intelligence. In G. H. Bower (Ed.), *The psychology of learning and motivation* (Vol. 7). New York: Academic Press, 1973.

Hunt, E., Lunneborg, C., & Lewis, J. What does it mean to be high verbal? *Cognitive Psychology*, 1975, *7*, 194–227.

Jordan, T. C. Characteristics of visual and proprioceptive response times in the learning of a motor skill. *Quarterly Journal of Experimental Psychology*, 1972, *24*, 536–543.

Kahneman, D. *Attention and effort.* Englewood Cliffs, N.J.: Prentice Hall, 1973.

Kandel, E. R. *Cellular basis of behavior.* San Francisco: Freemont Co., 1976.

Keele, S. W., Neill, W. T., & de Lemos, S. M. *Individual differences in attentional flexibility.* Center for Cognitive and Perceptual Research Technical Report No. 1, University of Oregon, 1978.

Kinsbourne, M. The mechanism of hemispheric control of the lateral gradient of attention. In P. M. A. Rabitt & S. Dornic (Eds.), *Attention and performance V.* London: Academic Press, 1975.

Klein, R. M. Attention and visual dominance: A chronometric analysis. *Journal of Experimental Psychology: Human Perception and Performance*, 1977, *3*, 365–375.

Kraut, A. G. Effects of familiarization of alertness and encoding in children. *Developmental Psychology*, 1978, *12*, 491–496.

LaBerge, D., & Samuels, J. Toward a theory of automatic information processing in reading. *Cognitive Psychology*, 1974, *6*, 293–323.

Lewis, M., & Brooks-Gunn, J. *Social cognition and the acquisition of self.* New York: Plenum Press, 1979.

Lewis, T. L., Maurer, D., & Milewski, A. E. The development of nasal detection in young infants. *ARVO Abstracts*, May 1979, 271.

Mackworth, J. F. *Vigilance and habituation.* Harmondsworth, England: Penguin Books, 1969.

Mates, J. W. B. *Patterning of eye movements in the chameleon.* Unpublished doctoral dissertation, University of Oregon, 1973.

McLean, John P., & Shulman, Gordon L. On the construction and maintenance of expectancies. *Quarterly Journal of Experimental Psychology*, 1978, *30*, 441–454.

Mendelson, M. J., & Haith, M. M. The relationship between audition and vision in the human newborn. *Monographs of the Society for Research in Child Development*, 1976, *41*(4, Serial No. 167).

Morais, J. & Bertelson, P. Laterality effects in dichotic listening. *Perception*, 1973, *2*, 107–111.

Mountcastle, V. B. Brain mechanisms for directed attention. *Journal of the Royal Society of Medicine*, 1978, *71*, 14–27.

Nebylitsyn, V. D. *Fundamental properties of the human nervous system.* New York: Plenum Press, 1972.

Neely, J. H. Semantic priming and retrieval from lexical memory: Roles of inhibitionless spreading activation and limited-capacity attention.

Journal of Experimental Psychology: General, 1977, *106*, 226–254.

Neisser, U. *Cognition and reality*. San Francisco: Freeman, 1976.

Nickerson, R. Intersensory facilitation of reaction time energy summation or preparation enhancement. *Psychological Review*, 1973, *80*, 489–509.

Oldfield, R. C. Memory mechanisms and the theory of schemata. *British Journal of Psychology*, 1954, *45*, 14–23.

Paivio, A., & Ernest, C. H. Imagery ability and visual perception of verbal and nonverbal stimuli. *Perception & Psychophysics*, 1971, *10*, 429–432.

Papousek, H. From adaptive responses to social cognition: The learning view of development. In M. H. Bornstein & W. Kessen (Eds.), *Psychological development from infancy: Image to intention*. Hillsdale, N.J.: Lawrence Erlbaum Associates, 1979.

Pavlov, I. P. General types of animal and human higher nervous activity. In *Selected works*. Moscow: Foreign Language Publishing House, 1955. (Originally published, 1935.)

Pederson, F. A., Anderson, B. J., & Cain, R. L., Jr. *A methodology for assessing parental perception of infant temperament*. Paper presented at Southeastern Conference on Human Development, April 1976.

Perenin, M. T., & Jeannerod, M. Visual function within the hemianopic field following early cerebral hemidecortication in man. I. Spatial localization. *Neuropsychologia*, 1978, *16*, 1–13.

Posner, M. I. *Chronometric Explorations of Mind*. Hillsdale, N.J.: Lawrence Erlbaum Associates, 1978.

Posner, M. I. Mental chronometry and the problem of consciousness. In R. Klein and P. Jusczyk (Eds.), *Structure of thought: Essays in honor of D. O. Hebb*. Hillsdale, N.J.: Lawrence Erlbaum Associates, 1980.

Posner, M. I., & Cohen, Y. Attention and the control of movements. In G. E. Stelmach & J. Roquio (Eds.), *Tutorials in motor behavior*. Amsterdam: North Holland, 1980.

Posner, M. I., Cohen, Y., & Shulman, G. *Exogenous control of orienting*. Paper presented at meeting of the Psychonomic Society, Inc., Phoenix, Arizona, November 1979.

Posner, M. I., & Keele, S. W. On the genesis of abstract ideas. *Journal of Experimental Psychology*, 1968, *77*, 353–363.

Posner, M. I., Nissen, M. J., & Klein, R. M. Visual dominance: An information-processing account of its origins and significance. *Psychological Review*, 1976, *83*, 157–171.

Posner, M. I., & Snyder, C. R. R. Attention and cognitive control. In R. Solso (Ed.), *Information processing and cognition: The Loyola symposium*. Hillsdale, N.J.: Lawrence Erlbaum Associates, 1975.

Rao, S. L. *Similarity in sensory sensitivity between the auditory and visual modalities*. Unpublished doctoral dissertation, Delhi University, Delhi, India, 1978.

Remington, R. W. Attention and saccadic eye movements. *Journal of Ex-*

perimental Psychology: Human Perception and Performance, 1980, *6*, 726–744.

Resnick, L. B. (Ed.). *The nature of intelligence*. Hillsdale, N.J.: Lawrence Erlbaum Associates, 1976.

Revelle, W., Humphreys, M. S., Simon, L., and Gilliland, K. The interactive effect of personality, time of day, and caffeine: A test of the arousal model. *Journal of Experimental Psychology: General*, 1980, *109*, 1–31.

Rosch, E., & Lloyd, B. B. *Cognition and categorization*. Hillsdale, N.J.: Lawrence Erlbaum Associates, 1979.

Rothbart, M. K. *Longitudinal home observation of infant temperament*. Paper presented at the International Conference on Infant Studies, New Haven, April 1980.

Rothbart, M. K., & Derryberry, D. Theoretical issues in temperament. In M. Lewis & L. Taft (Eds.), *Developmental disabilities: Theory, assessment and intervention*. New York: S. P. Medical and Scientific Books, in press. (a)

Rothbart, M. K., & Derryberry, D. Development of individual differences in temperament. In A. Brown & M. Lamb (Eds.), *Advances in developmental psychology* (Vol. 1). Hillsdale, N.J.: Lawrence Erlbaum Associates, in press. (b)

Rothbart, M. K., Furby, L., Kelly, S. R., & Hamilton, J. *Development of a caretaker report temperament scale for use with 3, 6, 9 and 12 month old infants*. Paper presented at meetings of the Society for Research in Child Development, New Orleans, March 1977.

Russo, J., & Rosen, L. An eye fixation analysis of multialternative choice. *Memory and Cognitive*, 1975, *3*, 267–276.

Salapatek, P. Visual scanning of geometric figures by the human newborn. *Journal of Comparative and Physiological Psychology*, 1968, *76*, 247–258.

Sawusch, J. R., & Jusczyk, P. W. Adaptation and contrast in the perception of voicing. *Journal of Experimental Psychology: Human Perception and Performance*, in press.

Schiller, P. H., True, S. D., & Conway, J. C. Effects of frontal eye field and superior colliculus ablations on eye movements. *Science*, 1979, *206*, 590–592.

Schnur, P., Lubow, R. E., & Ben-Shalom, H. *Stimulus repetition effects in choice reaction time*. Paper presented to the Psychonomic Society, Inc., Phoenix, Arizona, November 1979.

Sekuler, R. Spatial vision. *Annual Review of Psychology*, 1974, *5*, 195–232.

Shulman, G. L. *Spatial determinants of attention allocation*. Unpublished doctoral dissertation, University of Oregon, 1979.

Sokolov, E. N. *Perception and the conditioned reflex*. New York: Macmillan, 1963.

Stechler, G., & Latz, E. Some observations on attention and arousal in the human infant. *Journal of the American Academy of Child Psychiatry*, 1966, *5*, 517–525.

Sternberg, R. J. The nature of human abilities. *American Psychologist,* 1979, *34,* 214–230.

Stone, L. J., Smith, H. T., & Murphy, L. B. *The competent infant.* New York: Basic Books, 1973.

Strauss, M. S. Abstraction of prototypical information by adults and 10 month old infants. *Journal of Experimental Psychology: Human Learning and Memory,* 1979, *6,* 618–632.

Tennes, K., Emde, R., Kisley, A., & Metcalf, D. The stimulus barrier in early infancy: An exploration of some formulations of John Benjamin. In R. R. Holt & E. Peterfreund (Eds.), *Psychoanalysis and contemporary science* (Vol. 1). New York: Macmillan, 1972.

Teplov, B. M. Problems in the study of general types of higher nervous activity in man and animals. In J. A. Gray (Ed.), *Pavlov's typology.* New York: Macmillan, 1964.

Thomas, A., Chess, S., & Birch, H. G. *Temperament and behavior disorders in children.* New York: New York University Press, 1968.

Thomas, A., Chess, S., Birch, H. G., Hertzig, M. E., & Korn, S. *Behavioral individuality in early childhood.* New York: New York University Press, 1963.

Thompson, R. F., & Spencer W. O. Habituation: A model phenomenon for the study of neuronal substrates of behavior. *Psychological Review,* 1966, *73,* 1–15.

Trevarthen, C. The tasks of consciousness: How could the brain do them? In *Brain and mind* (CIBA Foundation Symposium 69). New York: Excerpta Medica, 1979.

Tyler, L. E. The intelligence we test—an evolving concept. In L. B. Resnick (Ed.), *The nature of intelligence.* Hillsdale, N.J.: Lawrence Erlbaum Associates, 1976.

Tyler, L. E. *Individuality.* San Francisco: Jersey-Bass, 1978.

Underwood, B. J. False recognitions produced by implicit verbal responses. *Journal of Experimental Psychology,* 1965, *70,* 122–129.

Warren, R. E., & Warren, N. T. Dual semantic encoding of homographs and lomophones embedded in context. *Memory and Cognition,* 1976, *4,* 486–492.

Weiskrantz, L., Warrington, E. K., Sanders, M. D., & Marshall, J. Visual capacity in the hemianopic field following a restricted occipital ablation. *Brian,* 1974, *97,* 709–728.

Wilson, G. O., Tunstall, O. A., & Eysenck, H. J. Individual differences in tapping performance as a function of time on the task. *Perceptual and Motor Skills,* 1971, *33,* 375–738.

Wilson, W. R., & Zajonc, R. Affective discrimination of stimuli that cannot be recognized. *Science,* 1980, *207,* 557–558.

Witkin, H. A., Dyk, R. B., Faterson, H. F., Goodenough, D. R., & Karp, S. A. *Psychological differentiation.* New York: Wiley, 1962.

Witkin, H. A., & Goodenough, D. R. Field dependence and interpersonal behavior. *Psychological Bulletin,* 1977, *84,* 661–689.

Wurtz, R. H., & Mohler, C. W. Organization of monkey superior colliculus: Enhanced visual response of superficial layer cells. *Journal of
Neurophysiology,* 1976, *39,* 745–765.

Unitization and Automaticity in Perception[1]

David LaBerge
University of Minnesota

*T*HE purpose of this paper is to attempt to clarify and deepen our understanding of the notions of unitization and automatization in perception of stimulus patterns. I will mainly be concerned with a type of stimulus which apparently is processed in sizable units and automatically by a large majority of humans, that is, the class of familiar visual linguistic stimuli. To achieve a fluent skill of understanding written and spoken language apparently requires that perceptual information be processed in large units and automatically. Yet it is instructive parenthetically to note that there exist other types of stimuli, perhaps equally as familiar as linguistic patterns, which we may not wish to unitize or automatize as we perceive them. For example, it seems likely that the random details of some natural scenes may provide a healthful resistance to unitization. In fact, much of our enjoyment in viewing flickering flames, breaking waves, and the random arrangements of branches and leaves in a forest might well be lost if we succeeded in fusing the detailed components of these scenes into large perceptual units.

The perceptual appeal of orthography, on the other hand, is rather scant, with the possible exception of pictograms and ideograms of East Asian languages. A page of English text seems pale beside a painting or a shoreline seen through a window. Therefore, when considering the perceptual learning of written language, we usually feel little loss when lines and angles of print are fused into letters and words, and when words themselves are

1. This research was supported by a grant from the National Institute of Mental Health (5–R01–MH16270) and by grants to the Center for Research in Human Learning of the University of Minnesota from the National Science Foundation (NSF/ BNS–77–22075) and from the National Institute for Child Health and Human Development (HD–01136).

eventually ignored while they are being processed automatically, as in the reading of a novel or the daily newspaper. One could almost say that perceptual details of nature can help us come to our senses, while the semantic demands of language induce us to leave our senses.

This paper falls into three main parts. The first part will describe the process of perceptual unitizing and one way to measure it; the second part will do the same for automatization; and the third part will deal with the problem of acquisition of these two processing skills.

Unit and Unitization

It is difficult to image how scientists, or nonscientists for that matter, could talk to each other about what they see and hear without using units. The vast array of stimulation before our eyes and ears somehow becomes chopped up into the kinds of pieces that permit us to point them out to other people with remarkable consistency, accuracy, and interobserver agreement. At the same time, by selecting a small subset of these pieces for momentary consideration, we manage to reduce the potentially overwhelming amount of stimulus information to a size appropriate to the task at hand. For example, faced with a page of text, we can easily isolate a sentence, a phrase, a word, a spelling pattern, or a letter for our consideration, and we can also draw another person's attention to these items by pointing with our finger or by "pointing" with a spoken description. Letters, words, and sentences are therefore useful means of classifying instances of graphemic patterns, and are commonly called units. This use of the term *unit* is relatively objective, and it is also quite useful in denoting the particular level of description of the visually presented text that is being considered.

This view of the term *unit* emphasizes the external aspects of the bounded perception item, by separating the item from nonitem information, much in the sense that a figure is separated from its ground. The success of a pointing event usually depends upon how well the boundaries of a perceptual item are marked. But the success of perceptually processing the item depends on more than the saliency of its boundaries. In fact, the item information may often be successfully processed even when the perceptual boundaries are not clearly detectable, as in certain cases of perceiving syllables in a stream of speech (Studdert-Kennedy, 1976, pp. 243–293). When one considers the nature of the internal aspects (e.g., components and relations) of an isolated perceptual item, as opposed to its external aspects, then issues of perceptual processing arise other than the problem of merely isolating or selecting a bounded item. The manner in which one observer perceives the information within the boundary of an item is assumed to vary from person to person and from time to time for a given person. It is commonly believed that the optimum manner of perceiving the internal information of a linguistic item such as a letter or a word is as a "unified whole." Hence, the term *unit* has also been used to describe one way that the objectively designated classes of items are processed by observers. This second use of the term is regarded as somewhat less objective than the first in practice, probably because it is based on inferred properties of perception that are less widely agreed upon than figure-ground properties.

A third way that the term *unit* has been used is as a synonym for perceptual code or representation. When a person learns to perceive a word as a whole, the person is said to have formed a *perceptual unit*, which is activated whenever that word is displayed. The properties of this inferred representation usually correspond closely to the properties of the processing assumptions of the second use of the term *unit*. In summary, we recognize three uses of the term *unit*: (1) an objectively specified class of items, (2) a mode of processing an item, and (3) a perceptual representation of an item.

In this chapter I will focus the discussion on the second and third uses of the term *unit*. The extension of the term to its verb form, *unitizing*, seems appropriate here because the second and third uses of the term *unit* deal with dynamic aspects of a mode of processing, and of the acquisition of the capability of a mode of processing, in contrast to the static taxonomic property of the first use of the term.

One way to approach the problem of characterizing unitary processing is to contrast it to nonunitary processing. For example, a word display can be regarded as an ordered group of letter items. When the observer processes the display letter by letter, or as a group of spelling patterns, we would call his processing mode *nonunitary* or *component processing*. When the observer processes the display as a whole, we would call his processing mode *unitary*. In a technical sense, units are being processed in both cases, but in the first case there is no unit as large as the bounded word in the display, while in the second case it is presumed that there is such a unit.

A Measure of Unitization: Reaction Time to Words as a Function of Number of Component Letters

It is not a trivial matter to determine whether a unitary or component mode of processing is being employed by a person for a given display. This is especially the case when subjects apparently have the option of processing a given pattern such as a word or a face in terms of parts or wholes.

One indicator of unitary processing, developed by Terry, Samuels, and LaBerge (1976), asks the subject to categorize single words as being a member of the class of animals. In their study the subject pressed one button for the judgment of animal words, and made no response to nonanimal words. The nonanimal words usually differed from animal words by one letter (e.g., *turnkey*). The main independent variable was word length, which varied from three to six letters. A second independent variable involved degrading the letters of the words by erasing portions of the lines which made up the letters. Tests of the degraded letters presented alone confirmed that subjects could accurately identify each letter given sufficient exposure time. The degraded and normal conditions were run on separate groups of college-age subjects.

It was expected that unitary processing of the word displays would show no effect of word length on reaction time, while component processing (by letters, spelling patterns, or a combination of the two) would produce an increase in reaction time as word length increased. Moreover, if subjects process these words in terms of letter units, then degradation of the letter information should interact with word length in determining reaction time. Specifically, degraded letters should show a larger slope than normal letters under the assumption of letter-by-letter processing.

The results from both the normal and degraded conditions showed no hint of a change of mean reaction time with word length. Moreover, the absolute difference in mean reaction time between degraded and normal conditions was very small and not significant. Therefore, we tentatively concluded that subjects were not sensitive to the number of components nor the quality of the letter components in this task.

As it stood, this set of findings was not conclusive because (1) the findings were based on acceptance of the null hypothesis of zero slope of the curve relating word length to reaction time, and (2) there was no independent evidence that the letter degradation condition was sufficiently strong to provide a clear test of the effect of letter quality. A third manipulation attempted to resolve these two uncertainties by inducing subjects to use component processing in this task.

It seemed plausible that subjects could be induced to process words in component fashion if the words were presented in mirror image. Therefore two additional groups of college subjects were run in which the same set of words was presented in mirror image, but for one group the letters were degraded as before, and for the other groups the letters were undergraded.

The results showed a clear and substantial word-length effect on mean reaction time for both groups. Furthermore, the degraded letter group showed a significantly greater slope than the normal letter group. This result indicated that the degradation of the letters was sufficiently strong for present testing purposes.

These results seemed to indicate that words displayed in mirror image induced subjects to adopt a processing mode that was sensitive to the number of components in the display and to the quality of these components considered separately.

Taken together, the results of the four groups supported the hypothesis that college students process normally presented words in a unitary manner in categorization tasks. Furthermore, the word-length variable used in this study gained promise as a useful indicator of unitary and component modes of processing a word.

One comment is in order pertaining to the interpretation of a zero word-length slope as an indicator of unitary word processing. It may seem equally plausible to assume that parallel processing of component letters and/or spelling patterns could also produce a zero word-length slope. If the parallel processing of each of these components of a word were the only operation necessary to categorize the word, then the reaction time of a subject should be determined by the time needed to process the longest component. But the likelihood of encountering a component producing a long reaction time increases with the number of components sampled. This consideration leads to a prediction of an increase in reaction time as a word length increases. However, it could be argued that the processing times of the components of a word are highly homogeneous, so that the component producing the longest reaction time is only negligibly longer than that of the other components. This strong assumption concerning the distribution of processing times of components would seem to predict a negligible word-length slope.

Regardless of the foregoing line of reasoning, however, the parallel processing model must also address the problem of combining the letter and/or spelling patterns after each has been separately processed. The link between the processed components and the category meaning of the word can hardly be activated by each component separately (LaBerge, 1979). It is not the components which uniquely determine the selection of the category of the word, but the combination information arising from the components considered together. Therefore, the components must be combined in some way before the associated meaning can be accessed. The computation of this combination information takes time, and it would seem that the larger the number of components, the longer the time required for this operation. In view of these considerations, it would seem that a straightforward parallel model applied to a component hypothesis of word processing would have difficulty accounting for a zero word-length effect.

With this promising indicator of processing mode in hand, we turned to a population of children to see whether they might show different word-length effects than college students (Samuels, LaBerge, & Bremer, 1978). The category task was the same as the one used by Terry et al. Word lengths varied from three to six letters. The subjects were representative samples of students from second, fourth, sixth, and college grades.

The results of this developmental study showed a large slope effect for second-grade students, ad a diminishing slope as grade increased, with college students again showing no word-length effect. It was not possible with these data to rule out the possibility that significant word-length slopes represented a mixture of component and unitary processing because there is no a priori value to assume for the slope which indicates pure component processing, as there is for the case of unitary processing. Therefore, the existence of a word-length slope for some groups of students allows the interpretation that some students may be using unitary processing, and others component processing, or that some students may be shifting from one mode to another from display to display. The progressive flattening of the word-length slope as grade increases also leads to alternative explanations. The students may learn to process more of the words as units, or they may also learn to use larger components (shifting from letter units to spelling patterns) as they progress through the grades. In any case, the data indicate an increase in unitary processing with developmental level.

The foregoing experiments employed a categorization task in an attempt to determine the relative contributions of component and unitary modes of word processing. Other tasks, however, apparently do not produce word-length effects that are strictly comparable to those obtained with categorization tasks. For example, tasks which require the subjects to perform a physical match of two words yield significant and substantial increases in reaction time with word length for displays which simultaneously position one word above the other (Eichelman, 1970; Bruder, 1978) and for displays which show one word beside the other (LaBerge & Lawry, in press). We have attempted to eliminate the slope of reaction time with word length by cueing the matching words semantically or physically (by presenting the identical word itself), but have never succeeded, although we have managed to reduce the slope somewhat. Even using mismatching pairs of words which were highly dissimilar did not produce a zero word-length slope in the matching task.

We have tentatively concluded that the matching task by its nature requires even the advanced reader to process components of a word. However, this does not rule out the possibility that within a given trial, subjects may process words in a unitary manner at one stage of the matching operation and process them in a component fashion at another stage (LaBerge & Lawry, in press). What contrasts the matching task with the categorization task is the likelihood that the advanced reader can perform the categorization task without processing components at any stages between the onset of the display and the response.

Like the matching task, the lexical-decision task apparently also produces nonzero word-length effect for familiar words. Experiments in our laboratory indicated that the magnitude appears to be somewhat less than that obtained from matching tasks. But we have not been able to reliably eliminate the word-length effect by semantic cueing of the lexical-decision task.

Therefore, it appears that, of the three simple word tasks considered, only the categorization task provides a relatively reliable indicator of unitary processing of a word because it is the only one that has yielded zero word-length slope effects under normal display conditions. The fact that the indication of unitary processing depends on a zero effect can make an experimenter nervous about being on the wrong side of the null hypothesis, but this statistical uncertainty seems to be largely dispelled when studies show mean latencies which fall within a few msec of each other across word length under appropriate conditions, while under other conditions the latencies show a substantial increase with word length (Terry et al., 1976; Samuels et al., 1978).

One implication of the finding that a categorization task produces a zero slope word-length effect for familiar words is that this task should serve as a more appropriate training procedure for word recognition than other tasks which may not require unitization. It is clear that simple physical matching tasks can be performed successfully by a components matching strategy. Naming words aloud is also a task which can be performed by parts: the subject can simply sound out the word syllable by syllable. One might argue that categorizating a word could be done by sounding out visual spelling patterns and then blending the syllables into one phonological unit before accessing the semantic category. The reply to this comment is that this processing sequence could well be used by the beginning reader in the categorization task, but it should be noted that perceptual unitization is required in the phonological system before the category is determined. This phonological unitization presumably can feed back to the visual system to help form visual units of the same size (Petersen & LaBerge, 1977). In contrast, naming the word aloud can be carried out without using whole word units at either the phonological or visual system.

Another advantage of using a categorization task as a training method is that it requires the subject to associate the visual pattern with the semantic system, while matching and naming do not. The link between perceptual and semantic systems is important in a word-training task because this link more closely approximates the role a word plays in the context of reading.

The component-length indicator of unitary processing has not been used yet for testing the processing of single letters. Words can easily be divided into component letters or spelling patterns because the boundaries of these parts are marked by spatial separation. Single letters, on the other hand, have no such clearly marked boundaries for their internal parts, so that the number of component features in a letter is not easily estimated. Yet estimates have been made (Gibson, 1969), and one could attempt tests of letter unitization with these estimates.

Levels of Units

It is generally agreed that objectively defined units can be ordered in a systematic hierarchy. At the lowest level we identify features of letters, such as lines and angles. At the next levels are letters, then spelling patterns, and then words. At still higher levels, we point to groups of words extending from phrases to sentences.

This hierarchical ordering of physically defined units has been adopted for the theoretical domain where each physically defined unit has its counterpart as a perceptual representation or code (e.g., Estes, 1975; LaBerge & Samuels, 1974; McClelland, 1979). Thus, physical features such as lines activate line detectors in the visual system, letters activate letter codes, and words activate word codes. The hierarchical property relating one level to another in the physical domain is also carried over into the theoretical domain by these theories. For example, combinations of feature-detector outputs activate letter codes, and letter codes in turn feed into spelling-pattern codes, which combine their outputs to activate word codes. Thus, the same combinatorial principle is used to account for the activation of a code at level n using the outputs of codes at level $n-1$, regardless of the level under consideration. This general combinational assumption is an attractive one because it keeps the hierarchy theory of perceptual processing simple.

The hierarchy theory is also economical in accounting for the large number of codes stored in the visual system which represent the vast number of patterns we recognize. With a relatively few feature detectors, the theory apparently can generate a large number of higher order pattern codes, and when assumptions about position of component features and codes are incorporated into the hierarchy model, it would seem to have no trouble accounting for all of the patterns we identify.

Certainly it is desirable in reading and listening to build codes of a large size to increase the rate of perceptual information processing. What is the upper limit on the size of perceptual codes acquired by mature readers and listeners? I do not know of any evidence which bears directly on this question, but one might reason that progress toward an answer could be given by looking at the time needed to categorize phrases of varying length. One might expect that the slope of the curve relating latency to phrase length would be nonzero because one would not expect subjects to perceptually unitize a typical string of words. Instead one expects component processing of a phrase because it is necessary to maintain the semantic information of each word in order to arrive at the meaning of the phrase. In contrast, unitizing a string of letters into a word usually presents no such problem. When units less than a word carry no semantic information, the identity of these smaller units can be lost in the perceptual unitizing of the word. When words do contain segments that are semantically meaningful, readers may resist unitizing them under certain circumstances, and a "length" effect may show up. Examples of such words are *spacecraft* and *aftershock*. There may also be special cases of word groups which are treated as one semantic unit, and perhaps may show no word-group "length" effect. Examples are *red tape* and *hot dog*. These conjectures need experimental verification.

Automatic Processing

There seems to be general agreement concerning the general definition of automaticity. The term simply denotes processing without attention. But not everyone agrees upon the characteristics of attentional processing, so that the boundary between attention and automaticity may not be widely accepted when it is considered in some detail. In this paper we will assume that attention is a single-channel process which can operate at perceptual or semantic levels, but can be directed at only one unit or attribute at a time.

Currently the notion of automaticity is applied to information processing in at least two different ways. In the first application of the term, the subject's attention is focused *elsewhere* than the item being processed. For example, when the mature reader's attention is at the semantic level, perceptual material is assumed to be processed automatically. Another example is found in the Stroop test (Stroop, 1935). The subject's attention is directed to the attribute of the color of ink, while the words (color labels) are processed automatically. In the second type of application of automatic processing the subject's attention is focused on the code being processed, but is not involved in processing operations which activated the code. For example, we may focus attention on a face or a word, but the unitization of the face or word occurs without attention. This application of automaticity is often used to account for some of the difference in recognition latencies for familiar and unfamiliar patterns. Displays of either a familiar or an unfamiliar word apparently will draw attention to the perceptual word, but the unfamiliar word presumably requires attention to achieve unitization, while a highly familiar word does not.

A Measure of Automaticity: The Flanker Test

This method of measuring automaticity attempts to direct the attention of the subject to one item or attribute and then measures the processing of another item. It is therefore closer to the first type of situation in which automaticity is investigated.

Eriksen and Eriksen (1974) asked subjects to identify target letters which were presented with noise letters to the right and left of the target letter. The letters *H* and *K* were assigned to one hand, and the letters *S* and *C* were assigned to the other. The finding of main interest here was that the latency to a given target letter was increased when the flanking letters were assigned to a different response than the target letter's response. The mean difference between responses to compatible flanker displays and incompatible flanker displays was about 80 msec at the smallest spacing between the target and flanking letters.

This finding suggested strongly to me that the flanking noise letters were being processed automatically because subjects were instructed to fixate on a point where the target letter appeared, and were not encouraged to observe the flanking letters. This procedure seemed to be an attractive way of measuring automaticity because it was simple in design, and had the unusual feature of showing evidence of automaticity by a decrement in performance rather than by an increment in performance.

The question of automatic processing in this task pertains not only to the visual processing of the stimulus pattern but also to the association between this pattern and the appropriate response assignment (Greenwald, 1970; Flowers, Warner, & Polansky, 1979). For the Eriksen and Eriksen (1974) task, the perceptual processing of the highly familiar letters was presumably carried out automatically. However, the association to the response (pressing a lever) had to be learned during laboratory sessions, and practice trials were given to establish a high level of accuracy of response selection. In fact, it would seem that the response associations had been learned to an automatic level because the flanker effect was real. The question of interest is whether the category of the flanker item would also show evidence of automatic processing in this task. The method used to answer this question involved displays containing items from the two categories of letters and digits.

The items *G S 4 8* were assigned to one hand and *J H 5 6* were assigned to the other. An additional set, *C T U D 2 7 3 9*, served as catch items. Displays were constructed so that the target item was in the center flanked by two distractors. There were five types of displays, each labeled according to the relation of the flanker item to its target item: Identical (I) (e.g., *SSS*); Compatible response–Same category (CS) (e.g., *GSG*); Compatible response–Different category (CD) (e.g., *4S4*); Incompatible response–Same category (IS) (e.g., *HSH*); and Incompatible response–Different category (ID) (e.g., *6S6*). Each of the 48 subjects received a block of 72 practice trials with a prompt card in view showing the response assignments of the stimuli. The test block which followed contained 144 trials without a prompt card.

Table 1

Mean Reaction Time for Target Identification for Letters and Digits as a Function of Flanker Condition

Target Set	Flanker Condition				
	I	CS	CD	IS	ID
Letters	669	623	653	666	681
Digits	664	608	656	653	653

The results are shown in Table 1 for letter and digit targets under the five flanker conditions. The error term for paired comparisons was 8.0, and the overall mean error rate was 2.5%.

The planned comparison between conditions CD and ID showed significance only for the letter targets. But more substantial and significant differences showed up in ad hoc comparisons between condition CS and conditions CD, IS, and I. A replication of this study with 16 other subjects confirmed this pattern of differences. In particular the comparison of CD and ID mean latencies again showed a significant 28 msec for the letter targets, but no significant change for the digit targets. Apparently with these stimuli, there is a more consistent and generally larger flanker effect produced by shifting category than one produced by shifting responses, as shown by the comparisons of conditions CS and

CD. This unexpected finding suggested that the category of an item, as well as the item itself, may be automatically processed in this task. Moreover, the fact that flanker and target items were associated with the same response in conditions CS and CD implied that the locus of the interference between flanker and target information was not at the overt-response selection stage, but rather at an earlier stage at which the category is selected.

Before leaving this study, it should be pointed out that there is a paradoxical finding in the fact that the mean latency for the Identical condition (I) is substantially longer than for the Compatible—Same category condition (CS). Since both conditions involve compatible responses and compatible "categories," one would expect no difference in latency, as was found in the Eriksen and Eriksen (1974) study. A possible explanation for an elevation of Identical displays over compatible category displays is that inputs to the same stimulus code produce interference (Bjork & Murray, 1977). However, other experiments in our laboratory using letters and digits did not always produce a difference between an Identical flanker display and a Compatible flanker display. Therefore, it seems that this effect still stands in need of explanation. Another unexplained finding in Table 1 is the interaction of the ID-CD difference with type of item, a pattern which reappeared in the word flanker experiment to be discussed later.

With the result in hand that letter and digit categories apparently produce flanker effects, the next important step was to see if these effects would show up with semantic categories of words. There was also a methodological advantage implied in the category experiment that would make it possible to test the automatic perceptual processing of many items without requiring subjects first to laboriously associate each item with a response. All that was needed was merely to assign a category to a response, and then one could use as many members of that category as one wished. This procedure would also have the advantage of using a particular item only once or twice in a block of trials, in contrast to the letter-digit experiments which persented a given item a great many times in a block of trials.

William Shaffer and I (Shaffer & LaBerge, 1979) used four categories of words (metals, clothing, trees, and furniture) in this design. We assigned two categories (e.g., metals and clothing) to one hand, and two (e.g., furniture and trees) to the other. Stimulus displays were constructed of three words arranged one above the other, with the target word between the two flanking words. Displays occasionally contained neutral items in flanker positions, to serve as a baseline to assess the degree of facilitation or interference produced by other flanker conditions. The main flanker conditions were Identical (I) (e.g., *lamp, lamp, lamp)*; Compatible response–Same category (CS) (e.g., *desk, lamp, desk*); Compatible response–Different category (CD) (e.g., *pine, lamp, pine)*; and Incompatible response–Different category (ID) (e.g., *gold, lamp, gold)*.

The results showed significant flanker effects both for competing categories and for competing responses. The comparison of neutral flankers with the CD and CS flanker conditions yielded a 31 msec interference effect and a 12 msec facilitation effect. But the most interesting finding concerned the overall category effect. Not only were subjects apparently processing word items automatically, they were also apparently processing the category of these items automatically as well.

This category flanker test has been simplified for purposes of measuring automatic processing of words for beginning readers. Only two categories are needed to measure a flanker effect. For example, one may assign articles of clothing to the left button and names of animals to the right button. Then any display in which the target and flanker items come from different categories is a measure of possible interference effects, and any display in which the target and flanker items come from the same category is a measure of facilitation effects. The difference between the two measures presumably increases with increased automaticity. One attractive feature of this method, along with other variants of the Stroop task (e.g., Rayner & Posnansky, 1978, Willows & MacKinnon, 1973), is that the interference of the distracting information increases as the subject's degree of automaticity progresses. Recall that in the measure of unitization discussed in the first part of this paper, the slope of the word-length measure decreases as the subject's unitization progresses.

In the flanker method of measuring automaticity, the subject's attention is quite probably focused at the perceptual level of word processing. In normal fluent reading, on the other hand, attention is presumably focused at the semantic level. However, the normal reading situation has been modified slightly to include a flanker type of condition by Willows and MacKinnon (1973). Using paragraphs of text, these authors occasionally placed between the lines a word which could be substituted for a particular word in a sentence. When good readers were later asked questions about the semantic context of the text, they sometimes gave answers based on the inserted ("flanker") words. The answers of poor readers showed less evidence of such semantic intrusions. It would seem that the good readers processed some of the "flanker" words automatically while their attention was required for semantic aspects of reading.

Acquisition of Unitization and Automatization

The perceptual learning of patterns does not seem to be a one-stage affair (LaBerge, 1976, 1979). Prior to the achievement of unitization, we can identify other perceptual learning phenomena such as discrimination of features and grouping of components of a pattern. The purpose of this section is to briefly describe four proposed stages of perceptual learning, in order to fit unitization and automaticity into an appropriate context.

The first stage of perceptual learning of a pattern proposed here is *feature selection*. Following E. J. Gibson's (1969) notions of distinctive-feature discovery, we assume that the person must first discriminate the stimulus pattern from other patterns. Probably the most effective way to do this is to show subjects displays in which pairs of patterns are presented simultaneously. By comparing similar displays, the subject learns to select the feature or features by which the target pattern differs from others. Progress in this stage of learning is usually measured in terms of a reduction in errors. Some methods of teaching people to discriminate patterns present only one pattern at a time and ask the person to name the pattern. This method would seem to place a needlessly high burden on the attention of the learner, since in this task he must both discriminate the pattern from others and also associate the right response to the pattern. It would appear to be more efficient first to use a matching task to teach the relevant features of the pattern, and then to wait until confusion errors are minimal before attempting to associate a response to the pattern.

After the subject has learned to select or to become sensitive to the features which distinguish the given pattern from other patterns, he usually finds that more than one feature is required to identify a pattern uniquely. For example, the letters h and n may be distinguished by the length of a vertical line, but the letters h and d or h and k are distinguished by other features. Thus the letter h represents a group of features.

When the subject combines a group of features in order to uniquely identify (e.g., name) a pattern, he is at the second stage of perceptual learning. Not only are features assumed to be grouped to perceive a letter, but also a string of letters may be regarded as grouped at the second stage of perceptual learning of a word pattern. At this stage attention is normally necessary to scan the components of the group, noting position and/or order information as well as item information. Therefore it may be more appropriate to label this stage *ordered grouping*.

It should be pointed out that continued use of a matching task may well maintain perceptual learning at the grouping stage because subjects may match patterns component by component. Even pronouncing a word may keep the pattern at a component (spelling pattern) grouping stage when the person sounds out words syllable by syllable. Probably it is better to shift the subject to a word categorization task, which requires him to combine all the component information before responding.

When the subject is induced by an appropriate task to combine or consider more than one component at a time, it is likely that relations between components will also be perceived. But to perceive relations between two components normally requires that the subject "widen" his focus of attention from encompassing a single component to include both components so that the relation is perceived. For example, the letters b, d, p, and q may each be considered to contain a vertical line and a closed loop. But it is the particular relationship between the line and loop which uniquely determines one of these four letters. In order to perceive this relationship most clearly, the subject must attend to both of the features simultaneously. Similarly, to perceive possible internal relations of a word pattern, the "width" of attention probably includes first and last letters simultaneously. The relational features that stretch across many components have been termed *global information*, while the components are termed *local information* (e.g., LaBerge & Lawry, in press).

At some point the features and the relations spanning the entire pattern are "fused" or reintegrated into a single unit. Attention that was formerly directed successively to component features and to relations between features now is directed to one entity. This is the *unitization* stage. Attention is probably still required for maintenance of this new unitization, but the nature of its focus has changed from one perceptual level to a higher level. What it is that produces the shift from component grouping to unitization is not clear, but it probably involves a widening of the spatial extent over which information leading to higher order codes is integrated.

With additional experience with the pattern, less and less attention is needed to maintain unitization, and the process becomes more and more *automatic*. This moves the perceptual learning into the fourth stage.

Some Comments about Individual Differences in Perceptual Learning

For the person seeing a new orthography or hearing a new language, it is difficult to find what in the array of stimulation to pay attention to. Once the relevant features of a set of patterns are learned, however, the problem shifts to combining or integrating features of a given pattern into higher order codes or units. The formation and activation of visual word codes is currently viewed either as a combination of letter code outputs (Estes, 1975; LaBerge & Samuels, 1974; McClelland, 1979) or as a combination (Johnson, 1975) or integration (LaBerge & Lawry, in press) of feature detector outputs which bypass letter codes.

The position taken on the issue of how a unitary word code receives its activation from lower levels may influence where in the system one looks for the causes of individual differences. It is quite likely that not everyone needs to go through the same set of stages to achieve unitization and automaticity in the processing of a given pattern. Moreover, the speed at which learning progresses at a given stage apparently differs across people. Developmental level and the acquired knowledge base may drastically change the rate at which a new word or a new melody is first perceived, and may substantially shorten the time required to incorporate the perception of these patterns into a skill such as reading or listening to music (Gardner, 1979).

How might developmental and knowledge base factors influence the acquisition of unitary codes in the case of the component combination models as opposed to the reintegration-of-features models? This question can hardly be answered in a conclusive way at our present state of knowledge of perceptual unitization. The purpose of raising the question here is to remind us that the theoretical position we take about a topic usually influences where we look for answers to important questions such as those dealing with individual differences.

REFERENCES

Bjork, E. L., & Murray, J. T. On the nature of input channels in visual processing. *Psychological Review*, 1977, *84*, 472–484.

Bruder, G. A. Role of visual familiarity in the word-superiority effects obtained with the simultaneous matching task. *Journal of Experimental Psychology: Human Perception and Performance*, 1978, *4*, 88–100.

Eichelman, W. H. Familiarity effects in the simultaneous matching task. *Journal of Experimental Psychology*, 1970, *86*, 275–282.

Eriksen, B. A., & Eriksen, C. W. Effects of noise letters upon the identification of a target letter in a non-search task. *Perception and Psychophysics*, 1974, *16*, 143–149.

Estes, W. K. Memory, perception, and decision in letter identification. In R. L. Solso (Ed.), *Information processing and cognition: The Loyola symposium*. New York: Wiley, 1975.

Flowers, J. H., Warner, J. L., & Polansky, M. L. Response and encoding factors in "ignoring" irrelevant information. *Memory and Cognition*, 1979, *7*(2), 86–94.

Gardner, H. E. *The acquisition of song: A developmental approach*. Ann Arbor Symposium paper, University of Michigan, July 1979.

Gibson, E. J. *Principles of perceptual learning and development*. New York: Appleton-Century-Crofts, 1969.

Greenwald, A. G. A choice reaction time test of ideomotor theory. *Journal of Experimental Psychology*, 1970, *86*, 20–25.

Johnson, N. On the function of letters in word recognition: Some data and a preliminary model. *Journal of Verbal Learning and Verbal Behavior*, 1975, *14*, 17–29.

LaBerge, D. Perceptual learning and attention. In W. K. Estes (Ed.), *Handbook of learning and cognitive processes* (Vol. 4). Hillsdale, N.J.: Erlbaum Associates, 1976.

LaBerge, D. The perception of units in beginning reading. In L. Resnick & P. Weaver (Eds.), *Theory and practice of beginning reading instruction*. Hillsdale, N.J.: Erlbaum Associates, 1979.

LaBerge, D., & Lawry, J. A. Explorations of changing perceptual modes due to attentional factors induced by task demands. In D. Speer (Ed.), *Attention: Theory, brain function, and clinical application*. Hillsdale, N.J.: Erlbaum Associates, in press.

LaBerge, D., & Samuels, J. J. Toward a theory of automatic information processing in reading. *Cognitive Psychology*, 1974, *6*, 293–323.

McClelland, J. L. On the time relations of mental processes: An examination of systems of processes in cascade. *Psychological Review*, 1979, *86*, 287–330.

Petersen, R. J., & LaBerge, D. Contextual control of letter perception. *Memory and Cognition*, 1977, *5*, 205–213.

Rayner, K., & Posnansky, C. Stages of processing in word identification. *Journal of Experimental Psychology: General*, 1978, *107*, 64–80.

Samuels, S. J., LaBerge, D., & Bremer, C. D. Units of word recognition: Evidence for developmental changes. *Journal of Verbal Learning and Verbal Behavior*, 1978, *17*, 715–720.

Shaffer, W. O., & LaBerge, D. Automatic semantic processing of unattended words. *Journal of Verbal Learning and Verbal Behavior*, 1979, *18*, 413–426.

Stroop, J. R. Studies of interference in serial verbal reactions. *Journal of Experimental Psychology*, 1935, *18*, 643–662.

Studdert-Kennedy, M. Speech perception. In N. Lass (Ed), *Contemporary issues in experimental phonetics*. New York: Academic Press, 1976.

Terry, P., Samuels, S. J., and LaBerge, D. The effects of letter degradation and letter spacing on word recognition. *Journal of Verbal Learning and Verbal Behavior*, 1976, *15*, 577–585.

Willows, D. M., & MacKinnon, G. E. Selective reading: Attention to the "unattended" lines. *Canadian Journal of Psychology*, 1973, *27*, 292–304.

Motivated Retrieval from Archival Memory

Raymond S. Nickerson
Bolt Beranek and Newman, Inc.

*M*Y title demands an explanation, if not an apology. So I will begin by trying to explain what I mean first by *archival memory* and then by *motivated retrieval*.

The term *archival memory* was selected by default. The fact is, I am not sure how to characterize my interest precisely with a single term or phrase. *Long-term memory* will not do because it is used in the literature in too many ways. In particular, while it is sometimes used to refer to the retention of information over a period of years (which is appropriate for my purposes), it also is sometimes used to refer to information that has been retained for only minutes or even seconds (as, for example, when in a probe-recall task one refers to words recalled from more than six or eight positions back in the list as being recalled from long-term memory). Nor does *semantic memory* suffice, at least insofar as that term is used to represent something distinct from episodic memory, because I do not wish to rule out memory for events. *Lexical memory* is even more narrow, and therefore also inappropriate.

I was tempted to use the term *natural memory*, but decided not to because that suggests that I consider the type(s) of memory with which this paper does not deal to be unnatural, and I do not mean to suggest that. *Archival memory* seemed right when I first thought of it because it conveys the notion of relative permanence, which is intended; but it may, for some people, be suggestive of "dead storage," which is not. On balance, however, of the several possibilities that were considered, *archival memory* seems to come closest to capturing the essence of what I have in mind, so I will use it until a better term comes along.

What I mean by the term, as it is used in this paper, is memory for information that is acquired in the normal course of life and retained more or less indefinitely. It is our memory for words, for facts, for names, for places, for events, for procedures, and for that

73

portion of the information we acquired in school and forgot to forget. One might be tempted to equate it with one's knowledge of one's private life and of the world in general, but that would not be quite right because one's knowledge of oneself and the world goes considerably beyond the contents of one's memory. Knowledge includes not only information that one has explicitly acquired but also what one can infer from that information; in other words, what one remembers hopefully does not come close to exhausting what one knows. The problem of telling the difference between what is remembered, in any particular case, and what is inferred, is a nontrivial one, but that fact does not invalidate the distinction.

There are at least four questions one might like to ask about archival memory: (a) What is stored in it? (b) Why is what is stored stored? (c) How is what is stored stored? and (d) How is what is stored accessed and used? I have referred to these four questions as questions of content, selectivity, representation, and retrieval (Nickerson, 1977). This paper relates primarily to the fourth of these questions, the question of retrieval.

At the risk of oversimplification—which is perhaps less a risk than a surety in any effort to understand human memory—we may distinguish two kinds of retrieval: that which is passive, spontaneous, and automatic versus that which is active, effortful, and consciously directed. It is undoubtedly wrong to draw a sharp distinction here; retrieval can be more or less active, more or less effortful, more or less directed; but the difference is clear in prototypical cases. Examples of the first kind of retrieval include assigning names to common objects during conversation, remembering one's destination while driving a car, recognizing the voice of a friend on the telephone, remembering the rules of a familiar game. Examples of the second type might include trying to recall the elusive name of an acquaintance of many years ago, trying to recollect when and where one first ate pizza, trying to think of a familiar word containing the letter sequence *HTH*, generating as long a list as possible of animal names. It is the second kind of retrieval that is referred to in this paper as *motivated retrieval*.

Note that the two concepts, archival memory and motivated retrieval, are orthogonal. Often information may be retrieved from archival memory quite effortlessly; conversely, considerable directed effort may sometimes be required to retrieve information from memory that would not be considered archival as the term is used here—which is why both concepts are required to delimit the focus of this paper. It is the active, effortful, consciously directed retrieval of information that has been acquired in the natural course of life and is retained more or less indefinitely—motivated retrieval from archival memory—that will be the primary focus of attention in what follows.

I will describe four approaches that my colleagues and I have taken to explore certain aspects of motivated retrieval from archival memory. Three of these approaches will be mentioned only briefly; the bulk of the paper will be devoted to the fourth. Most of the work that will be discussed is currently in progress and is reported here in the spirit of raising questions and suggesting possible directions for further research. The experiments that will be mentioned have not been theory driven. They represent efforts to observe memory in operation under a variety of conditions, the hope being that such observations will provide some clues regarding how memory is structured and how it works. My purposes in writing the paper will be well served if readers are left with some interesting researchable questions about archival memory that they did not already have.

Memory for Common Objects

A paper illustrating one approach to the study of motivated remembering from archival memory has recently been published (Nickerson & Adams, 1979). Subjects were given a variety of tasks that were designed to assess the degree to which they could remember the visual details of an object they would have seen many times in their lives and with which they would undoubtedly have claimed to be familiar—in this case, a U.S. penny. Inasmuch as it seemed safe to assume that all of our subjects would probably have been willing to say that they would recognize a penny if shown one, the study was calculated to raise a question regarding what it means to be able to recognize something, or more particularly, what the ability to recognize something implies regarding what is stored about that something in memory.

Our subjects—all adult U.S. citizens—were asked to draw a penny from memory, to draw a penny given a list of its visual features, to distinguish among a list of features those that do appear on a penny from those that do not, to indicate what was wrong with an erroneous drawing of a penny, and to select the correct representation of a penny from a set of drawings containing many incorrect representations.

Performance was surprisingly poor on all of these tasks. Lest the reader think our subjects were unusual in this regard, he may check his own ability to draw a penny or, alternatively, to perform the easiest of our tasks by selecting the correct representation from the several candidates shown in Figure 1.

FIGURE 1. Which is the correct drawing of the U.S. penny?

We interpreted our results to be consistent with the notion that the ability to recognize objects in real-world contexts is not good evidence that the memory representations of those objects are accurate in much detail. It may be that relatively little stored information suffices to support the kind of recognition capability that everyday life typically requires us to have. Perhaps what we remember about "familiar" objects is what we must remember in order to distinguish them from other objects, from which it is important that they be distinguished, and this may not be so very much as we might have supposed.

Estimates of Unknown Quantities

In this case, we have asked people to estimate certain quantities the values of which they are unlikely to know explicitly.[1] The purpose is to explore how people make use of what they do know to make inferences about things they do not know.

Figure 2 shows data obtained from twelve people who were asked the questions shown in Table 1. Answers were converted into "factuality," or F, scores defined as

$$F = \log_{10} (S/T)$$

where S represents the answer given by the subject and T represents the correct answer (truth).

Table 1

Examples of questions used in experiment on quantity estimation

1. How many pounds of cane sugar did the average American consume in 1974?
2. How many registered pet cemeteries are there in the U.S.?
3. What is the average number of people per sq. mile in India?
4. How long is the Amazon River?
5. How many commercial airline pilots are there in the U.S.?
6. How many Americans died through combat in the U.S. Revolutionary War?
7. How much does a U.S. dime weigh?
8. How many live chickens are there in the U.S.?

The use of the S/T ratio follows from the view that "closeness" to truth should be defined not in terms of the absolute magnitude of an error, but in terms of the magnitude of the erroneous response relative to the magnitude of the correct response. An error of 5 miles in estimating a distance of 1,000 miles is, for most purposes, much smaller than an error of 5 feet in estimating a distance of 50 feet. The rationale for the logarithmic transformation is the assumption that underestimation that yields an answer that is 1/x of the correct one is, in some psychologically meaningful sense, an error of about the same magnitude as an overestimation by a factor of x. Note that, given the log-ratio measure, a precisely correct answer results in a score of 0; underestimations yield negative scores, and overestimations, positive ones.

1. The work mentioned in this section was done in collaboration with Marilyn J. Adams.

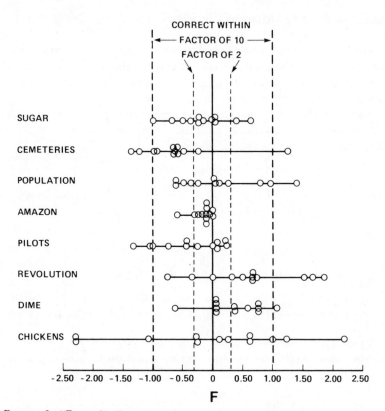

FIGURE 2. "Factuality" scores (see text) for each of 12 subjects who attempted to answer the questions in Table 1.

About 83% of the F scores shown in Figure 2 fall between −1 and +1, indicating that these subjects were able for the most part to infer answers to these questions that were correct to within an order of magnitude. About 40% of the scores were between −0.3 and +0.3, indicating correctness within a factor of 2.

Tape recordings of people "thinking aloud" while trying to estimate the answers to questions such as those in Table 1 are being studied for hints regarding the information that people retrieve from memory to provide a basis upon which to make their estimates, and the kinds of inferential procedures they apply to that information.

A generalization that our results lead us to state as a conjecture is that, as a consequence of their ability to use information in memory inferentially, people have a very great deal of approximate knowledge about the world. We would also state as a conjecture that approximate knowledge is quite adequate for a large percentage of real-life situations. Indeed the need for precise knowledge may be relatively rare. When precision is required, one typically resorts to sources of information other than one's head.

Introspective Observations

A third approach to the study of motivated remembering from archival memory that I will mention is not a very respectable one among many investigators, but I think it can be useful nonetheless. It involves introspecting on one's own efforts to recover information that memory seems reluctant to deliver up.

I have on occasion attempted to record the process of trying to retrieve some information from memory that was proving to be difficult to find. Inasmuch as the recording is done after the retrieval effort has been made, there is the risk of misremembering the process of remembering. But inasmuch as we are only looking for hints, the risk is probably acceptable. An example should suffice to illustrate the approach.

Consider the following effort to recall the name of a street that is located a few blocks from where I live. The name would not come to mind, but I did know it to be the name of a friend. The name Elliott suggested itself, but did not seem to be correct. I thought the name I was looking for was a first name, and although Elliott can be either a first or last name, it is in fact the last name of a friend of mine. I also was fairly sure the sought-for name was the first name of a female, and the Elliott in mind was a male. (In retrospect, I do not know whether I was aware of this constraint before or after thinking of Elliott, but I believe it was after. Was it the retrieval of the male-name candidate that brought this fact to mind?) As the search continued, the name Cellier surfaced, the last name of a close friend of Elliott's, who was also a friend of mine. Next came Emil, the first name of Cellier; then Hilda, wife of Emil. Hilda was immediately recognized as the name of the street. I have tried to represent the relationships involved in this retrieval effort graphically, and the best I can do is shown in Figure 3.

There are several aspects of this example that are especially interesting; I will mention two. First is the question of why, in looking for Hilda, I first found Elliott. It is not difficult to find a plausible path from one concept to the other, but getting first to Hilda and from there to Elliott seems a much more likely associative

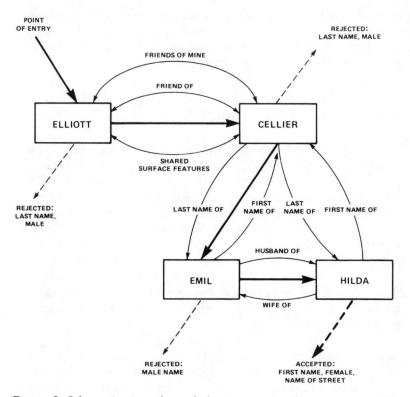

FIGURE 3. Schematization of search for street name that was not readily accessible. Sought name was "Hilda," which was eventually retrieved after "Elliott," "Cellier" and "Emil" were considered—in that order—and rejected.

sequence than the reverse, given the nature of the retrieval goal. The fact that the search for Hilda yielded Elliott first, invites the use of a spatial metaphor: It is almost as though the search for Hilda was begun in the right "region" of memory but at not quite the right spot.

A second interesting aspect of this example is interesting on the assumption that the phonemic similarity between Elliott and Cellier facilitated that association, an assumption that is strengthened by the fact that Elliott was not the only name of a mutual friend that could have led to Cellier, but was probably the only one that sounded quite so similar. To suggest that the structural similarity between Elliott and Cellier played a role in this retrieval process is to suggest that the structural similarity of two words, neither of which is the target word, can facilitate an associative sequence by which the target word may be found.

I do not mean to suggest that introspective data of the kind alluded to here should be used as a basis for evaluating theories of memory. I believe they do, however, suggest some questions about memory that otherwise might not be asked, and that they can provide some useful hints regarding some aspects of the way memory works. Such hints must be pursued experimentally if they are to eventuate in anything more substantive than conjectures. But to ignore such hints may be to overlook a major source of testable hypotheses.

A limitation of the introspective approach is that it can yield information only about those aspects of remembering that are available to consciousness, which, to the extent that such aspects are the focus of interest, need not be a limitation at all.

List Generation

The fourth approach that we have taken to explore motivated re-membering, and the one on which the remainder of the paper will be focused, involves a method that several investigators have used to study memory retrieval, namely that of having people attempt to generate lists of words that satisfy various criteria. The criterion may be semantic (names of vegetables), phonemic (words that rhyme with *pair*), orthographic (words with *c* in the third-letter position), or compound (five-letter names of animals). We had people generate such unlikely lists as words whose meanings change as a function of which syllable is stressed (*object, invalid*), words that contain the letters *p, d,* and *r* in any position (*ripped, dapper*) and palindromes (*tenet, radar*).

It should be noted at the outset that interest in the list-generation task is not based on the assumption that the way in which subjects perform the task is necessarily indicative of the way in which words are retrieved from lexical memory in language production. As Indow (1980) has pointed out, when people talk for the purpose of communicating, they usually are not conscious of scanning memory for words, as they are when attempting to gen-erate lists. There are exceptions to this rule: People do, now and then, find themselves searching for a word; and they do some-times have occasion to generate lists for purposes of communica-tion. The writing of poetry, and similar activities that involve the creation of linguistic structures that satisfy certain constraints, also may engage search processes not unlike those involved in the production of lists. By and large, however, the processes that underlie the production of words in conversation seem unlikely to be precisely those involved when an individual generates a list for the sake of generating a list. At least our reason for studying the latter process is not what we hope to learn thereby about the former one.

Several aspects of the performance of list-generation tasks are of interest, but perhaps the greatest amount of attention has been given to certain temporal relationships, and in particular to the way in which the rate of word production depends on such factors as the nature of the criterion and the time on the task. By studying the time course of the list-generation process as it relates to a variety of production criteria, one hopes to learn something about the way in which memory is organized and the relative ease with which it can be accessed by different routes. The task is attractive because of its pure-production nature, which means that the interpretation of its temporal characteristics is not complicated by considerations of input-processing requirements.

The curve showing the relationship between the cumulative number of items recalled and time on the task typically is a negatively accelerated one, as is idealized by the top graph of Figure 4. Individual subjects do not typically produce such smooth curves; however, this idealization does reflect a main characteristic of performance, namely the fact that the rate at which words are produced tends to decrease fairly regularly over time (as idealized by the bottom graph of Figure 4). Figure 5 shows some curves representing the performance of several subjects on two different list-generation tasks.[2] Results are shown for the best (most productive), the worst (least productive), and two intermediate subjects from each of two sets of 20 subjects who attempted to generate lists of bird names in one case and names of countries in the other. Figure 6 shows the results for the best, the worst, and an intermediate subject from each of four sets of four subjects who attempted to generate lists of words satisfying the orthographic criteria indicated on the graphs. (Only the best and worst subjects are represented on the graph for words ending in PT because the performance of all four fit within such a narrow range.) The same

2. The data represented in this figure were collected in collaboration with Edward Smith and Roger Wallach; those represented in Figures 6, 9, and 11 were collected in collaboration with Ann Rollins.

type of curve has been obtained when the material to be recalled consists of items presented during the experiment (Roediger & Thorpe, 1978) as when the task requires that items belonging to some specified category be recalled from archival memory (Rundus, 1973; Shiffrin, 1970).

A point that deserves some emphasis relates to the variability in performance across subjects that is illustrated by these graphs. Typically, the rate of word production and the total number of words produced during a given time vary considerably with the nature of the criterion for list inclusion. It is also the case, how-

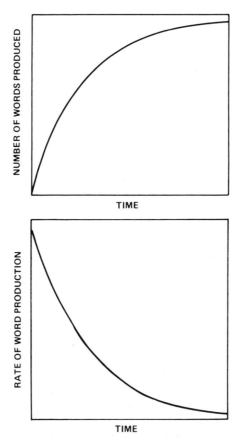

FIGURE 4. Curves showing idealized performance on word-production or list-generation tasks. The top curve shows cumulative number of words produced, and the bottom one rate of word production, as functions of time on the task.

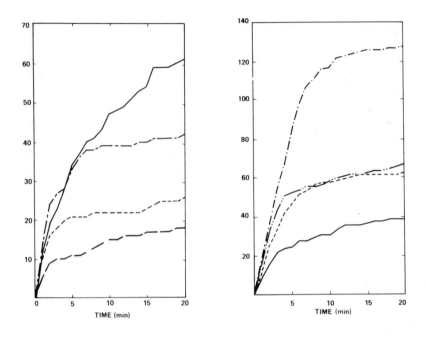

NUMBER OF BIRD NAMES PRODUCED   NUMBER OF COUNTRY NAMES PRODUCED

FIGURE 5. Performance of several subjects, including most and least productive, generating names of birds in one case and names of countries in the other. (Note difference in scale.)

ever, that for a given criterion, one frequently gets large performance differences across subjects. This being so, pooling data across subjects and drawing "average" curves is a questionable practice. This is especially true if one wishes to fit the data with an equation and draw some inferences from the values of its parameters. Pooling for the sake of smoothing may be justified when the subjects are very similar in their performance, but it is risky when they are not.

The fact that the rate of word production typically falls off as time goes on is not surprising. Even in the absence of an explicit model of how the task is performed, one would probably predict that as the subject uses up more and more of the supply of target

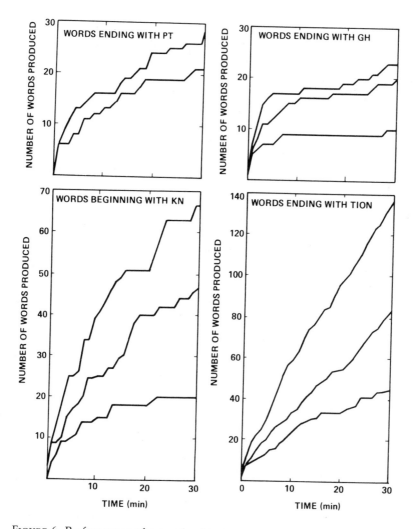

FIGURE 6. Performance of several subjects attempting to generate lists of words satisfying various orthographic criteria.

words, the identification of words that have not already been produced will become increasingly difficult, and time consuming.

One plausible answer to the question of *why* the rate of word production decreases is that producing a word involves a search process, the productiveness of which varies with the ratio of targets to nontargets among the items through which the search is being made, and that finding a target effectively decreases this ratio. This conjecture involves an assumption about the nature of the search process. If the search were random and if items (both targets and nontargets) were removed from the search space as they were considered, then the ratio of targets to nontargets would remain constant over time, and consequently the word-production rate should remain constant until the set of possibilities had been exhausted, at which time it would be zero. Thus, if one is to attribute the decreasing rate of word production to a decreasing target-to-nontarget ratio, one must assume either that the search is not random, or that items are not eliminated from the candidate set when they are considered during the search process.

Another plausible way of explaining the decreasing word-production rate is to assume a redistribution of processing capacity in response to the changing demands of the task. Initially, the subject's entire capacity can be devoted to word production. But as one produces more and more words, an increasing proportion of this capacity must be used to keep track of the words that have already been produced, if repetitions are to be avoided. If the words are produced orally, the keeping-track task will impose a load on short-term memory. If they are written, the subject need not remember them, but if he does not, he must continually scan the list in order to verify that a "new" word he thinks of is not one that has already been produced. In either case, the demands of the keeping-track task would increase with the size of the set of words that have already been generated, and the increasing demands of the keeping-track task could affect adversely the primary task of producing new words.

These two explanations of decreasing word-production rate—decreasing target-to-nontarget ratio and redistribution of processing capacity—are not mutually exclusive possibilities. Both could be at least partially correct. The second explanation has not been articulated in a very precise form. A very simple model has been suggested, however, that assumes a decreasing target-to-nontarget ratio and that predicts a relationship between word-production rate and time on the task, of the following form:

$$n(t) = n(\infty) (1 - e^{-\lambda t}) \qquad (1)$$

where n(t) is the total number of words produced by time t, $n(\infty)$ is the total number that can be produced in an unlimited time, and λ

is a growth parameter that determines the rate at which the curve approaches asymptote. By differentiating Equation 1, we obtain

$$\frac{dn(t)}{dt} = n(\infty)\lambda e^{-\lambda t} = \lambda[n(\infty) = n(t)] \tag{2}$$

as the rate of word production as a function of time. The first of these equations, which describes the curve in the top graph of Figure 4, is the more convenient of the two and has been the more frequently used by investigators working in this area. (Equation 2 describes the curve in the bottom graph of Figure 4.) Beginning with Bousfield and Sedgewick (1944), several investigators have obtained results that could be described reasonably well by this function (Indow & Togano, 1970; Johnson, Johnson, & Mark, 1951; Kaplan, Carvellas, & Metlay, 1969; Metlay, Handley, & Kaplan, 1971).

A Possible Interpretation of Equation 1

Assume there exists in that portion of memory that is being searched a set of N items, $n(\infty)$ of which would be recognized as satisfying the criterion for membership on the list the subject is attempting to generate. A random draw from the search set, therefore, would produce a target item with probability $n(\infty)/N$.

Suppose that in each unit-time interval, the subject draws (in parallel, or serially without replacement)[3] a random sample of S items from the N-item set. On the average, the number of targets contained in such a sample will be

$$\tau = S\frac{n(\infty)}{N}$$

Suppose that all of the items sampled during one interval are replaced before the next interval's sample is drawn (that is, although the sampling within an interval is done without replacement, sampling across intervals is done with replacement). The average number of *new* targets contained in one unit-time sample will be the difference between the average number of targets in the sample and the average number of *old* (previously discovered) targets

3. If S is very small relative to N, the error resulting from using $Sn(\infty)/N$ for the case in which items are sampled with replacement within the unit interval, will be negligibly small.

in the same sample. Since n(t) represents the number of targets found by time t, the number of undiscovered (new) targets at time t is $n(\infty) - n(t)$ and the average number of new targets in a sample will be

$$r_{new} = \frac{S[n(\infty) - n(t)]}{N}. \tag{3}$$

Equation 3, then, represents the rate at which new targets should be found, according to this random-sampling-with-replacement model. And with λ substituted for S/N, it is equivalent to Equation 2, which represents the empirical results that have typically been obtained.

This model was first proposed by Kaplan, Carvellas, and Metlay (1969) and has been referred to by Indow and Togano (1970) as the Constant Rate and Exhaustive Scanning (CRES) model. Note that it is the rate of sampling items for inspection (S/N) that remains constant, not the rate of discovery of new targets. The latter rate changes proportionally with the ratio of the number of remaining undiscovered targets to the total number of candidates in the set, and of course this ratio diminishes as new targets are found.

An Alternative Representation of the CRES Model

Equations 1–3 describe the prediction of the CRES model with respect to the relationship between the number of words produced and the amount of time the subject has been working at the task. Alternatively, we might derive the expected number of "trials" required to yield a given number of target words. We define a trial as the drawing at random of an item from the search set, and assume that each item, whether a target or not, is replaced before the next draw. Let N represent the total number of candidates within the search set, T the number of targets within this set, and F the number of targets that have been found by any given time. (T and F are equivalent, respectively, to the $n(\infty)$ and $n(t)$ of Equations 1–3; the change in notation is for the sake of convenience.) Letting p_F represent the probability that a randomly drawn item will be a new target, given that F targets have already been found, we have

$$p_F = \frac{T - F}{N}$$

The probability of drawing a target on the first trial is

$$P_0 = \frac{T}{N} .$$

The probability that the first target will be drawn on the ith trial is

$$p_0(i) = (1 - p_0)^{i - 1} p_0 .$$

The expected number of trials required to produce the first target is

$$E(1) = \sum_{i = 1}^{\infty} p_0(i)i = \sum_{i = 1}^{\infty} p_0(1 - p_0)^{i - 1} i = \frac{1}{p_0} = \frac{N}{T} .$$

The expected number of trials required to produce the $(F+1)^{th}$ target, given that F targets have already been found, is

$$E(F+1 | F) = \sum_{i = 1}^{\infty} p_F(1 - p_F)^{i - 1} i = \frac{1}{p_F} = \frac{N}{T - F} .$$

The expected number of trials required to produce a total of k targets, therefore, is

$$E(k) = \sum_{F = 0}^{k - 1} E(F+1 | F) = \sum_{F = 0}^{k - 1} \frac{1}{p_F} = \sum_{F = 0}^{k - 1} \frac{N}{T - F} . \qquad (4)$$

Figure 7 shows the cumulative expected number of trials to find k targets for several values of T, given $N = 100$.

If the axes of this figure are reversed to show number of targets as the dependent variable and expected number of trials as the independent one, as in Figure 8, the curves look very much like cumulative exponentials, which indeed they approximately are. Letting E represent the expected number of trials, we may approximate the curves of Figure 8 by

$$k = T(1 - e^{- \lambda E})$$

where $\lambda = .01$, the probability of drawing any given item of the 100-item set on a single trial.

Several properties of the curves of Figure 8 are worth noting at this point. First, given fixed N, the rate of word production (or the

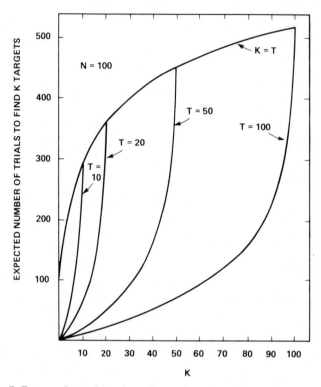

FIGURE 7. Expected number of random selections with replacement to find k targets within search set of 100 items. The parameter, T, is the total number of targets within the 100-item set.

number of words produced by a given number of trials) is directly proportional to T. That Equation 1 predicts this relationship is obvious by inspection. Second, the expected number of trials to produce a given percentage, P, of T targets is relatively independent of T, except when T is quite small or P is close to 1. This point is illustrated by the constant-proportionality lines in Figure 8, which show the expected number of trials required to produce any given proportion of the targets for target sets of widely different sizes. For example, given a search set of 100 items, it should take approximately 65 trials to find 50% of the targets when there are 10 of them, and about 69 trials to find the same percentage when there are 100 of them. In other words, the time required to find a given *percentage* of targets is a function of the size of the search set and relatively independent of the number of targets in the set. (The same point could be made from Equation 1: It is clear from that equation that

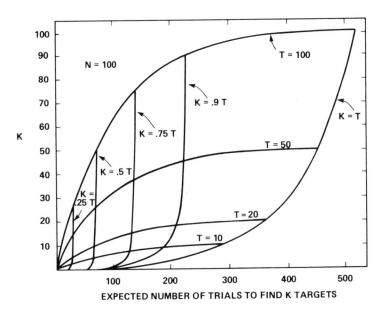

FIGURE 8. Figure 7 with axes reversed, showing k as a function of the expected number of trials to find k targets. The curves showing k as different proportions of T indicate the expected number of trials required to yield specified proportions of the total number of targets.

the rate at which the asymptote of the n(t) curve is approached is independent of what the asymptote is and is strictly a function of λ, which, by assumption, is the rate at which items are sampled from the entire search set.) One *would* expect a strong relationship between the number of trials required to yield a given percentage of the targets and the number of targets in the search set *if* the number of targets varied directly with the total number of items in the set; but the important variable in this relationship is the total number of items in the search set and not the total number of targets.

The third thing to note from Figure 8 is not obvious from Equation 1, and that is that the expected number of trials to produce *all* T targets, again given fixed N, does increase with increasing T. In particular, given N of 100, the expected numbers of trials to produce all 10, 20, 50, or 100 targets for these different values of T are 293, 360, 450, and 519, respectively. The reason this relationship is not apparent from Equation 1 is that that equation describes a continuous function that of course never does reach asymptote.

A fourth implication of the CRES model is also clarified by Figure 8. Note that on the assumption of random sampling with replacement, it takes very many more trials to find all the items of a target set than to find a relatively large proportion of them, and that this disparity increases both with the size of the search set (N) and with the proportion of the search-set items that are targets (T/N). To illustrate, with a search set of 100 items, it takes over 6 times as many trials to find all the items in a 50-item target set as it takes to find half of them. If all the items in a 100-item search set are targets (top curve in Figure 8), it takes about 7.5 times as many trials to find them all as it does to find half of them, and over twice as long to find them all as to find 90% of them. With smaller search sets and target sets the disparity is not so great, but it is still remarkable. With a search set of 20, for example, half of a target set of size 10 will be found in about 13 trials on the average, whereas it will take about 56 trials to find all 10, a ratio of about 4 to 1. When all the items of a 20-item search set are targets, it will take about 13 trials to find 10 of them and about 72 trials to find all 20, a ratio of about 5.5 to 1.

The CRES model has the virtue of simplicity, and it predicts not only the exponential relationship between number of words produced and time, but several other results that have been obtained. I believe the model to be incorrect, for reasons that will be given later, but it provides a frame of reference in terms of which to discuss experimental tasks and findings until a more generally adequate model is proposed. Moreover, given that it does a good job of accounting for several findings, there may be something of value to learn by attempting to understand *why* it fails to account for others.

Interpretation of n(∞)

According to the CRES model, the asymptote, n(∞), represents the number of target words a subject would produce given unlimited time, which is to say, all the target words in the search set. In practice subjects are never given unlimited time, and the asymptote is estimated by fitting a curve to data obtained during a relatively short period. The period often is long enough, however, that subjects are producing words at a very slow rate by the end of it.

Sometimes n(∞) is taken as an indication of the total number of words in a subject's vocabulary that satisfy the criterion for inclusion on the list. This is tantamount to assuming that the search set includes either the subject's entire vocabulary or at least that portion of it that contains all the target words that he knows. That this is not a generally valid interpretation of $n(\infty)$ is shown by two facts: First, subjects often can recognize as bona fide members of a criterion set, words other than those they have produced; and second, when asked to produce lists satisfying the same criterion on several different occasions, they typically produce a few more items on each successive attempt.

While $n(\infty)$ cannot, in general, be taken as the number of target words in the subject's vocabulary, it seems reasonable to assume that these two variables are highly correlated. That is to say, the larger the number of target words in the subject's vocabulary, the larger we would expect $n(\infty)$ to be. Why subjects fail to produce *all* the target words in their vocabulary when attempting to generate lists is an interesting question. The fact that they do fail to do so suggests that either (a) the assumption that the search is a random-sampling-with-replacement process is wrong, or (b) the search set does not contain all the target items in the subject's vocabulary.

There is another possibility, however, that is suggested by the fourth property of the curves of Figure 8, and it relates to motivation. Recall that on the assumption of random sampling with replacement, it takes very many more trials to find the last X percent of the targets than to find the first X percent. If one is willing to assume that the sampling process is a cognitively demanding task, one might speculate that as the sampling begins to return a vanishingly small percentage of new targets, the subject simply becomes less willing to persevere. Moreover, given that the diminution of the rate of return is the greater the larger the sizes of both search set and target set, one might expect the percentage of targets found to decrease as these variables—and especially the former—increase.

Interpretation of λ

According to the CRES model, λ reflects the ratio of the subject's sampling rate to the size of the set through which he is searching. There are two things, therefore, that could change the value of λ: a change in the number of items sampled per unit time, or a change in the total number of items in the search set. A change in the ratio of targets to nontargets should have no effect on λ. Therefore to the extent that the random-sampling-with-replacement model is taken as a representation of the process by which people produce word lists, a change in λ must be taken as reflecting either a change in sampling rate or a change in the size of the set of items from which the sampling is being done.

Some Results with a Word-Production Task

One of the things that makes it difficult to test the adequacy of any hypothesis relating to the notion of target-to-nontarget ratios is the fact that for most list-generation tasks, neither the number of targets nor the number of nontargets that lie within the search space is known. Kaplan, Carvellas, and Metlay (1969) have used a task, however, for which, given some plausible assumptions, these numbers may be estimated. Subjects were asked to generate as many four-letter words as possible from a set of L letters. L was an experimental parameter and was varied from 5 to 10. The data were well described by Equation 1. Kaplan, Carvellas, and Metlay's curves were based on data pooled over subjects; however, we have used their task and found that the performance curves of individual subjects typically can be fitted reasonably well by Equation 1. Figure 9 shows the data from three individual subjects we ran on Kaplan, Carvellas, and Metlay's task, using only 10-letter sets. These subjects were all professionals with presumably well-developed verbal skills, which may account for the high percentage of target words two of them produced in 30 minutes relative to the numbers reported by Kaplan, Carvellas, and Metlay. The data were fitted by exponential functions that were forced to coincide with the data curves at the 30-minute point.

In addition to yielding data that could be described by Equation 1 Kaplan, Carvellas, and Metlay's experiment had the following results: (a) The total number of words produced after an unlimited time increased as L increased; (b) the cumulative number of words produced *by a given time* also increased with L; and (c) the ratio of number of words produced per unit time to the total number of words produced after an unlimited time *decreased* as L increased. These results may be described in terms of Equation 1 by saying that (a) $n(\infty)$ varied directly with L; (b) for any given value of t, $n(t)$ varied directly with L; and (c) the rate at which $n(t)$ approached

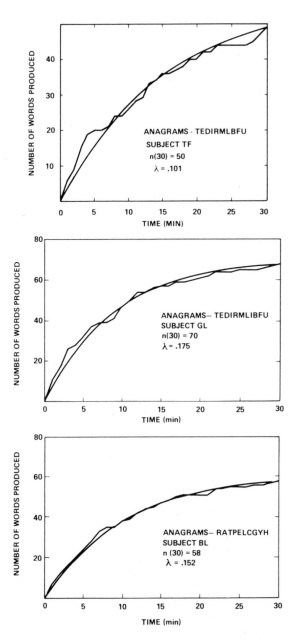

FIGURE 9. Performance of three subjects trying to list four-letter words that can be made with the specified sets of ten letters.

asymptote decreased as L increased (i.e., λ decreased as L increased).

Each of these findings can be accounted for by the random-sampling-with-replacement (CRES) model described above. That the total number of words produced in an unlimited time, $n(\infty)$, increases with L is a consequence of the fact that the larger L is, the greater is the number of words of a given length that can be formed, which is to say, the greater is the number of targets in the search set. (At least this must be true when a set of given size contains all the letters of sets of smaller sizes, as was the case in Kaplan, Carvellas, and Metlay's experiment.) The fact that the number of words produced by a given time increases with L is easily accounted for *if* one assumes that as L is increased, $n(\infty)$ varies with N in such a way that the ratio $n(\infty)/N$ does not decrease. (I will return to this assumption as it relates to Kaplan, Carvellas, and Metlay's experiment presently, but for the moment it is taken as valid.) For a given $n(\infty)/N$ ratio, the larger that $n(\infty)$ and N are, the smaller is the effect on $[n(\infty) - n(t)]/N$ of increasing $n(t)$. That is to say, for a given ratio of targets to nontargets in the candidate set, the probability of a randomly selected item being a new target will decrease the more slowly, the larger the number of items in the set. Finally, concerning the third finding, recall that the rate at which the curve approaches asymptote, λ, must decrease as the total number of candidates, N, increases. In the present case it seems reasonable to assume that N increased with L, so the change in λ is in the appropriate direction.

In short, the model appears to be able to account well, at least qualititatively, for the results that Kaplan et al. obtained. There are, nevertheless, several reasons to suspect that the model is not correct. First, consider the identification of the asymptote of the cumulative-response distribution ($n(\infty)$ of Equation 1) with the number of targets in a candidate set of items. As applied to the anagram task, the model defines $n(\infty)$ to be the number of target words that the subject would recognize among all possible four-letter permutations of the stimulus letters. The values of $n(\infty)$ that Kaplan et al. estimated from asymptotes of their cumulative-response distributions were 8, 14, 20.5, 28.4, 34.8, and 43.0 words for letter sets of 5 through 10 letters, respectively. If one exhaustively lists all of the four-letter words that can be formed from each of the stimulus sets that they used, one finds an average of about 11, 20, 33, 48, 68, and 91 words for sets of size 5 through 10, respectively. (See Table 2.) For the larger sets, therefore, subjects pro-

Table 2
Approximate number of four-letter words that can be formed from each of the letter sets used by Kaplan, Carvellas, and Metlay.*

Parent Letter Set	5	6	L 7	8	9	10
RATPELCGYH	14	26	37	46	63	84
LERDOPMNCH	8	18	31	48	63	85
TEDIRMLBFU	10	21	35	51	67	94
RADILGBNTW	11	17	29	49	74	100
Mean	10.75	20.50	33.00	48.50	67.75	91.00
T Values Estimated from Data	8.0	14.0	20.5	28.4	34.8	43.0
Percent of Target Words Produced	74.4	68.3	62.1	58.6	51.4	47.3

*The numbers in this table are unlikely to be precise. They are based on visual inspection of a computer-generated list of all possible four-letter permutations of the appropriate sets, and therefore subject to inaccuracies deriving from the author's limitations as a word recognizer.

duced only about half of the target words that could have been produced.

One possible way to account for this fact is to assume that not all of the target words were recognizable to the subjects as words; in which case, the *effective* number of targets for a given subject would have been smaller than the numbers in Table 2 suggest. The reader may judge the plausibility of this possibility from an inspection of one of the lists of target words, which is given in Table 3. I believe that people would recognize a much larger proportion of these words than they typically produce. Inspection of some of our own data, collected with the same task, reveals that literate subjects often fail to get quite common words. We conclude that the major reason that people do not produce more words than they do, given this task, is that they fail to consider all the possibilities, not that they consider them and decide that they are not words.

Another possible explanation of the failure of subjects to produce all the target words in their vocabularies is the one mentioned above that invokes the notion of motivation. This possibility gains some credence from the fact that the percentage of the

Table 3

Four-letter words that can be formed from the first L letters of LERDOPMNCH

		L			
5	6	7	8	9	10
DOER	DOPE	DOME	DONE	CERO	CHOP
DOLE	DORP	DORM	LEND	CLOD	ECHO
LODE	DROP	MELD	LONE	CODE	HELD
LORD	LOPE	MODE	LORN	COED	HELM
LORE	PLED	MOLD	MEND	COLD	HELP
REDO	PLOD	MOLE	MORN	COLE	HEMP
RODE	POLE	MOPE	NODE	COME	HERD
ROLE	PORE	MORE	HOEL	CONE	HERL
	PROD	OMER	NOME	COPE	HERN
	ROPE	POEM	NORM	CORD	HERO
		POME	OMEN	CORE	HOED
		PROM	OPEN	CORM	HOER
		ROMP	PEND	CORN	HOLD
			PEON	CROP	HOLE
			POND	ONCE	HOLM
			PONE		HOLP
			REND		HOME
					HONE
					HOPE
					HORN
					LOCH
					PECH
8	10	13	17	15	22

target words that were produced decreased regularly with the (assumed) sizes of the search and target sets. (See bottom row of Table 2.)

A second problem with the random-sampling-with-replacement model is one that Kaplan et al. themselves point out, and because of which they are led to reject the assumption that subjects find words by searching randomly through all possible four-letter permutations. The problem is that the estimate of λ that is obtained from fitting Equation 1 to their data is not sufficiently sensitive to changes in L. Recall that by definition, $\lambda = S/N$ where S is the number of items that the subject considers per unit time (which is assumed to remain constant) and N is the number of items in the search set. Now N changes by a factor of 42 (from 120 to 5,040) as L goes from 5 to 10; however, λ, as estimated from the data, changed by a factor of only 5.3 (from .487 with L = 5 to .092 with L = 10). Thus, Kaplan et al. concluded that the subject "can exclude many four-letter permutations from the category of potential words without explicitly examining them" (p. 380). In effect, this reduces N, the total number of candidate items.

The idea that a subject can exclude candidates from consideration without explicitly considering them seems to imply either a subconscious process that examines candidate solutions, eliminating some and presenting others for conscious consideration, or a procedure for generating candidates which simply fails to generate some of the possibilities. The first alternative assumes an explicit, albeit subconscious, process of exclusion; the second assumes that exclusion is accomplished indirectly, via the constraints of a generation process.

The question of which of these possibilities is the more plausible might appear to be a moot point because it is not clear that the exclusion assumption is very helpful. One might assume that given random sampling, the *proportion* of four-letter permutations that satisy any given criterion (form words, are pronounceable) to the total number of permutations that can be made should be independent of the number of letters, L, from which the four-letter subsets are drawn. Consequently, any reduction in N, resulting from the application of some criterion for exclusion, should be proportional to the size of the unreduced set, and the multiplicative effect on N of increasing L from 5 to 10 should remain the same. In fact, given the letter sets used by Kaplan et al., it is not the case that the ratio of permutations satisfying some criterion to the total number of permutations is independent of L. In particular, the proportion of permutations that form words varies inversely with L. (See Table 4.) This is because each of the 5-letter sets contained two vowels, and with one exception the letters that were added to these 5 to produce the 6-through 10-letter sets were all consonants.

For the same reason, it is undoubtedly the case that the proportion of the total number of permutations that are pronounceable also varies inversely with L. If this is true, and if the subject can exclude unpronounceable permutations from consideration, the multiplicative effect on N of increasing L from 5 to 10 would be

Table 4

Proportion of four-letter permutations that form words for each of the letter sets used by Kaplan, Carvellas, and Metlay

Parent Letter Set	L					
	5	6	7	8	9	10
RATPELCGYH	.116	.072	.044	.027	.021	.017
LERDOPMNCH	.067	.050	.037	.029	.021	.017
TEDIRMLBFU	.083	.058	.042	.030	.022	.019
RADILGBNTW	.092	.047	.035	.029	.024	.020
Mean	.090	.057	.040	.029	.022	.018

less than 42. Whether it would approach 5.3 could be determined empirically, with some patience. If one is willing to assume, however, that the number of pronounceable permutations is a constant proportion of the number of permutations that contain at least one vowel, an estimate of the expected multiplicative effect can be made in a straightforward way. The number of four-letter permutations containing no vowel is

$$\frac{C\,!}{(C - 4)\,!}$$

where C is the number of consonants in the set of L letters. Therefore, on the above assumption the expected number of pronounceable permutations that can be made from L letters, C of which are consonants, is

$$qN_v$$

where

$$N_v = \frac{L\,!}{(L - 4)\,!} - \frac{C\,!}{(C - 4)\,!}$$

is the number of four-letter permutations that contain at least one vowel, and q may be thought of as the probability that any given such permutation will be pronounceable.

Table 5 gives N_v as a function of L for the letter sets used by Kaplan et al. In three of the cases, N_v, and therefore qN_v, changes by a factor of 28 as L goes from 5 to 10; in the fourth case (that in which the tenth letter of the set is a vowel), the change is by a factor of 35. If our assumption about the constancy of q is valid, then the assumption that the effective set that was searched included only pronounceable permutations does not by itself explain why λ, in Kaplan et al.'s experiment, changed only by a factor of 5.3. It is possible that properties of letter strings other than, or in addition to, pronounceability (e.g., unlawful letter pairs or triplets) also reduced the size of the effective set. Such properties could have an effect on the multiplicative factor, however, only to the extent that they applied to different *percentages* of the permutations that can be made from the different-size letter sets. Whether properties can be identified that could account for the required reduction seems doubtful. Moreover, even if they could be identified, there remains the question of how the exclusion based on such properties is accomplished.

Table 5

Numbers and percentages of four-letter permutations formed from Kaplan, Carvellas, and Metlay's letter sets that contain one or more vowels.*

Number of Letters in Set (L)	Number of Four-Letter Permutations	Number with Vowel (N_v)	Percent with Vowel
5	120	120	100.00
6	360	336	93.33
7	840	720	85.71
8	1680	1320	78.57
9	3024	2184	72.22
10a(3)	5040	3360	66.67
10b(3)	5040	4200	85.54

*10a represents the 3-letter sets that contained only two vowels. 10b represents the one set that contained three vowels, the third of which was only in the 10-letter set.

If we accept the λ of Equation 1 as indicative of the probability that the permutations considered during any unit-time period will contain any particular one of the possible candidates, we must conclude that the effective size of the candidate set does not grow in proportion either to the total number of permutations, or to the subset of those permutations that contain at least one vowel. Apparently one is able to constrain the search so it is more efficient than if it contained all permutations, or perhaps even all pronounceable ones. And the larger the potential search space (the larger the number the permutations), the more it seems to be constrained. One seems to be able to search in a space where the hit rate is likely to be relatively high. How one delimits that space is not clear.

A Digression

The numbers in Table 4 provide an excuse, if not a reason, for a brief digression. The fact that only about 2% of the 5,040 4-letter permutations of each of the 10-letter sets used by Kaplan, Carvellas, and Metlay form words illustrates the very considerable orthographic redundancy of English even at the individual-word level. (A similar observation could be made with respect to phonemic representations and to alphabetic languages other than English.) The small percentage is not attributable to the specific letter sets selected by Kaplan and his colleagues. Kucera and Francis's (1967) 1,014,232-word corpus contains only 3,025 different (type) 4-letter words. This represents about 0.7% of the 456,976 4-letter strings that can be formed from the 26 letters of the alphabet. Even assuming that the Kucera-Francis sample contains only about 2/3 of the 4-letter words of the language, it would still be the case that only about 1% of all possible 4-letter strings form words.

Figure 10 shows more generally the relationship between the number of words (types in the Kucera-Francis count) and the number of possible letter strings, as a function of string length. The number of words increases as the number of letters increases up to 7, and then falls off gradually as the number of letters increases still further, but staying always between 1,000 and 10,000 for word lengths between 3 and 13 letters. The number of permutations of n letters increases exponentially with n. Consequently, the ratio of number of words to number of permutations falls off approximately exponentially as the number of letters increases; and for a moderately large n, that ratio is vanishingly small. For example, only about one 6-letter string in 100,000 forms a word, and for 8- and 10-letter strings the ratios are less than 1 in 10 million and 1 in 10 billion respectively. These ratios would be larger, of course, if the letter strings were constrained to have no repeating letters or to have wordlike properties (contain an admissible mixture of consonants and vowels, be pronounceable, etc.), but they

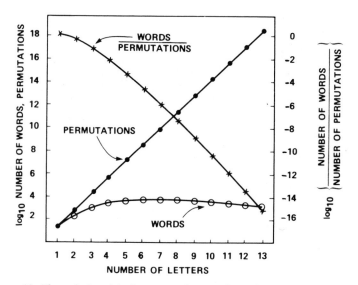

FIGURE 10. The relationship between the number of words of a specified length in the Kucera-Francis count and the total number of different letter strings of the same length that can be formed.

would still be small enough to demonstrate the very considerable redundancy of written English.

Relationship between N(∞) and λ

We have noted that according to the random-sampling-with-replacement, or CRES, model of the list-generation process: (a) n(∞) should vary directly with the number of targets in the search set (which presumably is roughly proportional to the number of targets in the subjects' vocabulary), and (b) (assuming a constant sampling rate) λ should vary inversely with the number of items in the search set and be independent of the number of targets.

What is of particular interest is the fact that n(∞) and λ are functions of different variables and that there is no a priori reason to expect them to be related in any systematic way. Indow and Togano (1970) have noted, however, that when exponential curves are fitted to list-production data obtained with a variety of list types, the parameters of the curves tend to be inversely related: As n(∞) increases, λ decreases. Figure 11 shows this relationship for the performance of a few dozen subjects on some of the tasks we have used. According to the model, this relationship suggests it must be the case that either the sampling rate or the size of the search set increases with the size of the target set. The latter possibility is an interesting one psychologically, and not altogether implausible. It suggests that the size of the "region" that is searched is somehow contingent on the size of the target set.

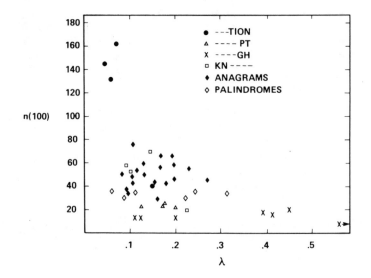

FIGURE 11. The relationship between the asymptote of word-production curves and the growth parameter for several types of list criteria.

To be more precise about what this possibility could mean is one of the challenges of this line of search. The suggestion is that the subject can restrict his search of memory for words to subsets of his lexicon, depending on what he is searching for. But if he can restrict his search, why does he not restrict it enough to consider *only* target items? It appears that the subject can restrict search, but only in certain ways and to limited degrees; the challenge is to be more specific about what can and cannot be done in this regard.

Evidences of Nonrandom Search

It has been known for a long time that people often organize their responses in terms of semantic categories in free-recall tasks when the situation permits them to do so. We have also observed several indications that the order in which words are produced is not random when the production criterion is not semantic. None of these indications has been verified statistically; they are noted here as possibilities for further exploration.

First, perusal of the lists of words produced by our subjects working on Kaplan, Carvellas, and Metlay's task (using only their 10-letter sets) made us suspect that words beginning with vowels were underrepresented. In fact, in each of several cases checked, a smaller percentage of the words produced by each subject began with vowels than would have been the expected had the words been produced by sampling randomly from the set of possibilities.

Second, we also had the impression that the frequency with which words were produced across subjects (in the same task), and the order in which they tended to be produced by individual subjects were related to the frequency of occurrence of the words in the language. While the number of subjects that we had do the task with a given letter set was too small to provide the basis for an analysis, I would state as a conjecture that (a) the greater the frequency of occurrence of a word in the language, the more likely that word is to be produced, and (b) the greater the frequency of the occurrence of a word, the sooner is that word likely to be produced on any given list. Such results would suggest that not only is the search for words not random but that at least one of the factors that give it its order operates with some consistency across subjects. Such results would also be consistent with other evidence that the frequency with which a word occurs in the lanaguage is an important determinant of how easily that word is perceived, remembered, and used. Table 6 gives the Kucera-Francis frequency count for each of the four-letter words that can be formed from the letters RATPELCGYH, on the chance that some reader may wish to check these conjectures.

A third bit of evidence regarding the nonrandom nature of the search process in this task is seen from an inspection of the lists that individual subjects produce. The list shown in Table 7 will serve to illustrate the point. The subject in this case generated 62 words in 30 minutes from the 10-letter set RADILGBNTW. The subject reported starting with a nonspecific approach, simply writing down words as they came to mind, and then adopting a more analytical attitude as the words began to come more slowly. It is apparent from even a casual inspection of the list that the order in which the words were written down is not random. In 17

Table 6
Four-letter words that can be formed from RATPELCGYH, listed in decreasing order of frequency of usage. The number following each word is its frequency in the Kucera-Francis count.

THEY	3,618	GATE	37	LACE	7	ARTY	1
EACH	877	TAPE	35	PREY	7	CLAP	1
YEAR	660	GEAR	26	PEAR	6	HARE	1
PART	500	TALE	21	CART	5	HARP	1
HELP	311	CAPE	20	CHAP	5	PEAL	1
REAL	260	TRAP	20	CHAT	5	PYRE	1
RATE	209	TRAY	18	PACT	5	RAPT	1
PLAY	200	RAGE	16	RAPE	5	CARP	0
TYPE	200	HEAP	14	ACHE	4	CRAG	0
LATE	179	LEAP	14	LACY	4	ETCH	0
CARE	162	ARCH	13	LEAR	4	GAPE	0
HEAR	153	HART	13	REAP	3	GELT	0
RACE	103	RELY	13	GALE	2	GHAT	0
CLAY	100	EARL	12	HALE	2	LYRE	0
HEAT	97	GREY	12	HEAL	2	PEAT	0
GRAY	80	PRAY	12	LATH	2	PELT	0
PAGE	66	PLEA	11	PARE	2	PLAT	0
PALE	58	TEAR	11	PATE	2	TALC	0
PATH	44	HALT	10	PERT	2	TARE	0
PACE	43	ACRE	9	RACY	2	TEAL	0
HATE	42	CAGE	9	YELP	2	TREY	0

out of 61 cases, a word differed from its predecessor with respect to only a single letter, and the remaining 3 letters occurred in the same order in both words (e.g., RAIL, WAIL, WAIT, GAIT). In 5 cases, a word had exactly the same letters as its predecessor, but in a different order. In 8 other cases, a word had three letters in common with its predecessor, but in a different order. Thus, these three relationships account for about half of all predecessor-successor relationships. In all but 8 of the remaining cases, the word had two letters in common with its predecessor. In general, it seems fairly clear that the probability of producing a particular word at a particular time was highly contingent on what word(s) had just been produced.

Table 7.

Words produced by one subject from the letters RADILGBNTW. Each cell represents one minute, and the order of the words in a cell reflects the order in which the words were produced.

1	2	3	4	5	6	7	8	9	10
RAIL	BAIL	NAIL	BRAN	RANG	DAWN	WART	GIRL	BRIG	
WAIL	BAIT	TAIL	GRIN	TANG	BIND	LINT	GIRD	BRAT	
WAIT	LAID	DIRT	GNAT	LAWN	BAND		BRAG	GRAB	
GAIT	DIAL	DART	RING		WANT			BRAD	
ARID	GLIB	BARN			WAND			DRAB	
GRID	BING				WIND			BIRD	
	BANG				WARD				
					DRAW				

11	12	13	14	15	16	17	18	19	20
GRIN	GLAD	WING	GRIT	DRAG		LARD	LAIN	LIAR	
GRIM			GRAD					LAIR	
BALD			DINT						

21	22	23	24	25	26	27	28	29	30
	DING						GARB		BAWL
							BARD		

Successive Attempts to Generate the Same List

When one is asked to generate a list of words satisfying a specified criterion, and then is asked to generate a list satisfying the same criterion a second time—minutes, hours, or even days later—the second attempt is likely to yield more words than the first. Indow and Togano (1970) report one experiment in which the same subjects were asked to generate a list of female names on four separate occasions at two- to three-month intervals. The total number of words produced increased, and the rate at which the cumulative-response curves approached asymptote decreased, with each successive attempt.

The fact that more words are produced on second or subsequent attempts to generate a specified list than on the first attempt has already been noted as one of the reasons why n(∞) cannot be taken as an indication of the number of target words in a subject's vocabulary. The finding is of interest in its own right, however, and begs an explanation. There are at least three possibilities.

1. It may be that the subject continues to attempt to generate words spontaneously following the termination of the first experimental session. Consequently, at the time of the second attempt, the number of recently activated words is greater than the number of words on the first list would indicate.

2. Perhaps the retrieval of some items primes, or in some other way facilitates, the retrieval of other associated items. In some cases the effect of the priming is sufficient to assure the retrieval of the primed items. In other cases, it is not. The state of the primed items that are not retrieved is changed as a result of the priming, however, such that on a subsequent attempt to produce words satisfying the same criterion, the probability that these items will be produced is increased. The effect would be expected to decrease as the time between the two attempts at producing the lists increases. This is the explanation proposed by Indow (1980), who suggested that during the first retrieval attempt some words are activated insufficiently to be evoked, but sufficiently to facilitate their evocation on a subsequent attempt. Indow's explanation does not necessarily involve associative priming, but is consistent with the idea; such priming could be one, but not necessarily the only, source of the hypothesized activation.

3. The third explanation is basically a statistical one. Assume that on any given attempt to generate a list, the subject produces a subset of the words in his repertory that satisfy the criterion, and

that the probability that a given word will be produced is a combination of several factors, one of which is the recency with which the word has been associated with the category criterion. On two efforts to generate the same list, sufficiently widely separated in time so the recency factor plays no role, one would expect the two lists to be nonidentical (although to have many items in common) but of equal size. When the two attempts are sufficiently close in time so that recency does play a role, one would expect the second list to be larger than the first because, although the set from which the items are selected is the same on this occasion as it was during the first attempt, the probability that some items will be selected (namely those items that appeared on the first list) is greater than it was during the first effort because of the recency effect. In other words, the probability of inclusion has not decreased for any item in the repertory, but for many items (specifically, those produced on the first attempt) it has increased; therefore, the expected number of items is greater for the second effort than for the first. Note that this explanation does not invoke the notion of interitem associations. In fact, it assumes that the probability of any given item among the set that was not produced on the first attempt being produced on the second attempt is precisely the same as the a priori probability that that item would be produced on the first attempt.

It is important to note that the second and third explanations differ fundamentally. The second one identifies unretrieved associates of the words that were produced on the first attempt as those for which the probability of being produced on the second attempt is increased. The third one identifies the words that were produced during the first attempt as those for which the probability of being produced on the second attempt is increased.

False Positives

One of the ways in which list-production tasks seem to differ from each other is with respect to the frequency with which subjects are aware of explicitly considering and rejecting items that do not satisfy the list criterion. In some cases few if any irrelevant items seem to come to mind (Indow & Togano, 1970). In other cases, subjects are keenly aware of thinking of, and rejecting, many irrelevant items. Indow (in press) refers to the kind of retrieval that is involved in the former case as *direct retrieval* and that involved

in the latter as *indirect*. It is of some interest to attempt to characterize the differences between the list criteria that yield these different effects.

It is also of some interest to consider how those irrelevant items
that do come to mind relate to the criterion for membership in the
target set. Certainly they usually are not random items from the
subject's vocabulary. They tend, in one way or another, to be
plausible candidates for inclusion on the list that is being produced. More often than not they seem to come "close" to satisfying the search crtierion, although what "coming close" means may
not be easy to specify, or may mean different things in different
contexts (e.g., "almost palindromes," words beginning with N or
GN when the criterion is KN, words with a CT in them *somewhere*
when the criterion is CT in the third- and fourth-letter positions).

It is clear that most searches are fairly constrained: When trying to
think of names of U.S. presidents, names of vegetables seldom
come to mind; when trying to produce four-letter words that begin
with P one generally is not bothered by eight-letter words or by
words that begin with K. It is the case, however, that when trying to
generate words satisfying an orthographic criterion, words that are
homophonic with the target words in the segment containing the
critical letters often come to mind. For example, efforts to produce
words ending in PT turn up false positives ending in PPED; efforts
to produce words ending in TION bring to mind words ending in
SSION; and, as noted above, when attempting to produce words
that begin with KN, one is quite aware of frequently considering
words that begin with N, or in some cases GN. However even here
it does not seem, introspectively, to be quite as simple as searching
on the N sound and then deciding to accept or reject on the basis of
inspection of the orthographic representation of the words that are
found. The ratio of N- words to KN- words listed in the eighth
edition of *Webster's New Collegiate Dictionary* is roughly 15 to 1. It
does not appear to be the case, again introspectively, that the
attempt to produce KN- words turns up 15 N- words for every KN-
word that is found.

How is memory search constrained? Why is it readily constrained on some dimensions and not on others? And what determines which dimensions will be *effective* constraints and which
will not?

If one is asked to think of a 4-letter word that is the name of a
fruit and rhymes with *bare*, one has little difficulty in quickly

producing an appropriate response. However, if asked to produce a word that contains the letter sequence WKW, it may take a while. Why does the one set of cues work so well and the other so poorly?

Strategies in Generating Lists

People undoubtedly can use a variety of strategies in generating lists. What strategies are used probably depends on the nature of the list that is being generated, and on the individual who is generating it, although any given individual may often resort to more than one strategy in the production of a given list.

In trying to think of names of vegetables, for example, one may try to visualize one's garden, and to name the vegetables that one "sees," by systematically scanning the rows of the visual image; or one may imagine oneself looking over the contents of a familiar roadside vegetable stand, or scanning a rack of packages of vegetable seeds, or looking over the contents of the family Thanksgiving table. In each of these cases, one is apparently making use of visual schemata stored in memory, and of the ability to generate visual images to facilitate the production of the words.

This description is an oversimplified one insofar as it suggests that a particular visual image is generated, scanned exhaustively, and then forgotten. There often appears to be a fair amount of skipping from image to image and returning to the same type of image, in some cases many times. For example, one might think of the Thanksgiving table and produce a few words, then imagine the rack of seed packages, and then return to the table again.

A second way in which the description may be misleading is in its implied one-way causal connection between image and word. While introspection suggests that images can be used to facilitate the production of words, words also can elicit the images; consequently, the tracking of a sequence of associative links involving both words and images becomes very difficult. One may, for example, think of the word *beans* for whatever reason, and be prompted to visualize beans in one's garden, which in turn may lead to visualization of other parts of the garden and to the elicitation of words associated with what one sees. Often, although one has a strong sense of the reality of the image that goes along with the word (e.g., it may be clear whether the peas that one is thinking of are growing in a garden, contained in a can, or sitting in a dish on a table), it is not always possible to say which came first—the word or the image.

Strategies for finding words can also be identified when the criteria for list inclusion are not semantic. Table 7 is suggestive of an approach in which the subject attempts to find a new word by making a minor modification in the word in hand.

Another example of strategizing can be drawn from the efforts of several subjects to produce lists of palindromic words. (A palindrome is a word, sentence, or sequence of sentences that reads the same backward as forward. The number of such words in English is relatively small; probably less than 100, excluding proper nouns. Table 8 gives a partial list.) The task of attempting to generate palindromic words is interesting because the types of features one usually thinks of as being helpful in limiting the search space are of questionable use in this case. There is no reason to expect that palindromic words will be more similar to each other than to other words, semantically, phonemically, or orthographically. So even if memory is organized in such a way as to facilitate search on one or more of these properties, this is not likely to simplify the search for palindromes.

Twelve subjects, all high-school graduates, were asked to list as many palindromic words as they could within thirty minutes. Half

Table 8

Some English Palindromes

A	EWE	NOON	REPAPER
AHA	EYE	NUN	REVIVER
BIB	GAG	PAP	ROTOR
BOB	GIG	PEEP	SEES
BOOB	HAH	PEP	SEXES
DAD	I	PIP	SIS
DEED	KAYAK	POOP	SOLOS
DEIFIED	LEVEL	POP	TAT
DID	MADAM	PULLUP	TENET
DUD	MAM	PUP	TIT
EKE	MINIM	RADAR	TOOT
ERE	MOM	REDDER	TOT
EVE	MUM	REFER	TUT
			WOW

of the subjects produced at least 28 words, and the most productive one listed 37. Introspective reports of our subjects give the following account of how at least some people go about trying to produce palindromes. One begins by just "trying to think of some words that fit" without attempting to follow any systematic approach for generating possibilities. Before long, however, one switches to a quasi-algorithmic procedure in which CVC, CVVC, or VCV combinations are considered systematically (e.g., *bab, beb, bib, bob* . . ., or *bab, cac, dad, faf* . . .). One individual wrote down the vowels and the vowel pairs *ee* and *oo* in a column, and then proceeded to bracket the column with each consonant in turn, looking for combinations that formed words.

This algorithm is not feasible for longer words because the number of possibilities quickly becomes unmanageable. So having exhausted the three- and four-letter possibilities, one must modify one's approach. The strategies at this point become less algorithmic and more idiosyncratic. One heuristic approach that was reported was to think of common word endings (e.g., *ed, er, ts*) and then attempt to think of words beginning with these letter sequences in reverse order. It also seems to be the case, however, that subjects often have a less clear idea of what strategy, if any, they are following in trying to produce longer words. Either they seem to be thinking of words more or less at random, or adopting a more passive attitude as though waiting for appropriate words to present themselves to consciousness. And, indeed, when such a word does make its appearance, one may be at a loss to say what elicited it. Some subjects reported that for days after working on this task, new palindromes would occasionally occur to them when they were not aware of intentionally trying to think of them.

An observation about strategy that cuts across the various types of criteria—semantic, orthographic, phonemic, or whatever—is the following one: Subjects often report being aware of adopting sometimes a passive, nonstructured approach and sometimes an active, structured one. Moreover, they report changing from one approach to the other while attempting to generate a particular list; the more typical case seems to be that in which the subject begins with a passive attitude, "just letting words suggest themselves," and then switches to a more structured approach, actively searching with the help of some rule or "map" (the garden or dining table) when the passive approach no longer yields a satisfactory return.

A Search Problem for the Reader

Much of what has been said in this paper could create the impression that searching memory for words that satisfy specified criteria is an easy task. An attempt to find words containing the letter clusters shown in Table 9 may suffice to convince the reader that this need not always be the case.

The list was given to me by a colleague in retribution for having talked him into donating a half hour of his life to the furtherance of science without telling him what he would be expected to do, and then having him spend the time trying to generate palindromes. I found the list to be a real challenge—not at all as easy as thinking of words that begin with KN, or that end with PT, or that have a CT in the third and fourth letter positions. For the compulsive puzzle doer who may find himself mentally crippled for some time by the challenge of Table 9, it is only fair to note that although all of the words given as answers in Table 10 are in the 1976 edition of *Webster's New Collegiate Dictionary*, a few of them are quite rare. However, at least some of the combinations also occur in words other than those listed in Table 10.

The exercise of trying to find the words containing the letter groups in Table 9 suggests a distinction that may be relevant to the

Table 9
WORD FUN.* *The following letter clusters are found in regular (uncapitalized) English words. Answers are given in Table 10.*

1. MKH	13. ODOD	25. KIU
2. YZA	14. TYT	26. XYM
3. SYT	15. OEI	27. MBM
4. LEK	16. EOI	28. KGO
5. FTB	17. HTH	29. UAGG
6. APLA	18. OKK	30. OCHL
7. ULOW	19. XII	31. APN
8. GHH	20. XIX	32. NYR
9. VEP	21. DAE	33. RDV
10. WKW	22. ZV	34. EREG
11. WZ	23. VZ	35. FGH
12. KST	24. XW	36. WW

*This list was given to me by a colleague who found it on a bulletin board. I have tried, unsuccessfully, to determine its origin.

question of why some words that satisfy a criterion tend to turn up on the lists that subjects generate, whereas other words that also satisfy the criterion do not. That is the distinction between word contexts in which certain letter sequences are part of the same phoneme and those in which they are not. Consider, for example, the different roles of the letter pair *ea* in *meat* and *create*, of *aw* in *awful* and *awake,* of *th* in *th* in *thigh* and *pothole.* This distinction is an important one for the task of developing computer algorithms that can translate orthographic representations of words into phonemic representations, as is done, for example, by reading machines for the blind. One approach to this problem is to de-compose the orthographic representation of a word into its con-stituent morphemes, from which a phonemic representation can be produced. The fact that a given letter combination sometimes is contained within a morpheme and sometimes spans two of them, as illustrated by the examples above, considerably complicates this task. Allen (1976) has estimated that a program has to be able to recognize about 12,000 morphemes to perform the word-decomposition task effectively.

For purposes of this paper, the question of interest is whether a search of memory for words containing a specified letter string is likely to be sensitive to the within- versus across-morpheme dis-tinction. My guess is that it is. More specifically, I would expect that, other things being equal, the probability that a word con-taining the string would be produced would be greater if the string were contained within a morpheme than if it spanned two of them.

Summary

It is time to attempt to summarize what has been learned about motivated remembering from archival memory as a result of ex-perimenting with list-generation tasks. I mentioned at the outset that this paper would be more likely to raise questions than to answer them, and that has certainly been the case. By way of summary, I will first list what seem to me to be the major findings from this line of exploration, and then mention some of the ques-tions that I think these findings raise. There are, in a few cases, some hints as to what the answers might be, but these hints will have to be pursued before we can be confident that definitive answers have been found.

Table 10

Words containing letter clusters listed in Table 9

1. MKH	gymkhana	19. XII	taxiing
2. YZA	analyzable	20. XIX	maxixe
3. SYT	forsythia	21. DAE	sundae
4. LEK	telekinesis	22. ZV	rendezvous
5. FTB	softball	23. VZ	evzone
6. APLA	seaplane	24. XW	boxwood
7. ULOW	paulownia	25. KIU	wickiup
8. GHH	roughhewn	26. XYM	oxymoron
9. VEP	stovepipe	27. MBM	entombment
10. WKW	awkward	28. KGO	ginkgo
11. WZ	blowzy	29. UAGG	guagga
12. KST	prankster	30. OCHL	pinochle
13. ODOD	rhododendron	31. APN	shrapnel
14. TYT	shantytown	32. NYR	pennyroyal
15. OEI	canoeist	33. RDV	aardvark
16. EOI	bourgeois	34. EREG	deregulate
17. HTH	eighth	35. FGH	afghan
18. OKK	bookkeeper	36. WW	glowworm

Major Findings

Lists can be generated in accordance with a wide assortment of criteria (semantic, orthographic, phonemic).

In almost all cases, word-production rate decreases gradually with time. Often the graph of cumulative number of words produced as a function of time is reasonably well fitted by an exponential equation.

Both parameters of the equation, the asymptote and the growth-rate parameter, vary depending on the nature of the list being generated.

It seems reasonably safe to assume that the asymptote of the word-production curve is positively related to the number of target words a subject knows. However, subjects typically reach asymptote—stop producing words—long before they have produced all the target words in their vocabularies.

How the rate at which the word-production curve approaches asymptote depends on the nature of the criterion for list inclusion, is not clear.

The two parameters tend to be inversely related across list criteria: the greater the asymptote, the more slowly it is approached.

False positives seem to occur frequently during the generation of some lists (e.g., palindromes) and hardly ever during the generation of others (e.g., animal names).

Successive attempts to generate the "same" list typically yield greater numbers of words and/or yield them at a greater rate.

There are several evidences of clustering (semantic, orthographic, phonemic) in the order in which words are produced.

A random-sampling-with-replacement model of the list-generation process can accommodate many, but not all, of the results that have been obtained.

In subjects' reports of how they perform list-generation tasks, there is often the suggestion of a dual-mode retrieval process: a relatively passive mode in which one waits for possibilities to come to mind, and an active mode in which one consciously attempts to "find" possibilities. It appears that subjects often use the passive mode until it no longer produces, and then switch to the second, more structured approach.

Some Questions

What makes words in some categories easier to retrieve than those in others? Is it strictly a matter of the ratio of the sizes of the target and search sets?

Why does the word-production curve typically reach asymptote long before the subject produces all the target words in his vocabulary?

If the asymptote of the word-production curve does not represent the total number of target words in a subject's vocabulary, what does it represent?

Assuming that the "search space" is seldom, if ever, the subject's entire lexicon, and that it varies with the nature of the criterion that defines membership on the list, what determines how the search space can be constrained? And given that it can be constrained at all, why can the subject not simply limit it to just the target set? How does the search space depend on the subject, on his vocabulary, and on his search strategy?

Why is the attempt to produce words from the same category more effective (efficient?) on successive efforts?

Why does the growth parameter of the word-production curve tend to vary inversely with the asymptote of the curve across different types of lists?

If the memory search is not random, how is it organized?

Assuming a dual-mode search process, one mode of which is relatively passive and the other relatively active, what are the defining characteristics and method of operation of each mode?

Why is it that false positives seem to occur very frequently in the generation of some lists and very infrequently in the generation of others?

To what extent is performance in the list-generation task (in particular the parameters of the word-production curve) dependent on the level of effort the subject is willing to devote to the task?

What are the implications of the fact that subjects can search memory for words that end with (or contain) specified letter sequences, as well as for words that begin with specified letter sequences?

REFERENCES

Allen, J. Synthesis of speech from unrestricted text. *Proceedings of the IEEE*, 1976, *64*, 433–442.

Bousfield, W. A., & Sedgewick, C. H. An analysis of sequences of restricted associative responses. *Journal of General Psychology*, 1944, *30*, 149–165.

Indow, T. Some characteristics of word sequences retrieved from specified categories. In R. S. Nickerson (Ed.), *Attention & Performance VIII*. N.J.: Lawrence Erlbaum Associates, 1980.

Indow, T., & Togano, K. On retrieving sequence from long-term memory. *Psychological Review*, 1970, *77*, 317–331.

Johnson, D. M., Johnson, R. C., & Mark, A. L. A mathematical analysis of verbal fluency. *Journal of General Psychology*, 1951, *44*, 121–128.

Kaplan, I. T., Carvellas, T., & Metlay, W. Searching for words in letter sets of varying size. *Journal of Experimental Psychology*, 1969, *82*, 377–380.

Kucera, H. G., & Francis, W. N. *Computational analysis of present-day American English*. Providence: Brown University Press, 1967.

Metlay, W., Handley, A., & Kaplan, I. T. Memory search through categories of varying size. *Journal of Experimental Psychology*, 1971, *91*, 215–219.

Nickerson, R. S. Some comments on human archival memory as a very large data base. In *Proceedings on Very Large Data Bases, Third International Conference on Very Large Data Bases*, Tokyo, Japan, 6–8 October 1977, pp. 159–168.

Nickerson, R. S., & Adams, M. J. Long-term memory for a common object.

Cognitive Psychology, 1979, *11*, 287–307.

Roediger, H. L., & Thorpe, L. A. The role of recall time in producing hypermnesia. *Memory and Cognition*, 1978, *6*, 296–305.

Rundus, D. Negative effects of using list items as recall cues. *Journal of Verbal Learning and Verbal Behavior*, 1973, *12*, 43–50.

Shiffrin, R. M. Memory search. In D. A. Norman (Ed.), *Models of human memory*. New York: Academic Press, 1970.

Concepts, Propositions, and Schemata: What Are the Cognitive Units?[1]

John R. Anderson

Carnegie-Mellon University

*I*T would seem that one of the surest advances of modern cognitive psychology over its behavioristic predecessor lies in its extensive postulation of mental structures and processes. Basically, cognitive psychology has reasserted the commonsense insight that if one's goal is to develop a theory of the connections between stimuli and responses, it helps to have a model of the structures and processes intervening between stimuli and responses. However, the radical behaviorist was guided by the motto "You cannot know what you cannot see." What goes on between stimulus and response takes place in the human black box which physiological psychology has not succeeded in effectively opening up. It seemed to the behaviorist that there was just no way of knowing what was going on in that box. However, at least some in cognitive psychology seem to have had greater faith in the powers of induction. Their faith is that by adding converging evidence upon converging evidence we should be able to uniquely identify what is going on in that box. If behavioral evidence is not enough, then there are additional constraints such as parsimony that can be called upon.

There are some modern cognitive psychologists who believe that the radical behaviorist was half correct, and I happen to be one who thinks so. If it ever really was in doubt, I think it can be shown (e.g., Anderson, 1976, 1978, 1979) that we cannot really know what is going on in a black box that we cannot open up. However, the radical behaviorist was also half wrong. Lack of unique identifiability is no reason not to postulate internal structure and represen-

1. Preparation of this manuscript and the research described herein is by grant BNS78–17463 from the National Science Foundation and Contract N00014–77–C–0242 from the Office of Naval Research. I am grateful to Lynne Reder for her comments and advice on this manuscript.

tations. I think that the success of cognitive psychology is a testimony to the importance of such structures in psychological theories. So, a recommendation I have made is to go ahead and get on with the business of science: Postulate some set of internal structures and processes that are consistent with the data and don't worry about unique identifiability.

It is not clear that anyone else is going to take my recommendation seriously, but I do. I face a certain dilemma in doing so: I have to choose some theory of internal structure. One important constraint on my choice is that the theory be consistent with the data. However, the conclusion about lack of unique identifiability implies that there will usually be multiple theories of internal structure and process that satisfy this constraint. Moreover, the problem of multiple theories of internal structure is not just an abstract metatheoretical dilemma. There are real options that I must choose between in trying to develop a theory. I suppose I could decide among the alternatives by tossing a coin, but I would feel unfulfilled as a scientist if I make my decisions this way. In fact I do make my choices in more principled ways than by tossing coins. I try to come up with constraints that serve to eliminate the ambiguity left by empirical data alone.

Among the additional constraints I have used are conventional ones such as parsimony, but I have found these to be not enough. In developing the ideas on representation in this paper, I have found two other bases to be particularly valuable. I would like to state them at the outset. One has to do with what I call "cognitive naturalness" (this is akin to an idea put forth by Pylyshyn, 1979, of "intended interpretations"). The idea is that while two explanations may be formally equivalent in accounting for behavior, one is a more natural interpretation of the behavior. Consider, purely for illustrative purposes, the equivalence between parallel and serial models (Townsend, 1974) for the Sternberg paradigm. The hallmark result of that paradigm is the set-size effect—that reaction time increases linearly with set size. That result is clearly more akin to a serial-search interpretation than a parallel-search interpretation. Therefore, were it not for the many other complications, the serial model would be preferable, not because of parsimony, but rather as a result of how we naturally think about processes. Thus, the issue is what is natural for our cognition as scientists. I think considerations of cognitive naturalness help one come to a conclusion about some important issues of representation.

A second constraint comes from efforts to come up with very

explicit process models. For me this has meant that my theories must be capable of implementation as computer simulations. Although any well-specified theory can be so implemented, some theories seem more satisfying when implemented than others. A computer simulation can be unsatisfying because of lack of parsimony, generality, or internal consistency, just as can nonsimulated theories. However, there is an additional potential problem with a simulation that does not really arise with a nonsimulated theory. This is efficiency of operation. To take an extreme instance, if I simulate a memory-retrieval process by a random search throughout all of long-term memory (e.g., Landauer, 1975), I would find that very unsatisfactory no matter how well it corresponded to the behavioral facts. It is probably upsetting as a theoretical proposal even without issues of simulation considered, but it is simply intolerable if one has to watch a simulation eating up CPU hours in grossly stupid search. I emphasize that the problem is not simply computation time, but computation time in conjunction with the nonoptimality of the computation. If there are obvious ways to be much more efficient, it seems too much to believe that the human brain would not have discovered these more efficient means through evolution. So, a second constraint is that the implemented theory not lead to gross inefficiencies.

In this paper I will be considering what a cognitive unit is and what evidence there is on whether propositions and schemata should be considered cognitive units. I will use as evidence both the conventional behavioral data and the less conventional criteria of cognitive naturalness and efficiency.

THE ISSUE OF THE COGNITIVE UNIT

It is typical to analyze cognition as a set of processes operating on mental data. It is also typical to think of the mental data as coming in *pieces* or *units* or *chunks*. These are the "packages" of data which the cognitive processes treat in an all-or-none manner. An important issue in cognitive psychology is determining what these units are, and considerable research can be seen as directed to this issue.

I would like to consider three levels of units that have been postulated—concepts, propositions, and schemata. Concepts are frequently taken as the unanalyzable building blocks or the primitives of cognitive representation. In semantic-network representations they are the nodes of the network. It is true that under some views (e.g., semantic features—Katz & Fodor, 1963) concepts might not be basic units. However, I will be assuming the semantic-network framework in which a concept is a basic unit or node. The meaning of the concept is attached to the concept node, but the concept can be accessed and processed as a unit independent of this attached meaning. Thus, in this framework the fact that concepts are units is given, and the question is whether propositions and schemata are units.

Propositions are composed from various configurations of the concepts. They are not arbitrary configurations, but have certain well-formedness constraints that derive from the logical notion of a proposition. That is, they are taken to be the smallest units of meaning that assert things about the world that might be reasonably judged true or false. Propositions have a "syntax" which can be used to determine what they assert about the world. There have been a number of proposals for propositional representations using semantic networks (e.g., Anderson, 1976; Anderson & Bower, 1973; Norman & Rumelhart, 1975; Schank, 1972; Simmons, 1972). In these proposals, propositions tend to be represented as configurations of nodes interconnecting more basic concepts.

A schema (Bobrow & Winograd, 1977; Rumelhart & Ortony, 1976) can be conceived of as a set of related propositions. Exactly what sets of propositions qualify as schemata is a little uncertain, but included are stereotyped sequences of events (typically called scripts—Schank & Abelson, 1977) or co-occurring descriptions describing various object concepts (most typically called frames—Minsky, 1975).

Much of our discussion of these units will be with reference to verbal experimental material. Hence, it is typical to correlate concepts with words, propositions with sentences, and schemata with passages. However, it should be kept in mind that concepts, propositions, and schemata are abstract mental constructs and that words, sentences, and passages are only operationalizations of ways to manipulate these abstract structures.

CRITERIA FOR A COGNITIVE UNIT

In defining what I mean by a cognitive unit, I need to assume a conception of cognition in which all processing takes the form of manipulating data structures in a *working memory* or an *active memory.* One prominent instantiation of this conception of cognition is the production-system architecture (Anderson, 1976; Newell, 1973; Rychener & Newell, 1978), but this conception is more general and does not imply a commitment to production systems. For our purposes, the two important cognitive operations are the formation of links to interconnect a set of elements in working memory and the retrieval of a set of elements into working memory. A type of structure, say a proposition, is to be considered a cognitive unit if: (a) Invariably, when any elements of the unit are interassociated, all elements are interlinked. Since formation of interassociations is the means for acquiring new information, this is the criterion of *all-or-none learning.* (b) Invariably, when some of the elements of the unit are retrieved into working memory, all are. This is the criterion of *all-or-none retrieval.*

ARE PROPOSITIONS COGNITIVE UNITS?

I have in the past claimed that while the proposition is an important theoretical construct, it is not a cognitive unit (Anderson, 1976; Anderson & Bower, 1973). To see what is meant by this, let us consider the ACT (Anderson, 1976) theory of memory representation. Figure 1 illustrates the semantic-network representation that we would assign to a sentence like *Caesar crossed the Rubicon.* This structure encodes a simple proposition and interconnects *Caesar, crossed,* and *Rubicon.* The top node represents the proposition. It is connected to its subject *Caesar* by an *S* link and to a predicate node by a *P* link. The predicate node is connected to the relational concept *cross* by an *R* link and to the argument of the relation, *Rubicon,* by an *A* link. ACT is relatively unique among semantic-network theories in that there is a clear semantics associated with such network structures. The predicate node is taken to reflect the set of people who crossed the Rubicon, and the proposition node encodes the assertion that the subject, *Caesar,* is a member of that set.

The proposition was not a cognitive unit in ACT because it was possible for such structures to be only partially encoded or only partially retrieved. For instance, according to the ACT theory, a subject upon hearing the sentence *Caesar crossed the Rubicon* might only succeed in encoding in memory a structure like that in part (b) of Figure 1. That is, he would have failed to encode the argument link. Thus, in ACT, propositions did not satisfy the criterion of

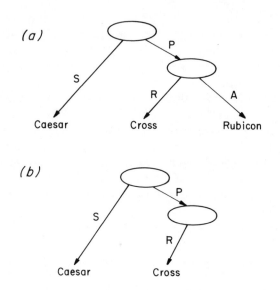

FIGURE 1. (a) The ACT network encoding of *Caesar crossed the Rubicon;* (b) A partial encoding of (a) that might be retrieved into working memory.

all-or-none acquisition. Similarly, even if the subject succeeded in encoding the complete proposition in part (a), he might only succeed in retrieving a fragment like part (b) when he later tried to retrieve that proposition back into active memory. Thus, in ACT the proposition failed the criterion of all-or-none retrieval. In ACT, propositions were conceived of as formed from associations that were at least somewhat independent. Propositions did not have the unitary character postulated of a cognitive unit.

Research on Single-Proposition Sentences

The issue of whether propositions are learned in an all-or-none manner has received considerable research and has been the subject of some debate. I think this research can be profitably divided into research that has tried to focus on sentences that assert a single proposition versus sentences that assert multiple propositions. One of the early single-proposition studies (Anderson & Bower, 1973) concerned location-subject-verb-object sentences like *In the park the hippie touched the debutante* or, to propose a sentence for the 1980s, *In the disco the Arab approached the actress.* We prompted subjects for recall of the sentences with location (L), subject (S), verb

(V), or object (O). To each the subject could recall zero, one, two, or three other words. There are three ways to recall one or two words of the three. Thus, to each of the four probes there are eight possible patterns of recall. Table 1 provides a classification of the data from the experiment. In the table, failure to recall an element is denoted by a bar over the letter corresponding to the element. So S$\bar{V}$O denotes that to a location cue, subject recalled subject and object, but not verb.

Table 1

Patterns of Recall to Location-Subject-Verb-Object Sentence

		Cued with					
	L		S		V		O
3 recalled							
SVO	93	LVO	87	LSO	78	LSV	95
2 recalled							
SV$\bar{O}$	17	LV$\bar{O}$	20	LS$\bar{O}$	18	LS$\bar{O}$	38
S$\bar{V}$O	33	L$\bar{V}$O	36	L$\bar{S}$O	30	L$\bar{S}$V	30
$\bar{S}$VO	33	$\bar{L}$VO	36	$\bar{L}$SO	21	$\bar{L}$SV	22
Total:	83	Total:	92	Total:	69	Total:	90
1 recalled							
S$\bar{V}\bar{O}$	41	L$\bar{V}\bar{O}$	43	L$\bar{S}\bar{O}$	24	L$\bar{S}\bar{V}$	41
$\bar{S}V\bar{O}$	23	$\bar{L}$V$\bar{O}$	19	$\bar{L}$S$\bar{O}$	16	$\bar{L}$S$\bar{V}$	29
$\bar{S}\bar{V}$O	37	$\bar{L}\bar{V}$O	36	$\bar{L}\bar{S}$O	30	$\bar{L}\bar{S}$V	31
Total:	101	Total:	98	Total:	70	Total:	101
0 recalled							
$\bar{S}\bar{V}\bar{O}$	461	$\bar{L}\bar{V}\bar{O}$	461	$\bar{L}\bar{S}\bar{O}$	521	$\bar{L}\bar{S}\bar{V}$	452

Note that 12% of the probes resulted in recall of all three elements, 11.3% resulted in recall of two items, 12.5% in recall of one item, and 64.2% in recall of no items. Clearly, with 23.8% partial recall, subjects are not encoding and retrieving these sentences in an all-or-none manner all the time. Moreover, every possible pattern of partial recall is represented with some respectable frequency in Table 1.

There are various challenges that can be made and have been made to this conclusion of partial recall. One challenge involves presenting another set of summary statistics about Table 1. Rather than considering absolute frequency of partial recall, consider probability of recall of one word contingent on recall of another word. For instance, contrast recall of V contingent on recall of O (denoted $P(V|O)$) with recall contingent on nonrecall of O (denoted $P(V|\bar{O})$)): $P(V|O)$ = .637, but $P(V|\bar{O})$ = .073. Similar patterns of contingency can be obtained by considering any other pair of words. The point is that recall of one term is much higher when conditionalized on recall of another. Thus, it might appear that propositional traces are much more unitary than would be expected by some notions of "chance."

R. C. Anderson (1974) has used such conditional-recall probabilities. He has also contrasted scoring subjects for verbatim recall versus a gist-scoring criterion. He counted subjects as correct in their recall if they recalled synonyms *(stone* for *rock)*, superordinates *(clothing* for *sweater)*, hyponyms *(sat* for *stayed)*, and cohyponyms *(rifle* for *pistol)*. Using a verbatim scoring, he found $P(V|O)$ = .634 and $P(V|\bar{O})$ = .084. Using his gist-scoring criterion and scoring for guessing, he found $P(V|O)$ = .951 and $P(V|\bar{O})$ = .049. So the all-or-none character of these conditional-recall probabilities becomes more extreme under a gist criterion. I have not always been able to find as extreme scores as Anderson, but I too find more extreme scores using a gist criterion. However, note that even with his extreme scores, Anderson still does find some evidence for partial recall (i.e., $P(V|O)$< 1 and $P(V|\bar{O})$ > O).

In Anderson (1976) I examined this issue in some detail and found it to be a real hornet's nest of details, complications, and multiple interpretations. This data cannot serve as the sole basis for coming to a conclusion about the unitary character of the proposition. However, we can emerge from this data with two loose and safe generalizations: (1) When a single-proposition sentence is presented to a subject, there is some probability that the sentence will be partially recalled. (2) This partial recall is much less than would be expected under many conceptions which see the proposition as a combination of independent concepts.

Multiple-Proposition Sentences

A second source of data concerns memory for multiple-proposition sentences. For instance, Anderson and Bower (1973) considered the following type of sentence: *The Arab approached the actress who drank in the disco.* Figure 2 provides an approximate ACT representation for such sentences. Notice that elements within a single proposition tend to be closer together than ele-

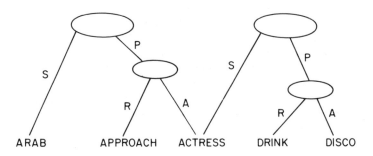

FIGURE 2. The ACT encoding for the multipropositional sentence *The Arab approached the actress who drank in the disco.*

ments between propositions. Excluding *actress,* which is shared by both propositions, the mean distance between concepts within a proposition is 2.5 links, while the mean between-proposition distance is 5.5 links. So, we would expect even on the ACT account that probability of recalling an element from one proposition given an element from the same proposition would be higher than given an element from another proposition. Anderson and Bower (1973) tried to fit the HAM theory (which involved representations like Figure 2) to the recall of such sentences. We found systematic misfits of the theory in the direction of there being greater tendency to recall an element from the same proposition as the cue. That is, even though the theory predicted within-proposition contingencies, it does not predict enough. Although it is undoubtedly the case that some process assumptions could be derived that would satisfactorily predict the data given the representation in Figure 2, this systematic failure of the ACT theory can be taken as some evidence for the unitary character of the proposition. Goetz, Anderson, and Schallert (1979) and Kintsch (1974) have reported similar studies of multiple-proposition sentences and have come to similar conclusions.

Ratcliff and McKoon (1978) report a different methodology for looking at memory for multiple-proposition sentences. They had subjects commit to memory sentences like *Geese crossed the horizon as the wind shuffled the clouds.* Since subjects memorized these sentences more or less perfectly, probability of recall was not the measure of interest. Rather, the subjects saw a series of words, and they were to respond *yes* or *no* whether each word was in one of the sentences they had studied. Ratcliff and McKoon were interested in the speed of this decision.

They contrasted three conditions under which the subject might have to decide whether he had studied a word like *horizon*. In the within-proposition condition, the preceding word to be judged had come from the same proposition—thus, the preceding word might be *geese*. In the between-proposition condition, *horizon* would be preceded by a word from the same sentence but from a different proposition—thus, the preceding word might be *wind*. In the unprimed condition the word would be preceded by a word from a different sentence. The mean response times in the three conditions are 709 msec for within-proposition priming, 752 msec for between-proposition priming, and 847 msec for the unprimed condition. So, there is a clear advantage for within-proposition cueing, although there is also a considerable between-proposition advantage among the propositions connected in a single sentence.

It would be wrong to conclude that any of these studies on multiple-proposition sentences clearly establishes the unitary character of the proposition. As we noted with respect to Figure 2, representational theories like ACT or HAM assume that the elements within a proposition are more closely connected than the elements between propositions. It is true that some of the within-proposition contingencies are stronger than predicted in the HAM model, but there are other non-HAM process assumptions that could be marshaled to predict this degree of contingency.

Conclusions about the Proposition as a Cognitive Unit

The fact of fragmentary recall of propositions, even if not a high-frequency occurrence, is the major argument against concluding that the proposition is a cognitive unit. The HAM theory makes certain predictions about fragmentary recall of propositions. For instance, verb and object are closer together in the network representation and should tend to be recalled together. Some of the early research had indicated that this fragmentary recall conformed to predictions derived from the HAM structure. However, subsequent research failed to support such conclusions. This research has found some systematic effects in fragmentary recall of propositions, but these turn out to be better predicted by closeness in the surface sentence than closeness in a deeper semantic representation. That is, the fragments that tend to be recalled together are close together in the surface sentence (see Anderson & Bower, 1973, for detailed discussion).

The above research suggests that when we observe fragmentary recall, we are not observing recall of single propositions, but recall of surface strings of words. Anderson and Paulson (1977), using verification times, provided evidence that memory for a sentence can rest either on an abstract proposition or a surface string. The resolution to the issue of partial recall of propositions may lie in the distinction between propositional and word-string representations for sentences. Perhaps the propositional representations are stored and retrieved in an all-or-none manner, while the word-linked-to-word sentence representations have the fragmentary character. This proposal would serve to account for the empirical data. The empirical data is sufficiently complex now that I do not think that there is a simpler explanation than this two-trace theory.

The strongest motivation for the two-trace proposal is not based on empirical data, but rather on five years of experience with a simulation of ACT that has had to work with representations of propositions or of word strings. We have found it extremely frustrating to work with a system where basic propositions can be partially encoded or partially retrieved. A partial proposition is virtually never of any use to the system, and effort that goes into partial encoding or retrieval is simply wasted. It makes the system much less efficient than it needs to be. Essentially, what was always happening is that the system would be looking for a proposition to guide its processing, retrieve only part of the required proposition, and so be delayed in its processing or, worse yet, be misdirected. The inefficiency associated with partial propositions is not just a consequence of ACT's implementation on a computer, but rather reflects a fundamental incompatibility between partial processing of a proposition and the all-or-none significance of a proposition in information processing. It is rarely the case that a partial proposition provides any guide to information processing. (What can we do with the partial proposition *Carter defeated*, and contrast this with the implications of *Carter defeated Kennedy!*) On the other hand, fragmentary processing of word strings is a necessity given the recursive or iterative character of the parsing that underlies sentence comprehension. One has to interpret word-string fragments of a sentence and then concatenate the interpretations of these fragments to come to the sentence meaning.

In summary, I think that the conjunction of the complex empirical literature with some clearer considerations about processing efficiency supports the conclusion that propositions are treated as cognitive units. It is also the case that the criterion of cognitive naturalness, discussed earlier, points in the same direction. Given the relative dominance of all-or-none recall, it seems more natural to think of the test results as being produced by a basically all-or-none process with a set of perturbating processes producing occasional partial recall, than to think of them as being produced by a basically partial process with various factors producing an enhancement of all-or-none recall. It needs to be emphasized that this is not a matter of parsimony.

ARE SCHEMATA COGNITIVE UNITS?

Schemata can be conceived of as being composed of propositions, just as propositions can be conceived of as being composed of concepts. For instance, consider one of the 16-sentence stories that we have used in some of our research:

1. Willa received a telephone message.
2. Willa was told that her father was dying.
3. Willa's father lived in San Francisco.
4. Willa had to get to San Francisco quickly.
5. Willa called up for a taxi.
6. Willa went to Kennedy Airport.
7. Willa purchased a ticket for San Francisco.
8. Willa got on board the plane.
9. Willa flew across the country.
10. Willa ordered four drinks on the plane.
11. Willa arrived in San Francisco Airport.
12. Willa was dizzy when she arrived in San Francisco.
13. Willa did not know her way around the Bay Area.
14. Willa was incoherent when she asked for directions.
15. Willa could not find her father's hospital.
16. Willa cried in the streets of San Francisco.

The middle six sentences (6–11) correspond to what most people would consider a script or schema about an airplane trip. They reflect a fairly stereotypic sequence of events on an airplane trip. (These six sentences were adapted from some unpublished research of Abelson and Reder.) The interesting question is whether these middle sentences form a "unit" in any interesting sense.

Figure 3 gives a network representation of the plausible inter-connections among the 16 sentences. For instance, consider sentence (9) about Willa flying across the country. It has connections of temporal adjacency with the immediately preceding and following sentences. It is connected with sentence (7) which indicates the destination of the flight and with sentence (11) which indicates the successful completion of the flight. Although this representation does not assign any special unit status to the plane-trip episode, the network does illustrate the fact that the material tends to be more interconnected within a schema than between schemata. For instance, each schema sentence in Figure 3 has a mean of 1.0 connections to nonschema sentences, but 3.3 connections to schema sentences.

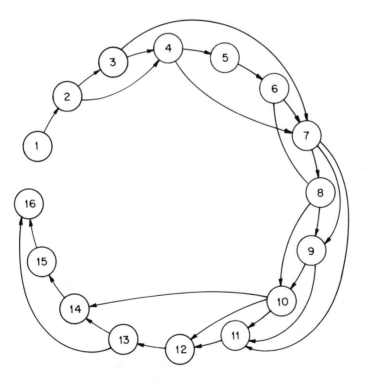

FIGURE 3. A diagrammatic representation of the relation among the sentences in the story about Willa.

This story representation has an important feature in common with our earlier ACT network representation of sentences (refer back to Figure 2). That is, in the story representation the elements composing a particular schema are more closely interassociated, just as in a sentence the concepts composing a proposition are more closely interassociated. Thus, even if we did not ascribe any special status to the schema, we would expect to see schema-defined contingency in story memory. Analogous to the propositional case, we can ask whether the contingency in schema recall can be explained solely in terms of this greater density of interassociations, or whether we will have to propose that schemata form special units. That is, are schemata encoded and retrieved in separate propositional units, or are they encoded and retrieved in an all-or-none manner?

General Schemata versus Instantiated Schemata

There is a fundamental ambiguity that lies in the use of schemata to refer to memory objects. On one hand, schemata can refer to general stereotyped patterns of propositions—for instance a general statement of what a dog looks like or what happens in a restaurant. This is probably their primary use. In such a case they are part of one's general semantic knowledge and are not the sorts of things that are generally learned in a memory experiment. Thus, the question of all-or-none learning does not arise experimentally. It is natural, however, to suppose that they gradually evolve through experience. The question of all-or-none retrieval is relevant. If a particular instantiation of such a schema is presented as to-be-learned material, and if the schema is retrieved to be put in correspondence with this experimental material, are the elements of that schema retrieved as a unit or individually?

The second use of schema is to refer to what is deposited in memory as a function of making the correspondence between presented material and a schema. According to schema theory this experimental material has somehow been organized to reflect the structure of the schema. For this use of the term *schema*, we can inquire whether it meets both defining features of a cognitive unit. Is the material within a schema interassociated in an all-or-none manner? Are its elements retrieved in an all-or-none manner? In this paper I am mainly concerned with this second use of schema and whether it can be considered a cognitive unit. However, I will also suggest that there might not be fundamental differences between these two types of schemata. Therefore, conclusions about the status of one sense of schema might generalize to conclusions about the other sense.

It would seem that typical discussions of schemata imply at least a partial commitment to their special status as cognitive units. This seems clearest in the writing of Schank and Abelson on scripts, which is the most explicit instantiation of a schema system. Mention of certain "header terms" like *restaurant* for the restaurant script caused the script to be invoked. When invoked, all the information in the script is available for processing a text. This would appear to be like having the script recalled in an all-or-none manner into working memory. While schemata appear to have a property of all-or-none retrieval, it does not seem that schema theorists are committed to all-or-none encoding of elements that conform to a schema. Schema theorists have not been explicit about what processes govern probability of encoding a fact except to suggest that facts which do not fit a script are less likely (or more likely—Schank, 1975) to be encoded. It is perhaps most in keeping with existing discussion of schemata to propose that facts which fit in a schema have an increased probability of recall, rather than to propose that they are remembered in an all-or-none manner. These two proposals can amount to quite different things, as a little thought should confirm.

Research on Schemata

There has been research showing distortions in memory such that subjects falsely think they studied things normatively part of a script and such that they transform other facts to fit the normative prescriptions of the script (Bower, Black, & Turner, 1979; Mandler & Johnson, 1977; Rumelhart, 1977; Thorndyke, 1977). While such studies may show the importance of schemata as explanatory concepts, they are not directly relevant to assessing whether schemata are cognitive units.

Black and Bower (1979) and Owens, Bower, and Black (1979) looked at the recall of multiepisode stories where each episode might be conceived of as a schema. They found that subjects recall facts from only some of the episodes, and from each of these they can retrieve a fair number of facts. This result is reminiscent of the some-or-none recall of instances from a category in a free-recall list (Cohen, 1963, 1966).

It is worth reviewing the basic phenomenon of some-or-none recall of items from a categorized list. If one plots the distribution of number of instances recalled from n-member categories, that distribution conforms to a binomial distribution except that there are too many cases of zero items recalled. It is as if the subject has one probability a of accessing the category and another probability b of retrieving instances for an accessed category. The 1-a probability of failing to access the category produces the concentration of zero recalls from a category, and the b probability, once in the category, produces the otherwise good fit to a binomial distribution.

Analogous to the situation of a categorized list, it might appear in script recall that there is one probability of retrieving the schema and then a second probability of retrieving the individual propositions organized by a schema. This implies, which is empirically the case, that all the facts are not recalled from a schema. Rather recall is some-or-none. However, this leaves open the issue of whether the failure of the "all" part of all-or-none recall occurs at encoding or at retrieval or at both. It should be kept in mind that there does not seem to be a commitment in current expositions of schema theory to all-or-none encoding. It might be that the information organized by a schema is partially encoded at study and that this partial encoding is retrieved in an all-or-none manner. This would produce the observed phenomenon of some-or-none recall.

An Experiment Looking for Schema-Units

We have recently performed a further study to determine whether there is all-or-none retrieval of schema-organized information. This study used a priming manipulation in a reaction-time paradigm. The study is analogous to the one by Ratcliff and McKoon described earlier. Such a methodology seems more appropriate than simple-recall studies for getting at the retrieval dynamics implied in the issue of all-or-none retrieval.

Our study used 16-sentence passages such as the Willa passage, where the middle 6 sentences corresponded to well-defined scripts (as determined in unpublished research of Abelson and Reder). We reasoned that if these scripts were to have a unitary quality, there should be a special facility for the sentences in one script to prime other sentences in that same script. We had subjects commit to memory six such stories. Then we used a sentence-recognition paradigm in which subjects had to decide whether a particular sentence came from one of the stories they had studied. Foils were created by re-pairing subjects with predicates. On most of the trials we avoided repetitions of sentences from the same story, but we created a few (10% of the trials) critical repetitions. These could involve pairs of sentences from inside the script or one sentence from outside the script and one from within. Always the second, primed sentences were from within the script. In fact these critical second sentences were the same in the outside-priming and inside-priming conditions. We were interested in whether there would be special priming and hence a special recognition advantage if the first sentence came from inside the same script as the second sentence. A special advantage for inside sentences seems implied from the viewpoint that the script is a cognitive unit. The principle of all-or-none retrieval implies that bringing one script sentence in working memory should bring the other script sentences in.

However, a priming advantage for within pairs might occur even if there were not special unitizing of the script. This can be seen from inspecting the greater interconnectedness of within-script sentences in Figure 3. The sentences within the script tend to be more related to one another, and priming might just reflect this greater relatedness. Therefore we had subjects rate pairs of sentences, either both from within the script or one from within and one from without. We chose pairs of sentences for our inside- and outside-priming conditions that were approximately equal in relatedness. Moreover, to assess whether there was an effect of relatedness, we divided the inside and outside pairs into two groups—those that received high relatedness ratings and those that received medium relatedness ratings.

Table 2 presents the recognition times for the second sentence in primed pairs, classified according to whether they were instances of outside or inside priming and according to the rated degree of relatedness for the pair. It is clear from Table 2 that there is little effect of either variable—certainly no significant effect. These times should be compared with subjects' response times to these same sentences when they were preceded by a sentence from another story—1,240 msec with a 6.9% error rate. Thus there is clearly priming relative to this control, but there is no effect of either priming variable in Table 2.

Our stories were deliberately constructed in this first experi-

Table 2

Recognition Times in Msec (and Error Rates in Parentheses) to Primed Members of Sentence Pairs

| | | Type | | |
		Inside	Outside	Average
	Hi	1078	1109	1094
Degree of		(.028)	(.038)	(.033)
Relatedness	Med	1071	1087	1079
		(.027)	(.035)	(.031)
Average		1075	1098	1086
		(.028)	(.037)	(.032)

ment to be thematically integrated. That is, the six-sentence script episode fit in as an integral part of the full story. This was to create examples of between-script pairs that were as related as within-script pairs. It seems like a fair test for whether there were unique properties associated with script processing. The story as a whole was not a stereotypic sequence of events, whereas the subset of script sentences was. If stereotypic sequences are specially processed as units, there should be special priming of the sentences within a script over and above sentences which are just thematically related.

The conclusion of this research seems to be that there is a special facilitating effect of thematic relatedness, but no special effect of the kind of stereotypic relatedness we associate with scripts. Note, however, there was not an effect of degree of relatedness. One might conclude that the thematic relatedness of the story had made the whole story a cognitive unit. To test this interpretation, we ran a second experiment in which the whole story was not thematically integrated.

An Experiment on Disjointed Stories

An example of the kind of stories used in this research follows:

1. Willa went to the sink to brush her teeth.
2. Willa picked up the tube of toothpaste.
3. Willa put some pepsodent on her toothbrush.
4. Willa cleaned her teeth in front and back.
5. Willa rinsed her toothbrush in cold water.

6. Willa went to Kennedy Airport.
7. Willa purchased a ticket for San Francisco.
8. Willa got on board the plane.
9. Willa flew across the country.
10. Willa ordered four drinks on the plane.
11. Willa arrived in San Francisco airport.
12. Willa entered the shoe store.
13. Willa found a shoe salesman.
14. Willa tried on a pair of shoes.
15. Willa said she would buy the shoes.
16. Willa took the boxed shoes home.

Note that the first five sentences are integrated, the next six are, and the last five are; but there are major "cognitive jerks" in the transition from one set to another. The central six sentences were the same ones as used in the previous experiment. We also used the same within-between manipulation in this experiment as previously. That is, in the critical pairs either both sentences came from within the critical six (within-primary condition), or the first came from without and the second from within (between-primary condition). As before, physical distance between the pairs, in terms of number of intervening sentences, was the same in both conditions.

We expected that if thematic relatedness was sufficient to create a cognitive unit, we should find priming within the six-sentence script and not between. The results were 1,134 msec (1.2% errors) for within-script priming, 1,240 msec (5.3% errors) for between-script priming, and 1,390 msec (6.4% errors) for the control case when the target sentence was preceded with a test item taken from a different story. Clearly in this experiment we have evidence for within-script priming. The between-script condition is still faster than the control condition. It is a little hard to know why the between-script condition remains better than the control. It may just reflect the benefit of repeating the person's name across the pair of sentences. In any case, we have obtained clear evidence for within-script priming when that script is thematically distinct from the rest of the passage. This reinforces the conclusion from the first experiment that what is important in determining the cognitive unit is thematic relatedness and not scriptal character per se.

Thus, it seems that we have evidence for cognitive units larger than the proposition. If we are to call these cognitive units schemata, we will have to change somewhat our interpretation of schemata away from the notion of a stereotypic set of facts or events to a notion of a thematically related set. This also carries with it the requirement that we become more precise about what we mean by "thematically related." I will attempt to do this after discussing some further research.

Cognitive Units and Interference

Another way to get at the issue of whether schemata are cognitive units involves the study of retrieval interference. The phenomenon of retrieval interference refers to the fact that as more items are associated to the same element, there is a loss in the facility to retrieve any of these items. This has been classically shown in a paired-associate paradigm where learning multiple responses to the same stimulus causes the responses to interfere with each other.

More recently the interference phenomenon has been studied in a sentence-recognition paradigm (e.g., Anderson, 1974, 1976; Hayes-Roth, 1977; Thorndyke & Bower, 1974). Subjects are asked to commit to memory a set of facts like: *The lawyer bought a pair of Adidas. The lawyer entered the restaurant. The doctor waited for the train.* Subjects are then asked to judge whether they have studied such sentences when they are mixed up with foils like *The lawyer waited for the train.* The more facts that a subject learns about a particular concept like *lawyer,* the slower he is to recognize any fact he has studied or to reject a fact he has not studied. This result is referred to as the *fan effect.* In the network representation of this information, more facts learned about a concept like *lawyer* means a greater fan of links leading out from the concept. Assuming that the rate at which activation spreads from the concept down the links is an inverse function of this fan, and assuming that retrieval depends on activating this structure, then recognition time will depend on fan.

Recently Smith, Adams, and Schorr (1978) uncovered an interesting situation where this fan effect does not hold. They presented subjects with a set of facts which could be unified into a schema. An example would be: *The lawyer christened the ship. The lawyer broke the bottle. The lawyer did not delay the trip.* As long as the facts could be organized into such a schema, there was no effect of number of facts on recognition time. Smith et al. suggest that such sets of facts are organized into script units. They suggest that while a script unit may take a long time to access, once it is accessed, its individual members can be scanned very rapidly. Thus, they are basically taking a variant of the schema-as-cognitive-unit approach. Translated into the terminology of activation or working memory, their assumption amounts to the claim that the time to activate a script or to read it into working memory is little affected by the number of facts contained in that script.

Some of our recent research (Reder & Anderson, 1980) has complicated in interesting ways the account of the Smith et al. result. It turns out that the Smith et al. result depends on the nature of the foils used. In various experiments Smith et al. created their foils by combining sentence subjects like *lawyer* with predicates that had not been studied of *lawyer*. They constructed their foils in two ways: (1) The predicate had been studied with some other character, but was not related to the script studied of the tested person. Thus, the subject might learn ship-christening facts about the lawyer and, say, restaurant facts about the dentist such as *The dentist ate the hamburger*. A foil would be *The lawyer ate the hamburger*. (2) The predicates had not been studied about another person, but were related to the script studied about the person. These predicates were derived by adding an extra word to a predicate that had been studied. So, whereas the subject had studied *The lawyer broke the bottle*, he would be tested with *The lawyer broke the champagne bottle*.

In our experiment we also used foils where (3) the predicate had both been studied about another person and was related to the original script. So the subject might have studied ship-christening facts about the doctor as well as the lawyer. For the doctor one of the facts might have been *The doctor waved good-bye*. The foil for *lawyer* would be *The lawyer waved good-bye*. We found that when we used foils like (3) the fan effect reemerged, whereas we were able to replicate Smith's result of a reduced fan effect with foils like (1). Subjects are also much faster at rejecting foils like (1) than foils like (3). It seems that subjects were able to use the lack of a relation to the script in foils like (1) to reject the foils quickly. Similarly, we suspect that they used the simple presence of a script relation to accept targets, thus avoiding the need for a search of the script. We did not try foils like (2), but we suspect that subjects used the lexical unfamiliarity of terms like *champagne* to reject these. Subjects appear to engage in a search of the script only with foils like (3) which are related to the studied script and which have no unfamiliar terms.

To summarize this aspect of our research, it seems that a revised interpretation of the Smith et al. research is necessary. It appears that the individual propositions can be unified into a schema, and that subjects can treat this schema in an unanalyzed fashion, provided they do not have to make fine discriminations between what they actually studied versus what is only related to the schema. However, if we force subjects to make such discriminations, then they must analyze the contents of their schema and the fan effect re-emerges.

There is another aspect of our experiment which is very relevant to the issue of schemata as cognitive units. We manipulated whether subjects studied one or two schematically organized clusters of facts, and the number of facts in each cluster. Thus, in the two-schema condition, subjects might study facts about the lawyer in the restaurant and the lawyer taking a train. We were interested in what the effects might be of learning a second schema, and of the number of facts in that schema, on time to verify facts from the first schema. Our results were quite clear: (1) Subjects were slowed by the presence of a second schema. (2) Subjects were not affected by the number of facts in that second schema. These effects held whether the foils were unrelated (type 1) or related (type 3). Both major results of our experiment are interesting. The first implies that while the facts in a schema do not interfere with each other at least under some circumstances, they can be interfered with by the presence of other unrelated facts. The second result implies that the interfering effect of these other unrelated facts can be minimized if they can be encapsulated into a schema themselves.

Figure 4 illustrates a slight adaptation of the knowledge structure proposed in Reder and Anderson. There is a node in memory corresponding to the lawyer. It is connected to what we called "subnodes" to represent the train and restaurant events. Directly attached to each subnode is an indicator of the schema it represents. Also attached to each subnode are the proposition nodes corresponding to the individual facts organized by the schema. Each of these proposition nodes is then connected to the individual concepts organized by the proposition. (Each of these propositions should include reference to the lawyer, but this is omitted for sake of simplicity.) What we have here, then, is a hierarchy of the sort seen many times in cognitive psychology. The lawyer can be seen as a cognitive unit that serves to organize its individual schemata. Each schema is a cognitive unit that or-

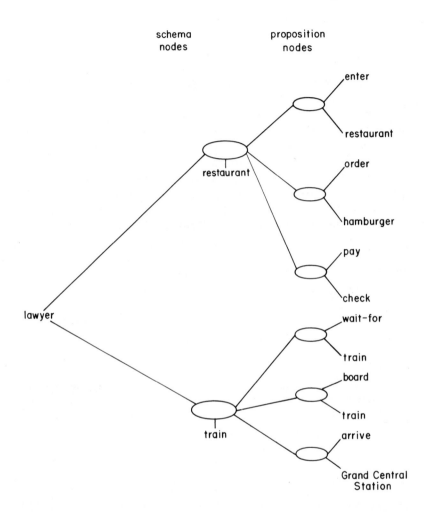

FIGURE 4. A representation of the hierarchical structure of schemata, propositions, and concepts attached to an individual in the Reder and Anderson experiment.

ganizes individual propositions. Each proposition is a cognitive unit that organizes individual concepts.

Faced with unrelated foils, subjects needed only to retrieve the schema nodes with their tags. They did not have to unpack each schema into its propositions. It is hypothesized that subjects can accept or reject probes by simply deciding if the probes were from the appropriate schema. This means that with unrelated foils, decision time should be a function of number of schemata but not number of propositions within a schema. This is just what we found. With related foils, subjects would have to inspect the individual propositions in the relevant schema. This would mean that decision time should vary with number of schemata, number of facts in the relevant schema, but not number of facts in irrelevant schemata. Again, this is just what we found.

An important issue in this proposal is how subjects decide whether a schema node is appropriate or not without inspecting the contents of the schema. There are two solutions that we have proposed. The first is that subjects retrieve a schema label from the predicate of a probe and match this to the labels stored with the schema nodes attached to the individual. There would be some implementation difficulties in achieving this, and even then the schema would have limited applicability. A basic problem is that a predicate may participate in many schemata, and it is not clear how to select the correct one without first considering all the information attached to the individual. A more reasonable solution in our view simply uses level of activation. The idea is that activation spreading from the individual node (e.g., lawyer in Figure 4) will quickly reach the schema node. Similarly, the predicates are strongly associated to the schema labels by prior knowledge. This is not shown in Figure 4, but there are strong preexperimental associations between propositions or predicates like *pay check* and schema labels like *restaurant*. Thus, activation will quickly converge on the schema node from the predicate. Because of this intersection of activation between the individual and the predicate, the node for the correct schema will be more active, allowing it to be selected.

Other Considerations about Schemata

So far I have presented some memory data in favor of the conclusion that schemata are cognitive units. For instance, we have shown in the experiment on disjointed stories that we can get within-script priming when the script has a sharp thematic contrast with surrounding information. The fact that the advantage of within-script priming (or the deficit of between-script priming) disappears when the thematic boundary is taken away, points to the fact that we need to liberalize the notion of a schema considerably over that of a script. With this liberalization the results are consistent with the schema-as-cognitive-unit view. Again the results of Smith et al. and of Reder and Anderson are nicely explained within the view that schemata are cognitive units.

While these results are conveniently explained in the schema-as-unit approach, they do not argue uniquely for this explanation. Indeed, in Reder and Anderson our analysis of these experiments did not invoke a units concept. My belief that schemata are cognitive units, as is the case for propositions, is bolstered by considerations of efficiency and cognitive naturalness.

Just as our efforts at simulation led us to dissatisfaction with the fragmented encoding of propositons, so too our efforts at simulation have led us to be dissatisfied with our inability to treat sets of propositions as units. Sometimes it proves desirable, and on other occasions it is essential to treat sets of propositions as units distinct from other related propositions. These are occasions when we need to treat sets of propositions as *patterns*. For instance, the set of propositions about a person's face may need to be treated as a pattern distinct from other propositions about the person. To take a more abstract example, the set of facts given in a geometry-proof problem needs to be treated as a pattern distinct from other related information in searching memory for solutions to similar proofs.

In the ACT system of 1976 there was already the facility to treat as a unit the propositions that made up the condition pattern of a production. These productions, however, were part of ACT's procedural knowledge of how to do things. What we are now finding is the need to deal with patterns in ACT's declarative-memory component.

The essence of a pattern is that it is to be put in correspondence with another object. By declaring a set of propositions a unit, we partition them as the elements for which a correspondence is to be found. This is the convenience of unitization. When patterns involve variables, partitioning is no longer a matter of computational convenience but rather is a necessity. The clearest argument for this point was developed by Hendrix (1975) in his discussion of partitioned semantic networks. For instance, consider the following information. *Labradors are large black dogs with floppy ears.* Figure 5 illustrates the network connections among the basic propositions that encode the sentence above. Here we have a set of propositions about a variable X which serves to stand for the defined labrador. The structure in Figure 5 might be translated, "If X is a labrador, then X is large, X is a dog, X is black, and X has Y, and Y are floppy

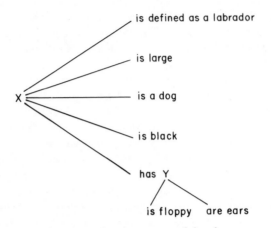

FIGURE 5. A network pattern for the concept labrador.

ears." It is essential that these propositions be partitioned off so that the system does not think X is a specific dog and so the system knows that the scope of variable X is limited to just this set of propositions. It is essential that the system realize that the variable Y, which also appears in Figure 5, is a variable which is in the scope of X. The proposition about Y in Figure 5 is not about ears in general, but is rather about labrador ears.

Part of the motivation for unitization of schemata can be seen to derive from their patternlike quality. Schemata frequently represent what can be thought of as patterns in that they use variables and can be invoked in the recognition of objects or situations. By making the schema a unit, one has a mechanism for indicating the scope of variables.

It is unclear how strongly one can go from the argument for pattern-units to the argument that sets of propositions should be treated as cognitive units in terms of encoding and retrieval. The fact that it is logically necessary to conceive of the propositions in a pattern as a unit distinct from other associated information does not imply that the information in the unit must be encoded in an all-or-none manner nor that it need be retrieved in an all-or-none manner. With respect to propositions it was argued that partial propositions were useless and therefore that it was essential that they be encoded in an all-or-none manner. A similarly strong argument cannot be made with respect to the sets of propositions in a pattern. It is frequently the case that patterns can only be partially matched to data. For instance, all the features of a face or of a typical restaurant episode may not be available in a specific case to be matched. Thus, it is hard to argue that there would be any disaster if only part of a pattern were retrieved from memory. All one can say is that partial encoding or retrieval would further degrade the reliability of the matching process.

It is at this point where cognitive naturalness comes in as a criterion for judging a representation. It is possible, as suggested above, that structures which need to be logically treated as units in pattern-matching will still be retrieved in a piecemeal manner. However, it is clearly unnatural to have this dichotomy between the pattern-matching processes and the retrieval processes. Again, while it is possible to come up with explanations that account for the memory phenomena that were presented as evidence for units interpretation without invoking the concept of a cognitive unit, there is something unnatural about explaining data suggestive of units with piecemeal mechanisms.

In conclusion, I think that the issue of whether schemata should be considered cognitive units is currently less decidable than the propositional case. We need more data and more quasi-logical arguments before enough evidence will be available on which to make a clear decision. However, I also think that the current state of evidence favors the cognitive-unit interpretation.

COGNITIVE UNITS: THEIR ENCODING AND RETRIEVAL

So, I have come to tentative answers to the questions set out at the beginning of the paper. It seems that propositions and schemata can be cognitive units by the encoding and retrieval criteria set forth at the beginning of the paper. I think that with more explicitly stated assumptions about encoding and retrieval, we can account for the apparent empirical contradictions to this conclusion. However, before developing the more explicit assumptions, I would also like to suggest that propositions and schemata not be seen as two different species of cognitive units, but rather that they be viewed as two manifestations of the same species. I do not think there will prove to be any useful distinction between propositions and schemata beyond size. The basic idea is that when elements in working memory can be put into correspondence with the elements of an existing knowledge structure, the working-memory elements will be unitized. The concepts in a proposition form a unit because they can be put into correspondence with various well-worn cognitive schemata such as *agent performing action on object* or *object in location*. Similarly, sets of propositions can be unitized when they can be put into correspondence with a cognitive schemata. Thus, I am treating cognitive units to have the same range of denotation as is exemplified by schemata in a system like KRL (Bobrow & Winograd, 1977). I will return later to a fuller discussion of what is meant by putting the elements in working memory in correspondence with the elements of an existing cognitive unit.

The idea that there is a general cognitive-unit structure that spans concepts, propositions, schemata, and other structures as special cases is appealing, of course, because of its generality. The generality of the idea is part of what leads me to venture a hypothesis about schemata in the face of insufficient evidence.

Encoding Assumptions

Now I would like to spell out more carefully what is meant by unitization and what the encoding and retrieval consequences are of unitization. Unitization occurs when a set of elements in working memory can be put into correspondence with an existing knowledge structure. Unitization involves creating a new node, let's call it the *chunk* node, and adding links to interconnect the previously unconnected working-memory elements. Also, an *index* tag is added to this chunk. This index points to the prior-knowledge structure with which it had been put into correspondence. The index provides a way to access the content of a chunk without actually inspecting the chunk. We discussed two ways we could do this with respect to Figure 4 for the Reder and Anderson experiment.

It is useful to contrast the encodings of elements that form cognitive units with the encodings of elements that do not. If elements cannot be put into correspondence with a cognitive unit, they still can be linked together to a node. However, each of the links must be formed independently. This gives us the contrast between all-or-none encoding and partial encoding. Secondly, there is no index that can be attached to guide access to these elements. This means, for instance, that one cannot reject these elements as a unit, and so one cannot reduce interference as in the Reder and Anderson study.

It should be emphasized that the contrast between the unit and nonunit is one of rate of encoding as well as all-or-none encoding.

The amount of effort (number of separate acts of association or time to interassociate) required in the case of a nonunit is linear with the number of elements being associated. In the case of the unit the effort is independent of the number of elements being associated. This accounts for the heightened level of recall typically associated with elements that organize themselves into well-formed cognitive units. It is interesting to speculate about the kind of mechanism that would find it easier to create structure given a corresponding structure. If we think of the links to be formed as complex and requiring some effort to create, then something of an explanation can be offered out of analogy to computer systems. As a rule it is much easier to create a data structure in a computer if the structure can be simply copied from an existing structure rather than if it has to be created anew. Perhaps the function of a correspondence is to enable the human memory system to create the new structure by the analog of a copy operation rather than having to perform the analog of creating structure by original computation.

One empirical difficulty with the all-or-none encoding assumption was the apparent result that multiproposition units in texts or stories are only partially recalled. I think this apparent contradiction can be explained away by assuming a difference between the operational definition of units and what is a cognitive unit for the subject. That is, there may be all-or-none encoding of multiproposition schemata, but these schemata do not always correspond to what the experimenter designates as units. A definition of what is and what is not a schema has not been as sharp as the definition of a proposition. Moreover, if we expect a subject's schemata to depend on his experience—what he has learned to be a unit—then we might well expect subjects to differ among themselves as to what the boundaries are for their schema units.

In particular I think there is very good reason to believe that the true cognitive schemata are much smaller than many of the schemata suggested in recent theoretical proposals. The size of any structure that can be unitized is limited by the number of propositions that can be kept active in working memory. It is the conventional wisdom to assign a relatively small number to working-memory capacity (e.g., four elements—Broadbent, 1975). This is much smaller than the number of elements that are listed in many schemata. The only way the large schemata can be organized is to have hierarchies of schemata with higher level schemata organizing lower level schemata. Indeed, this is what Schank and Abelson seem to be doing with their scenes within scripts. The hierarchical structure of many text units is explicitly recognized in the story grammars. It has also been very clearly acknowledged in some of the other discussions of schema theory (e.g., Bobrow & Winograd, 1977; Rumelhart & Ortony, 1976). Of course, if a text must be encoded into a hierarchy of cognitive units, it is possible to have partial encoding of the whole text, even if each of the cognitive units in the text is encoded in an all-or-none manner.

Retrieval Assumptions

When the cognitive unit is activated, the chunk node, its index, and its elements become available in working memory. This could be referred to as the *expansion* of the cognitive unit. The elements of a cognitive unit may themselves be cognitive units. However, when a cognitive unit is activated and expanded in working memory, the elements of the cognitive unit are not also expanded. Activation must spread from the chunk node to the element in order that the element be expanded. This means that, in the Smith et al. and the Reder and Anderson experiments, subjects were able to quickly identify the theme of their cognitive units but not their specific contents. The expansion of a cognitive unit is independent of the number of elements in that unit. The effect of number of elements comes in when activation must spread from the chunk node to the elements in order that the elements can themselves be expanded. So there should be an effect of number of elements in a cognitive unit only if it is necessary to inspect the content of these elements.

Establishing Correspondence with Old Knowledge

The key process in unitization is establishing a correspondence between a unit already in memory and some set of elements in working memory. The establishment of such a correspondence is far from a trivial process. The simplest case would be when the elements in working memory correspond exactly to the elements in the established knowledge unit. For instance, when we hear *George Washington crossed the Delaware,* presumably this proposition (and perhaps the exact sentence) corresponds to what we already have stored in memory. In this case it would not even be necessary to create a new unit. We could tag the existing memory unit. The many "chunking" proposals (Miller, 1956; Simon, 1974) advanced this role for old knowledge in encoding new knowledge. However, it is often the case that the elements in memory do not correspond exactly to the old knowledge unit.

Some potential for the lack of correspondence between old and new was foreseen in the use of variables in the various schemata proposals. Consider the following story:

Fred went to the movies.
Fred had a headache.
He bought popcorn and a drink.
Fred saw *Star Wars*.
After the movie he went to the coffee shop.

Presumably, this does not correspond exactly to anything that we have heard before, but it can be put into correspondence with a schema of the following sort:

= Person goes to movies
= Person enters to = theatre
= Person pays for = ticket
= Person buys = refreshments
= Person gives = ticket to = collector
= Person finds = seat
= Person watches = movie
  After = movie, = person leaves = theatre
= Person goes to = food establishment

Here = person, = theatre, = ticket, = collector, = refreshments, = seat, = movie, = food establishment, are all variables which can match a range of objects. The entire schema summarizes a set of events, none of which are identical. The variables denote places where one event might differ from another. Actually, in line with earlier remarks, this schema is probably too large to be a single cognitive unit and is better thought of as a hierarchy of units. Figure 6 illustrates a possible hierarchy.

Clearly, the problems of making correspondences with this structure are not so trivial. First, there is the problem of deciding whether the constants in the to-be-encoded structure can be put consistently in correspondence with the variables in the schema (i.e., Fred in correspondence with = person, popcorn and a drink in correspondence with = refreshments, *Star Wars* in correspondence with = movie, and coffee shop in correspondence with = food establishment). Moreover, we see that only some of the elements in the knowledge-unit are instantiated in working mem-

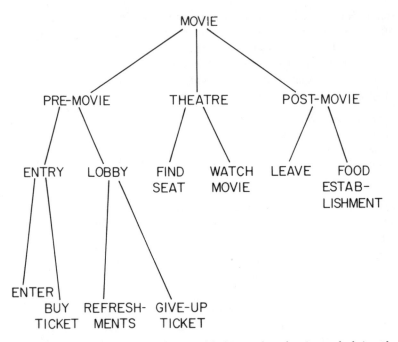

FIGURE 6. A representation of a possible hierarchy of units underlying the movie script.

ory. Moreover, there may be elements in working memory that do not correspond to the script (e.g., Fred had a headache). In its general form it is an extremely difficult matching problem to decide how to make the correspondence between such a variabilized pattern and the elements of working memory. A very good dissertation in computer science (Forgy, 1979) only solves part of the problem.

Related to the correspondence problem is the invocation problem. When should such a script be invoked. Presumably, when we hear "John bought popcorn and a drink," "John found a seat," we do not want to immediately invoke the movie script. Schank and Abelson make heavy use of certain key phrases like "went to the movies" to select a script. This seems related to the index in my proposal. However, this is only a partial solution.

For a long time we have suspected that the correspondence process might even be more complex than envisioned in the schema proposal with its variables and optional clauses. It seems that often correspondences are made with special cases rather than with general schemata. That is to say, oftentimes we spontaneously use analogies to make correspondence, Consider the following:

Ahero in Imaginaryland

This story is about Ahero who led his nation of Imaginaryland through a bitter civil war because of his belief in basic equality of all sexes. Women in the eastern states of Imaginaryland were bought and sold as wives and had few basic rights guaranteed. The economy of the East was heavily agricultural and some farmers had acquired hundreds of wives to work on their huge farms. The practice had been abolished in the West because of the decline of agriculture and greater contact with the liberal ideas of Europe. Ahero grew up in the southern wilderness area of Imaginaryland. He developed a strong moral commitment to abolish the wife-practices in eastern Imaginaryland. After a hard political struggle Ahero became prime minister of Imaginaryland. He immediately abolished wife-trade and guaranteed all women rights almost equal to those of men. After a few months of abortive parliamentary moves, the eastern states seceded from the confederation. There followed a long bitter civil war which finally reunited Imaginaryland. Ahero was assassinated just before the end of the war by a western actor sympathetic to the eastern cause.

Presumably, a reader of this story finds herself inevitably led to making correspondences with Abraham Lincoln and the Civil War, although the correspondences are hardly perfect. However, finding correspondences here differs from the schema-correspondence in at least two ways: (1) The knowledge structure being evoked, for instance about Abraham Lincoln, is not schematic. In no way could it be considered to contain variables which are filled by constants in making the correspondence. (2) There are failures of correspondence—for instance, Ahero abolished wife-practice before the war, while Lincoln abolished slavery at the end of the war. Still the correspondences are made almost irresistibly. It seems that such correspondence-by-analogy can be frequently involved in understanding texts, and we suspected that it might have beneficial effects on memory like those associated with other manipulations that enable subjects to unify information by making correspondence with past knowledge.

In a recent paper (Schustack & Anderson, 1979), we have explored the issue of the effects of such analogies on memory. We used texts such as the following which do not have such obvious analogies:

Yoshida Ichiro was a Japanese politician of the 20th century. He was chosen as national leader in his own right after having substituted for another. He was responsible for intensifying his country's involvement in a foreign conflict. He devoted much money and effort to eradicating economic and social injustices. He was made aware of rapidly worsening problems with his nation's energy supply, but he ignored them out of fear of political repercussions.

We contrasted four conditions—an experimental condition and three kinds of control. In the experimental condition the subject was told of the analogy between the fictional person and a well-known individual (in the case above, Lyndon Johnson). Such analogies were deliberately not perfect but are fairly close. Using a norming study, we had designed the material so that subjects would not spontaneously discover the analogies. In the first control condition subjects were not given any information about an analogy. The other two control conditions were used to assess the effects of having a name given as an analogy when no correspondence could be made. In the counterfeit condition subjects were given as an analogy a name of a person they did not know (e.g., Michael H. Donavan). The final condition, the inappropriate condition, was to test for the effect of providing as an analogy the name of a famous person. Here we provided an analogy that did not fit the fictional person well (e.g., Robert F. Kennedy for the Yoshida Ichiro character). The result was that subjects showed by far and away best memory for the material when they were given an appropriate analogy. This seems to support our suspicion that subjects find themselves able to establish loose analogical correspondences with past knowledge and that these correspondences really can help memory. The analogy helps because it allows the subject to inter-link all the elements for which correspondences have been made in a single step rather than having to separately encode each element.

Thematic Relatedness

Central to the discussion has been the idea of a correspondence between incoming data and existing knowledge structures. I have been arguing that such correspondences will be made and will have their impact on memory even in cases where the correspondence is hardly perfect. There are various kinds of "imperfection" that we have considered so far: (1) Certain pieces of the incoming data may not be matched in the existing structure and must be "skipped over." (2) Certain elements of the incoming data may be mismatched in the existing structure and require either the use of variables or of analogy. These are examples of where the data do not quite match the existing knowledge structures. There is another possibility, which is that no existing knowledge unit may adequately match a set of data elements, but that the combination of a number of existing knowledge units will match the data. This is what happens in the case of thematic relatedness. As we noted with respect to the stories like the one represented in Figure 1, these appeared to be unitized, although they corresponded to no single preexisting knowledge structures. Similarly, Reder and Anderson (in press) found the same effects for sets of facts that were instantiations of familiar sequences (i.e., scripts) versus sets which were only loosely and thematically related.

It remains unclear what exactly it takes for a set of facts to become thematically related. At one extreme the facts might only need to be related by interassociated structure. At the other extreme, the facts may need to be much more tightly interlocked by some plan. Schank and Abelson (1977) have considered such possibilities in their discussion of plans and themes. We have yet to do the research that will determine just how loose the thematic structure can be before it loses the ability to integrate incoming information.

I see the problem of computing this correspondence between existing knowledge and incoming data as part of a major issue for cognitive science: that of computing partial matches. A presupposition underlying information-processing work from Sternberg's analysis of memory scanning to production systems is that we detect perfect matches between structures or mismatches. However, it is perfectly clear that the human system operates in terms of partial matches, and any viable artificial system will have to also. The closest thing we have to this in psychology is the work on random-walk models of recognition (Link, 1975; Ratcliff, 1978); however, these are not up to the structural complexity of the input that need to be matched. We are currently working on a "partial" solution to this partial-match problem. As these ideas are not yet completely implemented, I don't think it appropriate to present them yet. However, until they are presented, there is a very big hole in the theory presented here. The basic claim of this paper is that the act of correspondence creates a cognitive unit. To have a real theory, then, one needs to specify the partial-match processes by which this correspondence is computed.

COMPARISON WITH OTHER THEORIES AND CONCEPTS

It is useful to consider how this proposal relates to other proposals that have been offered for knowledge representation and memory. The past proposals for which it is easiest to establish a correspondence are the ideas about how higher order concepts could serve to organize instances in a list. This is the work on categorized recall (e.g., Bower, Clark, Lesgold, & Winzenz, 1969; Mandler, 1967; Tulving, 1968). In this work one finds the proposals for a hierarchy of units, for all-or-none retrieval of units, and for the hypothesis that heightened recall results from unitization. These are all ideas that I want to emphasize in my proposal.

There are two principal differences between this proposal and standard discussions of categorized recall. One, of course, is the extension to propositions and other larger units of knowledge. The second is the explicitness of the mechanisms proposed. It has always been something of a mystery just why categorization produces the effects it does. If it produces better recall because it takes advantage of existing knowledge structures, as was commonly supposed, it becomes a mystery why there are not more intrusions of nonpresented members of the category. One solution to this mystery was the tagging proposal developed in the context of the FRAN model (Anderson, 1972; Anderson & Bower, 1972). This tagging proposal left open the issue of why it was easier to associate tags to elements in existing structures rather than simply interassociating them in new structures. While not denying the tagging mechanism, a rather different mechanism is being proposed here. The proposal here is that a new unit is created that organizes whatever elements are in working memory. The problem for this mechanism is to explain why there are any categorical intrusions rather than why there are so few. Perhaps this could be explained in terms of a guessing strategy.

The ideas in this paper have their strongest superficial similarity to the set of ideas that have developed in the past five years about frames, scripts, and schemata, and I have made constant reference to these ideas throughout the paper. There is a range of ideas that have been advanced in these other proposals, and I would not want to advance any aspect of my proposal as totally unique; but I would like to emphasize certain aspects that are relatively distinct: (1) Important is the concept of a hierarchy of units and the idea that the need for this hierarchy is forced by limits on the size of working memory. (2) Related to (1) is the conception of a cognitive unit as appropriate at many levels including the proposition and large story texts. (3) Also important is the extremely general notion of *correspondence* being advanced. Correspondences are not just calculated by fitting constants into variable slots but rather by a more general process of partial matching. (4) A fourth relatively unique aspect of the proposal is the explicitness with which the consequences of the cognitive-unit idea have been developed for mechanisms of encoding and retrieval (i.e., we have described the mechanisms that lead to all-or-none recall and heightened levels of recall.)

Another recent proposal, to which mine bears a superficial similarity, is the "cogit" model of Hayes-Roth (1977). In that model she proposed that elements could become unitized and that once unitized they would acquire an immunity to interference. The similarities here are quite superficial, and the two proposals are really quite orthogonal. It is important to state why they are orthogonal. First, Hayes-Roth proposed that the elements became unitized by dint of massive practice, while the proposal here is that unitization occurs after a single study when the elements are put in correspondence with an existing knowledge structure. Second, Hayes-Roth claimed that once knowledge was unitized in her sense, the knowledge unit became impervious to interference. When elements are unitized in the sense of this paper, the consequence for interference in many tasks is that the individual elements within the unit are no longer interfering or interfered with. However, the knowledge unit in which they are unitized still interferes and can be interfered with. These remarks are not meant to question the usefulness of Hayes-Roth's ideas, but only to question perceptions of their relevance to the current discussion.

The current proposal might seem to be in contradiction with another proposal I have put forth to account for the beneficial effects of prior knowledge in the acquisition of new knowledge. This is the elaboration proposal (Anderson, 1976; Anderson & Reder, 1979; Reder, 1979). The idea is that subjects generate additional redundant memory connections to encode a particular proposition. For instance, a subject given the sentence *The doctor hated the lawyer* might elaborate it: *The lawyer brought a lawsuit against the doctor for malpractice. When the doctor was on the witness stand, the lawyer assailed him with a stream of questions. The doctor glared at the lawyer. The lawyer continued to ask insulting questions. The doctor cursed the lawyer.* A subject, even if he could not remember the original sentence, might be able to infer it if he could retrieve a substantial amount of his elaboration. The elaboration proposal is that subjects use past knowledge to create inferential redundancies that help them remember new information. The unitization proposal claims that past knowledge helps retention of new information because the new information can be more rapidly encoded in terms of its correspondence to past knowledge. Thus one proposal emphasizes redundancy of encoding, while the other emphasizes increased rate of encoding.

While the two proposals sometimes can both account for the same memorial advantage of familar over unfamilar material, they extend to explain different phenomena. It is hard to make any firm connections between the elaboration proposal and any unitization phenomena such as all-or-none recall or within-unit priming. On the other hand, the unitization proposal cannot account for the effect of embellishment when these embellishments do not serve to establish correspondences with prior-knowledge units. For instance, it is hard to see why the doctor-lawyer elaboration given earlier would help according to the unitization proposals. Related to this is the fact that it is hard to extend the unitization proposal to account for effects of depth of processing or inferential intrusions in recall (see Anderson & Reder, 1979). So, my inclination is to consider both hypotheses as necessary to account for the complexities of human memory.

SUMMARY

In this paper I have reviewed the data and theoretical considerations that bear on the issue of whether propositions and schemata should be considered cognitive units. Assuming a certain general framework about working memory and long-term memory, the evidence tended to point toward a positive conclusion—that both can be cognitive units. Evidence for this comes from observations about all-or-none recall, heightened recall of units, associative priming, diminution of interference effects, considerations of implementation efficiency, and considerations of cognitive naturalness. This being said, I do not find the current picture so convincing that I would want to make a never-say-die commitment to the positive conclusion for cognitive units at all levels of knowledge structures. The idea seems sufficiently promising that it is worthwhile to develop a more explicit theory of what a cognitive unit would be like. So I have proposed a general notion of a cognitive unit that spanned propositions and schemata as special cases and specified the encoding and retrieval properties that such a cognitive unit would have. To be succinct, the important ideas associated with cognitive units are the following: (1) They can occur at multiple levels and enter into hierarchies. (2) If a set of working-memory elements can be put in correspondence with an existing knowledge structure, the elements can be joined in a cognitive unit by a single encoding act. (3) The elements in a cognitive unit are brought into working memory in a single retrieval act. (4) It is possible to evaluate general properties of a cognitive unit without having to expand it into its elements and inspect these. Perhaps this is done by measuring level of activation.

REFERENCES

Anderson, J. R. FRAN: A simulation model of free recall. In G. H. Bower (Ed.), *The psychology of learning and motivation* (Vol. 5). New York: Academic Press, 1972.

Anderson, J. R. Retrieval of propositional information from long term memory. *Cognitive Psychology, 1974, 5,* 451–474.

Anderson, J. R. *Language, memory, and thought.* Hillsdale, N.J.; Lawrence Erlbaum Associates, 1976.

Anderson, J. R. Arguments concerning representations for mental imagery. *Psychological Review, 1978, 85,* 249–277.

Anderson, J. R. Further arguments concerning representations for mental imagery: A response to Hayes-Roth and Pylyshyn. *Psychological Review, 1979, 86,* 395–406.

Anderson, J. R., & Bower, G. H. Recognition and retrieval processes in free recall. *Psychological Review, 1972, 79,* 97–123.

Anderson, J. R. & Bower, G. H. *Human associative memory.* Washington, D.C.: Hemisphere Press, 1973.

Anderson, J. R., & Paulson, R. Representation and retention of verbatim information. *Journal of Verbal Learning and Verbal Behavior, 1977, 16,* 439–451.

Anderson, J. R., & Reder, L. M. An elaborative processing explanation of depth of processing. In L. S. Cermak & F. I. M. Craik, (Eds.), *Levels of processing in human memory.* Hillsdale, N.J.: Lawrence Erlbaum Associates, 1979.

Anderson, R. C. Substance recall of sentences. *Quarterly Journal of Experimental Psychology, 1974, 26,* 530–541.

Black, J. B., & Bower, G. H. Episodes as chunks in narrative memory.

160

Journal of Verbal Learning and Verbal Behavior, 1979, *18*, 309–318.

Bobrow, D. G., & Winograd, T. An overview of KRL, a knowledge representation language. *Cognitive Science*, 1977, *1*, 3–46.

Bower, G. H., Black, J. B. & Turner, T. J. Scripts in memory for text. *Cognitive Psychology*, 1979, *11*, 177–220.

Bower, G. H., Clark, M. C., Lesgold, A. M., & Winzenz, D. Hierarchical retrieval schemes in recall of categorical word lists. *Journal of Verbal Learning and Verbal Behavior*, 1969, *8*, 323–343.

Broadbent, D. E. The magical number seven after fifteen years. In R. A. Kennedy & A. Wilkes (Eds.), *Studies in long-term memory*. New York: Wiley, 1975.

Cohen, B. H. Recall of categorized word lists. *Journal of Experimental Psychology*, 1963, *66*, 227–234.

Cohen, B. H. Some-or-none characteristics of coding behavior. *Journal of Verbal Learning and Verbal Behavior*, 1966, *5*, 182–187.

Forgy, C. L. *On the efficient implementation of production systems*. Ph.D. Dissertation, Computer Science Department, Carnegie-Mellon University, 1979.

Goetz, E. T., Anderson, R. C., & Schallert, D. L. *The representation of sentences in memory*. Unpublished manuscript, 1979.

Hayes-Roth, B. Evolution of cognitive structures and processes. *Psychological Review*, 1977, *84*, 260–278.

Hendrix, G. G. *Expanding the utility of semantic networks through partitioning*. Stanford Research Institute Technical Note 105, 1975.

Katz, J. J., & Fodor, J. A. The structure of a semantic theory. *Language*, 1963, *39*, 170–210.

Kintsch, W. *The representation of meaning in memory*. Hillsdale, N.J.: Lawrence Erlbaum Associates, 1974.

Landauer, T. K. Memory without organization: Properties of a model with random storage and undirected retrieval. *Cognitive Psychology*, 1975, *7*, 495–531.

Link, S. W. The relative judgment theory of two choice response times. *Journal of Mathematical Psychology*, 1975, *12*, 114–135.

Mandler, G. Organization and memory. In K. W. Spence & J. A. Spence (Eds.), *The psychology of learning and motivation* (Vol. 1). New York: Academic Press, 1967.

Mandler, J. M., & Johnson, N. S. Remembrance of things parsed: Story structure and recall. *Cognitive Psychology*, 1977, *9*, 111–151.

Miller, G. A. The magical number seven, plus or minus two: Some limits on our capacity for processing information. *Psychological Review*, 1956, *63*, 81–97.

Minsky, M. A framework for representing knowledge. In P. H. Winston (Ed.), *The psychology of computer vision*. New York: McGraw-Hill, 1975.

Newell, A. Production systems: Models of control structures. In W. G. Chase (Ed.), *Visual information processing*. New York: Academic Press, 1973.

Norman, D. A., & Rumelhart, D. E. *Explorations in cognition*. San Francisco: W. H. Freeman, 1975.

Owens, J., Bower, G. H., & Black, J. B. The "soap opera" effect in story recall. *Memory and cognition*, 1979, *7*, 185–191.

Pylyshyn, A. W. Validating computational models: A critique of Anderson's indeterminacy of representation claim. *Psychological Review*, 1979, *86*, 383–394.

Ratcliff, R. A theory of memory retrieval. *Psychological Review*, 1978, *85*, 59–108.

Ratcliff, R., & McKoon, G. Priming in item recognition: Evidence for the propositional structure of sentences. *Journal of Verbal Learning and Verbal Behavior*, 1978, *17*, 403–417.

Reder, L. M. The role of elaborations in memory for prose. *Cognitive Psychology*, 1979, *11*, 221–234.

Reder, L. M., & Anderson, J. R. A partial resolution of the paradox of interference: The role of integrating knowledge. *Cognitive Psychology*, 1980, *12*, 447–472.

Rumelhart, D. E. Understanding and summarizing brief stories. In D. La Berge & J. Samuels (Eds.), *Basic processes in reading: Perception and comprehension*. Hillsdale, N.J.: Lawrence Erlbaum Associates, 1977.

Rumelhart, D. E., & Ortony, A. The representation of knowledge in memory. In R. C. Anderson, R. J. Spiro, & W. E. Montague (Eds.), *Schooling and the acquisition of knowledge*. Hillsdale, N.J.: Lawrence Erlbaum Associates, 1976.

Rychener, M. D., & Newell, A. An instructible production system: Basic design issues. In D. A. Waterman & F. Hayes-Roth (Eds.), *Pattern-directed inference systems*. New York: Academic Press, 1977.

Schank, R. C. Conceptual dependency: A theory of natural language understanding. *Cognitive Psychology*, 1972, *3*, 552–631.

Schank, R. C. The structure of episodes in memory. In D. G. Bobrow & A. M. Collins (Eds.), *Representation and understanding*. New York: Academic Press, 1975.

Schank, R. C., & Abelson, R. P. *Scripts, plans, goals, and understanding: An inquiry into human knowledge structures*. Hillsdale, N.J.: Lawrence Erlbaum Associates, 1977.

Schustack, M., & Anderson, J. R. Effects of analogy to prior knowledge on memory for new information. *Journal of Verbal Learning and Verbal Behavior*, 1979, *18*, 565–583.

Simmons, R. F. Some semantic structures for representing English meanings. In R. Freedle & J. B. Carroll (Eds.), *Language comprehension and the acquisition of knowledge*. Washington, D.C.: Winston, 1972.

Simon, H. A. How big is a chunk? *Science*, 1974, *183*, 482–488.

Smith, E. E., Adams, N., & Schorr, D. Fact retrieval and the paradox of interference. *Cognitive Psychology*, 1978. *10*, 438–464.

Thorndyke, P. W. Cognitive structures in comprehension and memory of narrative discourse. *Cognitive Psychology*, 1977, *9*, 77–110.

Thorndyke, P. W., & Bower, G. H. Storage and retrieval processes in sentence memory. *Cognitive Psychology*, 1974, *5*, 515–543.

Townsend, J. T. Issues and models concerning the processing of a finite number of inputs. In B. H. Kantowitz (Ed.), *Human information processing: Tutorials in performance and cognition.* Hillsdale, N.J.: Lawrence Erlbaum Associates, 1974.

Tulving, E. Theoretical issues in free recall. In T. R. Dixon & D. L. Horton (Eds.), *Verbal behavior and general behavior theory.* Englewood Cliffs, N.J.: Prentice-Hall, 1968.

Organization of
Factual Knowledge

Edward E. Smith[1]
Stanford University

*F*OR the past decade, psychologists have been intensively studying how people represent and remember the factual knowledge they encounter in sentences. Perhaps the high-water mark of this research occurred in the first half of the 1970s with the publication of large-scale models, such as Anderson and Bower (1973) and Norman and Rumelhart (1975). This work deservedly became among the best known in cognitive psychology. Unlike some of its predecessors in the field of memory, the model of Anderson and Bower (1973), for example, was sweeping in scope yet precise in detail.

Despite their achievements, these models had a major difficulty that rapidly became apparent to many. The problem was that the models achieved their theoretical power by representing only those facts that were explicit in the input sentences, and failed to give serious attention to how people brought to bear other knowledge that elaborated the input facts. This was a serious omission, partly because such elaborations are often the hallmark of true comprehension of the input facts, and partly because these same elaborations organize the input facts and boost their memorability. To illustrate, suppose you read *Herb needed a diversion* and *Herb looked at the movie times.* In representing this information, you would presumably depict not only the facts explicitly stated but also something about going to a movie. The latter constitutes an elaboration of the input. From the point of view of comprehension, this elaboration is crucial because it provides a basis for integrating the input facts into a coherent scenario. From the point of view of memory, it is important because the elaborated facts turn out to be more retrievable than the unelaborated ones.

Lately there has been a lot of attention given to the above prob-

1. The author is now at Bolt Beranek and Newman, Cambridge, Mass. Preparation of this manuscript was supported by U.S. Public Health Service Grant MH-19705, and by the National Institute of Education under contract no. US-NIE-L-400-76-0116.

lem, much of it due to the same psychologists who produced the
first generation of sentence-memory models. Thus when Anderson (1976) proposed a revision of the original Anderson and Bower
(1973) model, he devoted much concern to how people elaborate
input propositions. Similarly, Bower (e.g., Black & Bower, 1980),
Norman (e.g., Norman & Bobrow, 1976), and Rumelhart (e.g.,
Rumelhart & Ortony, 1977) have all begun to study how people
use what they already know to organize new information. And
there are also many contributions from artificial intelligence dealing with the use of prior knowledge in representing and remembering new information (e.g., Adams & Collins, 1979; Minsky,
1975; Rumelhart & Ortony, 1977; Schank & Abelson, 1977; Winograd, 1972).

So everybody seems to agree that the early 1970s approach to
sentence memory needs to be altered so as to be consistent with
the fact that people use prior knowledge to process new knowledge. But in making such an alteration, certain questions arise.
The first is an empirical one: (1) Precisely what conditions lead
people to elaborate and organize input facts? The remaining questions are theoretical: (2) What are the mechanisms behind organization? Is there one basic one, or are there many? (3) How well can
these organizational mechanisms be intefaced with the original
theories of sentence memory? These questions form the focus of
my paper.

With this as background, let me lay out a more exact agenda. In
the next section I review some basics of how current sentence-
memory models represent and retrieve sentences, and then illustrate three conditions that lead to an elaboration of representations. In subsequent sections, I take up each condition in detail,
review the experimental data showing that the condition does
indeed result in an organization of the input, and try to spell out
the theoretical mechanisms involved. In the final section I summarize the main conclusions.

I. SENTENCE REPRESENTATIONS AND ORGANIZATIONAL POSSIBILITIES

A. Representation and Retrieval in Current Models of Sentence Memory

1. Representation and Retrieval of Single Sentences

Let me first illustrate how three different models would represent and retrieve the proposition in the sentence *Woody Allen makes movies*. Figure 1 contains the sample representations. In all three cases it is assumed that the representation corresponds to a network, where the concepts—"Woody Allen," "makes," and "movies"—are depicted as nodes, and the relations between concepts are given by labeled links between nodes.

Panel A of the figure is based on the ELINOR model presented in Rumelhart, Lindsay, and Norman (1972). This network is centered around the verb or action concept. The node for the action, "makes," is linked to the nodes for the other two concepts, "Woody Allen" and "movies," while the latter two have no direct

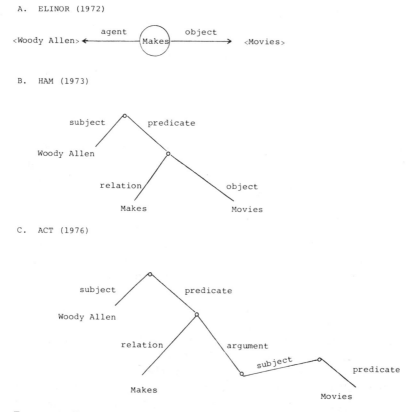

FIGURE 1. Propositional representations of *Woody Allen makes movies* based on (A) Rumelhart, Lindsay, and Norman (1972), (B) Anderson and Bower (1973), and (C) Anderson (1976).

connection. Each connection has a label that depicts the semantic relation operative: for instance, "Woody Allen" is the *agent* of "making," and "movies" is the *object*. To see how a retrieval process might operate on this representation, suppose that sometime after reading the sentence, you were presented it as a probe and asked if you had seen it before. According to the general ideas in ELINOR, you would form a representation of the probe identical to that in Panel A, and then use the concepts in the probe to directly access those in the representation of the memorized sentence. From the accessed memory nodes you would search for a path (i.e., a set of labeled links) that perfectly matches the path in the probe representation. If you found such a path, you would say you recognized the sentence; if you did not, you would call it a novel sentence.

Panel B contains a representation from the HAM model of Anderson and Bower (1973). The action concept has no privileged status here. Rather, the internal structure of the proposition is closer to that of a phrase structure. There is first a distinction between *subject* ("Woody Allen") and *predicate*, and then the predicate itself is divided into a *relation* ("makes") and an *object* ("movies"). Again we have concepts connected by labeled links, but now some nodes are higher order ones that stand for complex concepts, like that designating the entire predicate. It turns out, though, that the terminal nodes standing for specific concepts (e.g., "movies") do the bulk of the work in retrieval. And the retrieval process for HAM looks like the one I described earlier. So if later asked if you've ever seen the probe *Woody Allen makes movies*, you would form a representation of the probe just like that in Panel B of Figure 1, use its terminal nodes to directly access those of the memorized proposition, and search for a path connecting all nodes in the memorized proposition that would match the path in the probe representation.

Panel C of Figure 1 contains a third representation, one based on the ACT model of Anderson (1976). Its core is the subset of the network that relates "Woody Allen," "makes," and a node that eventually points to the concept of "movies." This subset is almost identical to the previously considered HAM representation, the only difference being that the label *argument* has replaced the label *object*. The rest of the present representation consists of a secondary proposition asserting that what Allen makes is a subset of the class of movies. While the latter is important for issues that Anderson (1976) was concerned with, it is not critical for what I will say and I ignore it in what follows.

What I cannot ignore about ACT is its retrieval process. The discrete search process of HAM has been replaced by a continuous, spreading activation process in ACT. When the probe *Woody Allen makes movies* is presented, each word activates its corresponding concept in a long-term memory network, and activation from each of these sources spreads along the links emanating from the source. The rate of spread on a given link increases with the strength of that link (an associative-strength idea) and decreases with the number of other links emanating from that source (an associative-interference idea). When the activation from the three sources intersect, say at the predicate node, the path leading to this intersection can be evaluated to see if its component links contain the same labels or relations as those specified in the probe. If the relations are the same, the probe would be recognized.

2. *Representation and Retrieval of Sentence Pairs*

So much for single sentences. From the perspective of organization, nothing really interesting happens until we consider at least pairs of sentences. Figure 2 contains representations of two facts about Woody Allen, the old one about him making movies and a new one about his living in New York. Panel A gives the ELINOR representation, Panel B a simplified HAM-ACT one.

In Panel A we have two propositions connected to the node for "Woody Allen." This should slow down the retrieval process in recognition. That is, when presented with the probe *Woody Allen makes movies*, one would again use the concepts in the probe to access those in the memorized propositions; but now the search process, which is looking for a path matching that in the probe, will have to consider two links off the "Woody Allen" node. And if the search process is limited in capacity, it will take longer when there are two paths from a node than when there is only one. Therefore, the time to correctly recognize a probe should increase with the number of links emanating from the relevant memory nodes.[2]

2. This prediction was not explicitly made by Rumelhart, Lindsay, and Norman (1972) or in any other paper on the ELINOR model that I know of. However, I believe it follows quite directly from what has been explicitly stated about the model's representations and retrieval processes.

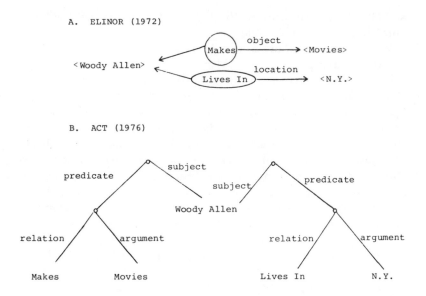

FIGURE 2. Propositional representations of *Woody Allen makes movies* and *Woody Allen lives in New York* based on (A) Rumelhart, Lindsay, and Norman (1972), and (B) Anderson and Bower (1973) and Anderson (1976).

This same prediction follows from HAM and ACT. In Panel B of Figure 2 there are again two links from the "Woody Allen" node. Given the probe *Woody Allen makes movies*, the three corresponding concept nodes will be activated, where the activation emanating from "Woody Allen" must be split between two links. This will slow the rate of activation on the critical link leading to "makes" and "movies." Consequently it will take longer to get an intersection that can lead to a correction recognition.

3. *The Fan Effect and Interference*

The three models agree that as one learns more facts about a concept these facts fan out from the concept node, thereby slowing any limited-capacity retrieval process that underlies recognition. Hence recognition time for a specific fact about a concept should slow down as we increase our knowledge about that concept. This effect, called the *fan* effect, has been extensively documented by recognition-memory studies showing that the time to decide whether a probe sentence is Old or New increases with the number of facts learned about each concept in the probe (Anderson, 1974, 1975, 1976; Anderson & Bower, 1973; Anderson & Paulson, 1978; Hayes-Roth, 1977; Hayes-Roth & Hayes-Roth, 1977; King & Anderson, 1976; Lewis & Anderson, 1976; Moesher, 1979; Reder & Anderson, 1980; Shoben, Wescourt, & Smith, 1978; Smith, Adams & Schorr, 1978; Thorndyke & Bower, 1974).

Thus one reason why fanning is important is that the fan effect on recognition latency is a common prediction of models with different representations. Another reason why fanning is important is that the basic idea behind it—that multiple facts learned about a concept interfere with one another during retrieval—may play a role in any memory task, not just speeded recognition. Thus an increase in fanning can lead to an increase in recognition or recall *failures* if we make the following two assumptions: (1) People continue to search the links from a memory node until they hit a stop rule, like "when the last *n* links examined have not led to a path matching the probe, call the probe a New item (if in a recognition test) or give up (if in a recall test)" (e.g., Rundus, 1973; Shiffrin, 1970); and (2) every time a particular link is examined, it increases in strength or accessibility and is therefore more likely to be examined again (Rundus, 1973). Now the more facts you learn about a concept, the more likely you will hit the stop point before finding a target fact, and hence the more likely you are to suffer a recall or recognition failure. Moreover, this can happen even when you have learned just a few facts, because if you sample the wrong link early, its accessibility will increase and you may continue to resample it.

Powerful as the idea of fanning is, in its unchecked form it has a paradoxical quality (Smith et al., 1978). The idea that the more we learn about a topic the more interference we suffer, seems at odds with our everyday experience that as we become increasingly knowledgeable about a topic we are often better able to answer questions about it. The way to reconcile everyday experience with the propositional representations and fan effects discussed is to invoke the organizational mechanisms alluded to earlier. That is, certain conditions lead us to alter the facts that we are explicitly given, resulting in a representation that allows us to store multiple facts about a topic without substantial increases in fanning. It is time to describe these organizational conditions.

B. Conditions That Foster Organization in Sentence Memory

1. *Facts That Subdivide into Distinct Groups*

The first condition fostering organization in sentence memory is that the facts to be learned come from distinct groups. In such a case, we may subdivide our memory representations and thereby boost retrieval. Figure 3 illustrates this subdivision.

Panel A shows a simplified HAM-ACT representation of four facts. (To expedite matters, relation names like *subject* and *predicate* have been replaced by the first letters of these names.) The

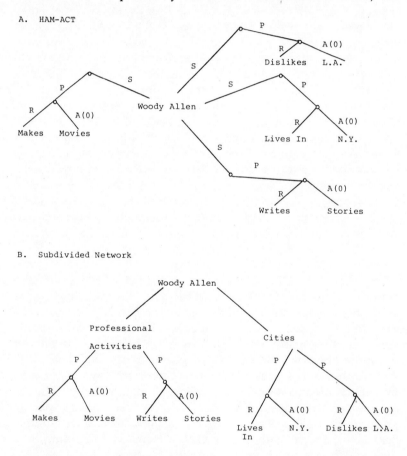

A. HAM-ACT

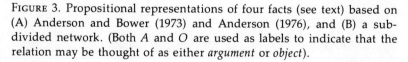

B. Subdivided Network

FIGURE 3. Propositional representations of four facts (see text) based on (A) Anderson and Bower (1973) and Anderson (1976), and (B) a subdivided network. (Both *A* and *O* are used as labels to indicate that the relation may be thought of as either *argument* or *object*).

facts correspond to the two sentences previously illustrated plus two additional ones: *Woody Allen writes stories* and *Woody Allen dislikes LA*. There are now four links fanning off the "Woody Allen" node, and this spells trouble for the retrieval process. Panel B shows how to get rid of the trouble. The representation there has been altered so as to take advantage of the natural division among the facts. The "Woody Allen" node now leads to two subnodes, one designating professional activities and the other experiences with cities. These subnodes are in turn connected to their relevant predicates: For example, the Professional subnode goes to the predicates concerned with making movies and writing stories. The major elaboration is thus to create two subnodes that were not explicit in the input facts, and to insert each subnode between the relevant subject and predicate nodes in what is called a *subdivided network*.

2. Facts That Can Be Integrated by Prior Knowledge

To illustrate this condition, consider the HAM-ACT representations in Figure 4. Panel A represents two sentences, *Herb needed a diversion* and *Herb waited in line*; Panel B represents the same two sentences plus two additional ones, *Herb went to a movie* and *Herb bought popcorn*. There is an increase in fanning off the "Herb" node from 2 to 4 as we move from Panel A to Panel B. This means that the models we reviewed earlier would predict that it takes longer to correctly recognize *Herb waited in line* if you learned the four sentences in Panel B than only the two in Panel A. Intuition suggests otherwise. The four facts in Panel B seem to make up a coherent unit, while the two in Panel A are more difficult to integrate. Here our sentence-memory models seem to be missing a critical point: facts integrable by some prior knowledge (like knowledge about going to a movie) may not function as independent propositions in memory.

3. Facts Containing Perfectly Correlated Predicates

The condition of interest is illustrated by the sentences in Table 1. On both the left- and right-hand sides, there is one fact about John, one about Ed, and three each about Woody and Mel. Furthermore, for both the sentences on the left and those on the right,

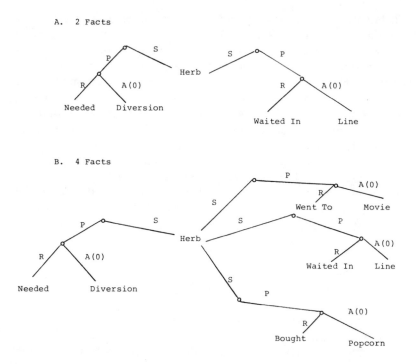

FIGURE 4. Propositional representations based on Anderson and Bower (1973) and Anderson (1976) for (A) two unrelated facts and (B) four integrated facts (see text).

each predicate is used twice, and the trio of predicates attributed to Woody or Mel are not readily integrated by any salient packet of prior knowledge. What then is the difference between the two sentence sets? The predicates on the left are perfectly correlated, whereas those on the right are not. Given the facts on the left, if someone makes movies, that same someone was born in Brooklyn and went to California; or if someone visited Virginia, that's all they did. In contrast, for the facts on the right, if someone makes movies, they may have been born in Brooklyn (like Woody) or they may not have (like Mel). Perfectly correlated predicates seem to provide some structure to the input facts. And people seem to use this structure: Though the variations in fanning are identical in the two sets of sentences in Table 1, only the sentences on the

Table 1
Sentences with Predicates That Vary in Correlation

Perfectly Correlated	*Less Than Perfectly Correlated*
John visited Virginia	John visited Virginia
Ed visited Virginia	Ed was born in Brooklyn
Woody was born in Brooklyn	Woody was born in Brooklyn
Woody makes movies	Woody makes movies
Woody went to California	Woody went to California
Mel was born in Brooklyn	Mel visited Virginia
Mel makes movies	Mel makes movies
Mel went to California	Mel went to California

right produce a fan effect on recognition latencies (Whitlow, Medin, & Smith, 1980).[3]

II. SUBDIVIDING FACTS FROM DISTINCT GROUPS

My first task will be to present empirical evidence about how facts memorized from distinct groups facilitates retrieval. I will start with research on the fan effect and then move on to other empirical phenomena. After that, I will discuss theoretical mechanisms.

A. Empirical Evidence

1. *Fan Effects on Recognition Latency*

A few experiments have dealt with recognition latencies for memorized facts from distinct groups. One of the simplest is by McClosky (1979). He first had subjects learn from one to six facts about various people identified by occupation terms, such as *the*

---

3. This brief review of conditions that foster organization has omitted Hayes-Roth's (1977) work, which indicates that practice can organize the constituents of a proposition into a single unit. The reason for the omission is that Hayes-Roth focuses on the organization of a single proposition, while I am concerned with organizing a set of propositions.

tailor. For each occupation term, some facts concerned animals, the rest countries. And for each occupation term, McClosky manipulated the fan level of the animal facts independently of the fan level of the country facts. This is illustrated in Table 2. For *the tailor* there are five facts about animals, but only one about countries, while for *the chemist* there is one fact about animals, but five about countries. After memorizing these facts, subjects were given an Old-New recognition test. The memorized facts were intermixed with a like number of distractors, where each distractor was constructed by repairing the occupation term from one learned sentence with the predicate of another (e.g., *The tailor likes Canada* [see Table 2]). The subject's task was to decide as quickly as possible whether each sentence—referred to as a probe—was Old (on the memorized list) or New (a distractor). The data of major interest were the average times needed for correct Old and New decisions.

To appreciate the results, note that any probe contains both an occupation and an object term from the memorized list. The occupation term is characterized by two fan levels, one designating the number of learned animal facts, the other the number of learned country facts. The object term of the probe, however, tells the subject which of these two sets of facts is relevant (e.g., if the object names an animal, only the animal facts are relevant). Thus, though a probe has two fan levels, one may be designated a *relevant* fan, the other an *irrelevant* fan. To illustrate with the items in

Table 2

Example of Sentences Used in McClosky (1979)

Facts about Animals	The tailor likes wolves The tailor likes rabbits The tailor likes bears The tailor likes tigers The tailor likes pigs	The chemist likes wolves
Facts about Countries	The tailor likes Portugal	The chemist likes Portugal The chemist likes Canada The chemist likes England The chemist likes Brazil The chemist likes Italy

Table 2, if the probe was *The tailor likes wolves,* the relevant fan would be 5 and the irrelevant fan 1. If McCloskey's subjects used the object term of the probe to decide which set of memorized facts was relevant, their recognition latencies should have systematically increased with the relevant fan, but not with the irrelevant fan. This is roughly what McClosky found. Recognition latency increased about 370 msec as the relevant fan increased from 1 to 5, but increased only about 100 msec as the irrelevant fan varied over this same range. While the 100 msec increase may suggest that subjects were considering the irrelevant facts, two points mitigate against this. The 100 msec increase did not reach a conventional level of statistical significance, and part or all of it may reflect the time needed to decide whether the object term names an animal or a country. All things considered, McClosky's results suggest that people can sometimes subdivide their knowledge and use information in the probe to direct their search to the relevant subgroup.

In the above study the subdivision was based on a semantic aspect: the object term named either an animal or a country. Anderson and Paulson (1978) looked at a different basis for subdivision. Using a paradigm like that described above, they showed that if some facts about an object are presented pictorially while others are presented as verbal descriptions, subjects may use this difference in mode of presentation as a basis for subdivision. When Anderson and Paulson's subjects were given a recognition test, if the probe was a verbal description of an object, for example, recognition latency increased substantially with the number of verbally presented facts about that object, but only minimally with the number of pictorially presented facts about the object.

The above studies have two limitations. First, the only bases for subdivision that have thus far been demonstrated are simple ones—the semantic category of a probe word and the modality of presentation. If subdivision is confined to such simple aspects, it could not play much role in real-life memory situations and hence could not be the only means of organization we use. Second, though the above results suggest that people can restrict their search to the subgroup deemed relevant by the probe, we will soon have cause to question whether search processes in recognition are usually this selective.

2. Free Recall of Categorized Lists

The previous studies make excellent contact with models of sentence memory because they focus on the fan effect. But while

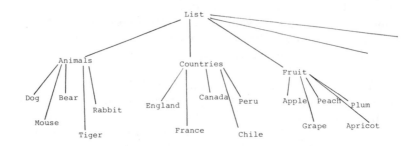

FIGURE 5. Example of a subdivided representation for a categorized list.

these studies are analytic, they provide too narrow a view of sub-division. For subdivision can have striking effects on recall, both the amount recalled and the structure of the recall. These effects have recently been demonstrated in prose recall (Black & Bower, 1979), but they have been most extensively documented in studies dealing with the free recall of word lists.

Those concerned with memory for word lists long ago dis-covered that recall improves when the words are drawn from a few semantic categories. Suppose subjects are presented a list of 40 words. They will recall more if the list consists of 5 instances from each of 8 semantic categories—just the instances, not the category names—than if all words are semantically unrelated (e.g., Cohen, 1963; Puff, 1970). This effect depends partly on subjects being aware of the categorical structure of the list at the time of input (e.g., Cofer, Bruce, & Reicher, 1966), which suggests that the effect depends on setting up a certain kind of representation. The obvi-ous possibility is a representation that is subdivided according to categories (e.g., Bousfield & Cohen, 1953). Figure 5 presents an example. Though the category terms—*animals, countries,* etc.—did not appear in the input list, they have been inserted in the repre-sentation as subnodes and are connected to nodes for words that did appear in the input.

This representation seems consistent with three important findings about recall from categorized lists.

(1) *Recall is clustered by categories.* Subjects recall a number of instances from one category in succession, then a number of in-stances from another category, and so on (e.g., Bousfield, 1953). This suggests that subjects retrieve a category subnode, search its links to instances, and move on to the next subnode.

(2) *Recall is "some or none."* Typically either several instances of a category are recalled or none are (e.g., Cohen, 1963). This suggests that if one can't get to a particular subnode, there is no other path to its instances.

(3) *Category cueing aids recall.* If recall is substantially less than perfect, giving subjects the category terms as cues will enable them to retrieve some of the missing items (e.g., Tulving & Pearlstone, 1966). The cues apparently allow subjects to retrieve subnodes they missed in their initial recall.

B. Theoretical Mechanisms

1. *Retrieval Processes for Free Recall*

To illustrate the mechanisms involved, consider Figure 6. It contains some facts that a devotee of Woody Allen might have stored. The top node designates the concept "Woody Allen." Then come two levels of subnodes. The first distinguishes "Personal" and "Professional Life," while the nature of the subnodes at the next level depends on whether they are dominated by "Professional" or "Personal-Life" subnodes. Subnodes under "Personal Life" designate periods or eras of life (Kolodner, 1978)—like "Early Childhood," "Boyhood," "Marriage," etc.—whereas subnodes under "Professional Life" designate different occupational and artistic roles—like "Gagwriter," "Storywriter," and "Filmmaker."

Consider how the information in the network might be retrieved during free recall. If the possessor of the above network

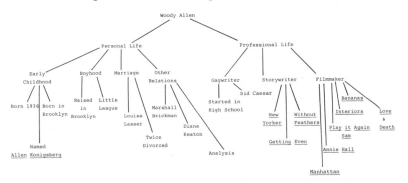

FIGURE 6. Example of a subdivided network for knowledge about Woody Allen.

were asked to say everything he knew about Woody Allen, he would presumably enter at the top node and traverse either the link to "Professional Life" or to "Personal Life," with the strength or accessibility of these links determining which one is chosen (Rundus, 1973; Shiffrin, 1970). Assume he took the path to "Professional Life." Then he would traverse one of the links leading to a more specific subnode, for example, "Filmmaker" (the choice again determined by link strength), and start searching paths from this specific subnode, emitting each fact he found, for example, *Woody Allen's films include Annie Hall and Manhattan*. Having done what he could with the facts under a specific subnode, our respondent would then presumably find his way back to the higher subnode that was activated, "Professional Life," trace a path down to another specific subnode, for example, "Gagwriter," and start searching paths from there to specific facts. Once he has done his utmost with the accessible subnodes under "Professional Life," our respondent would move on to "Personal Life" and the specific subnodes it dominates.

This scheme is consistent with the free-recall findings. Following the process just outlined, our respondent would cluster his recall by specific subnodes (e.g., he would recall Allen's movies in one group), as well as by higher level subnodes (e.g., he would recall Allen's movies closer to Allen's published stories than to facts about Allen's boyhood). His recall should also have a some-or-none character: For example, he would either not mention anything about Allen's marriages or mention most facts he has stored about them. And should our respondent fail to emit anything at all about a particular subnode like "Gagwriter," reminding him that Allen was once a gagwriter might bring forth the relevant facts.

2. Considerations of Efficiency

The above retrieval scheme is extremely efficient because each node has a relatively small number of links fanning off of it. I was able to depict over 20 facts about Woody Allen while keeping the maximum fan off a node down to 6. The largest number of links one would ever have to traverse is 8 (for a question about films made), while the smallest is 4 (for a question about gagwriting). High efficiency could be maintained even with a substantial increase in the number of facts by increasing the number of subnodes at each level and/or the number of levels.

However, research on the recall of categorized lists suggests a limit to the amount of subdivision possible. Mandler's (e.g., 1967) studies indicate that recall is maximal with 5±2 categories or nodes per level: If more than these are used to divide up a fixed number of facts, recall starts to decline. Since there is no reason to think otherwise, I assume that this 5±2 limit might hold at all levels. What about a limit to the number of levels? I don't know of any experimental work on this issue, but since no one seems to have worked with categorized lists using more than three levels, I suspect that this factor too is governed by some small number. If it is again about 5, an optimal subdivided network—5 levels with 5 nodes per level—could represent 3,225 facts without requiring the retrieval process to ever inspect more than 25 nodes. This remarkable efficiency may account for why hierarchical representations have been shown to be such powerful recall aids in general (e.g., Bower, Clark, Lesgold, & Winzenz, 1969; Nelson & Smith, 1972), and why they are so widely used as storage devices in computer systems (where they are referred to as *discrimination nets*).

3. Retrieval Processes for Recognition

For recognition, there is in principle no need to search the entire network. To illustrate, given the probe *Was Woody Allen ever married to Louise Lasser?*, our respondent could enter at the top of the network, use the probe to get to "Marriage." (Note that to use the probe to get to "Personal Life," our respondent must know that marriage pertains to personal life.) Under this view the search process is selective, in the sense that it uses information from higher level subnodes to select the appropriate lower level ones.

Problems for this view arise, however, if we alter our probe slightly to *Was Woody Allen ever involved with Louise Lasser?*. Now the analysis of the probe that gets our respondent to "Personal Life" must be quite complex. It can't simply use "involved with" as an access condition for "Personal Life," for the question *Was Woody Allen ever involved with Sid Caesar?* will get our respondent to the "Professional Life" subnode. It seems that to get to the "Personal Life" node for the Louise-Lasser question but not for the Sid-Caesar one, I have to consider the fact that Woody Allen is a notorious heterosexual, thereby making it plausible that *involved with* can be given a romantic reading with Louise Lasser but not with Sid Caesar. But Allen's heterosexuality is the kind of fact that is presumably represented at some lower level subnode, so how can I have access to it while still working at a top-level subnode? More generally, selection of a higher level subnode may sometimes rest on information at lower level nodes, which is at odds with the idea of a selective search where one only accesses lower level nodes by first going through higher level ones. It seems, then, that search processes in recognition are considering lower level nodes at the same time as higher level ones. To illustrate with the above example, we seem to search up from the nodes for Louise Lasser or Sid Caesar at the same time we search down the nodes of the hierarchy.

Considerations like these in a different domain led Anderson (1976, chap. 8; King & Anderson, 1977) to reject the notion of selective search altogether, and to opt for a spreading activation process that starts at the probe concepts and then searches blindly through a network. I think this a reasonable move, but there are two problems with it that have to be faced. First, we have to reconcile the lack of selective search in recognition with the idea that search appears directed in free recall, in other words, that in free recall one enters at the top of the hierarchy and searches systematically through it. (Direction is a necessary component for selection.) This reconciliation can be made by noting that there is typically only a single retrieval cue in free-recall—in our free-recall example, the only cue was the name *Woody Allen*—and that this cue permits access to only the top of the network. In contrast, a recognition probe typically contains multiple retrieval cues—for example, *Woody Allen, involved with,* and *Louise Lasser*—thereby permitting simultaneous access to multiple parts of the network. Under this view, which is essentially due to Tulving (e.g., 1974), people use whatever retrieval cues they can, and so-called directed search is what happens when they are forced to work with a single cue.

The second problem is that the fan experiments reviewed earlier, McClosky (1979) and Anderson and Paulson (1978), do provide evidence for selective search in recognition, which of course contradicts the generalization that such a search is not used in recognition. A resolution here may hinge on something I mentioned earlier: The fan experiments in question used very simple bases for subdivision, such as the semantic category of a probe word. Perhaps selective search is used when the basis for selection is easily computed from the probe, as when determining whether the last word of the probe names an animal or a country, but is not used when such computations become at all complex, as when determining that *involved with Louise Lasser* means something about romance.

4. The Status of Subdivided Networks as an Organization Device

Let me summarize the main points made above. Free-recall data provide good evidence that we can subdivide our knowledge, and that the concomitant reduction in fan level per node facilitates the retrieval process. Since we can subdivide when preparing for free recall, I assume we can also do so for recognition. In recognition, however, subdivision also has the potential to permit a selective search (as well as a reduction in fan level per node), but such selectivity may only occur in certain simple cases.

So at this point, subdivision without selectivity seems a reasonable organizational device, primarily because of its reduction in fan level. There is, however, a cost to subdivision that places limits on how widespread a device it can be. Dividing our knowledge into different chunks ignores existent relations between facts stored under different subnodes. Since people know these relations and use them in answering questions, subdivided networks cannot be the only way we represent substantial bodies of knowledge.

Let me again illustrate with the Woody Allen network. Under the "Personal Life" node we had a subnode for romantic relations that was connected to facts about Allen's relation with Diane Keaton, while under "Professional Life" we had a "Filmmaker" subnode connected to facts about Allen's movie *Annie Hall*. But as any devotee of Allen knows, his relation with Keaton formed the basis for *Annie Hall*. So to be true to our knowledge base, we need some sort of connection between these disparate subnodes. One way to do this is to insert a link between the film *Annie Hall* and the relevant facts about Allen's relation to Keaton. This move can substantially increase the number of facts fanning off the "Annie Hall" node, yet the whole point of subdivision is to keep the fanning down.[4] An alternative is to add a fact to the "Annie Hall" node, namely that it was based on Allen's relation to Keaton. This will increase the fanning off "Annie Hall" by only one fact. But this move is not really faithful to the knowledge base of a Woody Allen fanatic, who presumably knows how various aspects of

4. A substantial increase would occur if there were numerous facts stored about Diane Keaton.

Allen's personal relations mapped onto different aspects of the film in question. That is, part of what is known here is how one structure maps onto another. More generally, part of a rich knowledge base about any topic consists of relations between seemingly disparate facts, and subdivided networks seem more disposed to keeping such facts apart than to depicting their subtle connections.

III. FACTS INTEGRABLE BY PRIOR KNOWLEDGE

A. Empirical Evidence

Again I first consider findings about fan effects, then take up results with other memory measures, and lastly consider theoretical mechanisms.

1. *Fan Effects on Recognition Latency*

A few recent experiments demonstrate that learning new facts about a topic causes little fan effect when the propositions are integrable.

In the first set of studies (Smith et al., 1978), subjects learned either two or three facts about a person designated by an occupation term, such as *the banker*. Some subjects learned facts that were easily integrable by prior knowledge, like those at the top of Table 3. The two facts about *the banker* fit with what we know about christening a ship, and the three facts about the *accountant* are consistent with knowledge about playing a bagpipe. The remaining subjects learned facts that were not so integrable, as illustrated by the items at the bottom of Table 3.

For both the integrated and unrelated facts in Table 3, the fan off the "banker" node is 2 and that off the "accountant" is 3. This means that current models of sentence memory would expect comparable fan effects on recognition latency for both kinds of facts. When subjects in the Smith et al. study were given a recognition task after learning the facts, however, there was a substantial fan effect with the unrelated items but not with the integrated ones.

Apparently subjects given the facts in the top half of Table 3 used their world knowledge about ship christenings and playing a bagpipe to integrate the facts. That world knowledge was indeed activated showed up in other findings of Smith et al., specifically

Table 3

Example of Sentences Used in Smith, Adams, and Schorr (1978)

Integrated Facts

The banker was chosen to christen the ship	The accountant played a damaged bagpipe
The banker broke the bottle	The accountant produced sour notes
	The accountant realized the seam was split

Unrelated Facts

The banker was asked to address the crowd	The accountant painted an old barn
The banker broke the bottle	The accountant produced sour notes
	The accountant realized the seam was split

findings concerned with the distractors in the recognition task. Most distractors were formed by repairing the occupation term from one learned sentence with the predicate of another (call these *repaired* distractors); some distractors, however, were formed by changing one word in a learned sentence so that it remained consistent with the relevant world knowledge (call these *related* distractors). To illustrate with the distractors for *the banker* (see Table 3), a repaired distractor would be *The banker realized the seam was split*, while a related one would be *The banker broke the champagne bottle*. The findings of interest were that subjects who learned integrated facts responded more slowly and made more errors on related than on repaired distractors (presumably because related distractors were consistent with the accessed world knowledge), while subjects who learned unrelated facts did just the opposite. Hence one indication of the use of world knowledge is the difficulty of rejecting distractors consistent with the knowledge.

The relative lack of a fan effect with integrated facts has been replicated by Moesher (1979) and Reder and Anderson (1980). Both studies, however, revealed constraints on the power of integration to offset the fan effect. Moesher (1979) demonstrated that integrated facts are insensitive to fanning variations only when the facts are presented close together during learning. For example, if successive facts about christening a ship are separated by five irrelevant sentences, the christening facts will behave like unrelated ones. This suggests that at least a couple of the integrable facts must be in active memory at the same time in order to access the relevant world knowledge.

Reder and Anderson (1980) showed that the fan effect is diminished with integrated facts only when the distractors are not always consistent with the world knowledge needed for integration. To illustrate, suppose subjects first learned facts about a particular person that all dealt with skiing and then were given a recognition test. If the distractors on the recognition test (1) used recombined subject and predicate terms and (2) were always consistent with skiing, there was as substantial a fan effect as occurs with unrelated facts. My interpretation of this finding goes as follows. The representation that results when world knowledge is used to integrate input facts cannot adequately discriminate between the input and novel facts equally consistent with the knowledge, so when all distractors are consistent with the world knowledge, subjects are forced to use an unelaborated representation of the input.

In addition to varying the number of facts integrable by some packet of world knowledge or theme (e.g., skiing, washing clothes), Reder and Anderson also varied the number of themes learned about a particular person. Thus, subjects might have learned three skiing facts and one washing-clothes fact about a ficitious character named *Arnold* (i.e., two themes about *Arnold*), but only three skiing facts about a character named *Bruce* (one theme about *Bruce*). Even in conditions where recognition latency was unaffected by the number of facts within a theme, latency did increase with the number of themes learned about a person.

2. *Experiments on Recall and Recognition Accuracy*

Numerous studies show that when subjects use their prior knowledge to integrate some presented facts, recall accuracy of the learned facts is increased, but at the price of intrusions that are consistent with the relevant knowledge. In like vein, recognition studies show that integration via previous knowledge leads to better recognition accuracy of the learned items, but at the cost of more false alarms to distractors consistent with the knowledge. Representative studies of each type are described below.

a. *Integration and recall.* Bransford and his colleagues (e.g., Bransford & Johnson, 1973; Bransford & McCarrell, 1974) have performed several experiments that take the following form: (1) All subjects are presented some facts that appear to be unrelated; (2) one group of subjects are also presented a clue specifying a packet of world knowledge that can be used to integrate the presented facts, while the remaining subjects receive no such clue; and (3) subjects given the clue rate the presented facts as more comprehensible, and recall more of them on a subsequent recall test.

Let me illustrate with the Bransford and Johnson (1973) study. The seemingly unrelated facts comprised an obscure paragraph, whose first few lines were:

> The procedure is quite simple. First you arrange things into different groups. Of course, one pile may be sufficient, depending on how much there is to do. If you have to go somewhere else due to lack of facilities, that is the next step; otherwise you are pretty well set.

Subjects given the clue *washing clothes* at the time of input rated the paragraph more comprehensible and subsequently recalled more propositions from it than subjects lacking the clue. The power of the clue resides in its ability to access knowledge about the actions typically involved in washing clothes, where this knowledge can then be used to elaborate and integrate the input propositions.

The above shows the beneficial effects of integration but says nothing about its costs. The latter has been demonstrated by Bower, Black, and Turner (1979). They had subjects read stories about recurrent, stereotyped situations like going to a restaurant. Subjects presumably utilized their world knowledge about such situations in understanding the input stories. And in a subsequent recall test, the bulk of the intrusions were consistent with the world knowledge presumably accessed.

b. *Integration and recognition.* Some experiments on recognition have used a cueing variation similar to that employed in Bransford's studies. In Dooling and Lachman (1971), for example, all subjects were presented the following obscure paragraph:

> With hocked gems financing him our hero bravely defied all scornful laughter that tried to prevent his scheme. "Your eyes deceive," he had said, "an egg not a table correctly typifies this unexplored planet." Now three sturdy sisters sought proof, forging along, sometimes through calm vastness, yet more often over turbulent peaks and valleys. Days became weeks as many doubters spread fearful rumors about the

edge. At last from nowhere, welcome winged creatures appeared signifying momentous success.

One group of subjects was given the clue at the time of input that the paragraph was about *Christopher Columbus,* while the remaining subjects made do with no clues. At some later point, all subjects were given a recognition test. It included old sentences from the above paragraph intermixed with distractors, where some distractors were related to the Columbus saga. Subjects given the clue correctly recognized more old sentences than their nonclued counterparts, but the clued subjects were also more likely to false alarm to the related distractors.

B. Theoretical Mechanisms

Two different kinds of mechanisms need to be considered. The first involves an extension of subdivided networks. The second focuses on some new processes, namely inferences made during comprehension.

1. *Subdivided Networks*

The ideas here were developed by Reder and Anderson (1980) to account for why the fan effect on recognition latency is reduced if all facts learned about a character can be integrated by some prior knowledge. To extend an earlier example, if subjects already know that *The banker christened the ship* and *The banker broke the bottle,* then learning that *The banker did not delay the trip* does not slow them down in answering questions about *the banker.* According to Reder and Anderson, when learning the above facts, subjects presumably set up a subdivided network like that in Figure 7. "The banker" is the top node, "ship-christening" the only subnode, and the three specific predicates comprise the bottom nodes. This looks like the subdivided networks we considered previously. But there is something new here. In addition to the "ship christening" subnode being attached to the three specific predicates, it is also associated with concepts relevant to ship christening, such as "bottles," "trips," and "champagne." These connections constitute the subjects' prior knowledge about ship christening, and they play a critical role in Reder and Anderson's *subnode-activation* hypothesis. Specifically, when a probe is presented, for example,

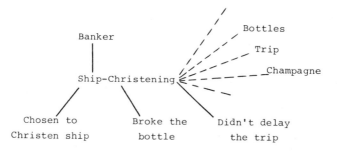
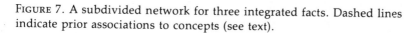

FIGURE 7. A subdivided network for three integrated facts. Dashed lines indicate prior associations to concepts (see text).

The banker broke the bottle, there is activation at the "banker" node as well as at the concept nodes representing the relevant prior knowledge. Activation from the latter nodes travels directly to the subnode along the pre-existent paths, while activation from the "banker" node goes to the subnode along the link created in the experiment. So the subnode is the first likely point of an intersection of activation, and such an intersection is assumed to be sufficient for recognition, in other words, sufficient for subjects to respond Old to a probe.

Thus even though search is not selective (all probe concepts are activated simultaneously), and even though there is a substantial fan off of the subnode, the subnode-activation hypothesis is consistent with organizational effects. There is no fan effect because the search process need not examine the learned predicates. Related distractors (e.g., *The banker broke the champagne bottle*) are difficult to reject because they contain terms that activate the prior knowledge concepts and consequently can lead to a spurious intersection at the subnode. If all distractors are related, as in some conditions of Reder and Anderson (1980), subnode activation is no longer a useful indicator of what facts were actually presented; hence subjects will be forced to search the specific facts, and the fan effect should reappear. Lastly, the hypothesis explains why recognition latencies increase with the number of themes learned about a character. Each theme requires a different subnode (as well as a different set of prior-knowledge concepts), and the more subnodes, the less activation to any one of them from the top node of the network. So the number of relevant themes slows recognition because it slows the rate of top-down activation, while the number of facts per theme has no effect on recognition because such facts need not be examined if the distractors are unrelated to any theme.

The virtue of the above hypothesis is that it explains the recognition results for integrable facts by the same kind of mechanism used to account for results with facts from distinct groups. Thus only one basic mechanism is needed to account for two seemingly disparate kinds of organizational effects, where this mechanism is readily interfaceable with Anderson's (1976) existent theory of sentence memory.

There are, however, two limitations of this subnode approach. The first is that while it can account for variations in recognition accuracy as well as in recognition latency, it is unclear how it would explain the comparable recall results. In the preceding accounts of fan effects, we assumed connections between a subnode and the specific concepts previously associated with it; but to account for recall we need connections between a subnode and entire propositions, as in a recall test people emit full sentences, not single words designating specific concepts. I will not dwell on this because it is unclear to me whether or not the needed modification of the subnode approach can easily be made. The second difficulty with the approach is that it focuses exclusively on *memory* for integrated facts and ignores pocesses involved in the *comprehension* of such facts. The exclusive focus on memory is problematic because it may turn out that the memory phenomena obtained with integrated facts are being mediated by comprehension effects. This leads me to a second kind of theoretical mechanism.

2. *Interconnecting Inferences by Schemas*

a. *World knowledge and comprehension.* Let me begin by elaborating on the above suggestion that the effects of prior knowledge on memory may be mediated by the effects of such knowledge on comprehension. Figure 8 provides an abstract illustration of what I have in mind. Suppose a reader is presented two input facts and accesses some relevant world knowledge to aid in understanding them. The world knowledge will be used to generate inferences. Some will establish direct relations between the input facts, illustrated in Figure 8 by the link between Input Facts 1 and 2. Others will result in inferred facts that yield a multilink relation between the input facts; this is illustrated by In-

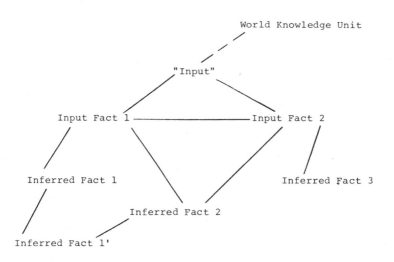

FIGURE 8. Abstract illustration of use of world knowledge in understanding two input facts.

ferred Fact 2, which creates a two-link relation between the input facts. And once a fact is inferred, it may lead to other inferences that create still other multilink relations between the input facts; thus Inferred Fact 1 leads to Inferred Fact 1', which in turn leads to Inferred Fact 2, thereby creating a four-link relation between the input facts. Lastly, there will be inferred facts that do not result in any connection between the input facts, as illustrated by Inferred Fact 3.

The result of all this inferencing is a representation that goes far beyond the input, one that shows enablement and causal relations between propositions and that can be used to answer all sorts of questions about the input. The construction of such a representation is what many people mean by *comprehension*. Under this account, the major purpose of contacting world knowledge during reading is to facilitate comprehension. But, and this is the critical point, note that in constructing this representation, many of the inferences have interconnected the input facts, and *interconnections per se are good for memory retrieval*. For having found one fact, the retrieval process can follow the path to a second one. So a side benefit of the inference process is that it facilitates subsequent retrieval. Hence my claim that many effects of world knowledge on memory are mediated by effects on comprehension.

Another consequence of accessing world knowledge is represented by the dashed line in Figure 8. It occurs whenever the relevant world knowledge forms a prepackaged unit of properties and actions—what Schank and Abelson (1977) call a *script*. In such cases the reader may establish a connection between some node standing for the input and the entire script. This connection can also benefit memory retrieval because it allows the reader to encode the input by constructing a single link to a pre-existent higher unit, and to subsequently retrieve the input by tracing that link and unpacking the constituents of the unit.

The above account can be made more precise by being more specific about the world knowledge involved and how it is used to generate inferences. To aid in this, we need the notion of a *schema*, which many have taken to be the basic form of representation for units of world knowledge (e.g., Adams & Collins, 1979; Rumelhart & Ortony, 1977). Roughly, a schema is a description of a particular set of interrelated concepts that may represent a specific situation, such as going to a movie, or a general activity that can occur in many situations, such as asking someone for a favor. The components of a schema (either other schemas or primitive concepts) are often only vaguely specified; this permits them to function as variables that can be filled in or instantiated by input information with certain properties. To see what these ideas buy us, we will look at a specific schema and see how it is used in understanding and remembering.

b. *Schemas for specific situations.* As developed by Schank and Abelson (1977), a script represents the objects and actions that typically occur in a recurrent, stereotyped situation. Figure 9 presents a hypothetical script for going to the movies.

Our script contains several components. First, there's the *header* or title, *Going to a Movie*, whose major function is to access the script. Anytime I read something that means movie going, I presumably retrieve the script. Second, a script contains a list of the objects, called *props,* and a list of the *roles* that are likely to be encountered in a situation described by the script (see Figure 9). Mention of these props or roles can also access the script. Third, a script contains *preconditions* and *outcome* conditions (see Figure 9), which can again access the script, and which are also plausible inferences given that the script has been accessed. For example, if I read *Herb went to a movie,* I can infer that Herb had some money before entering the movie and less of it when he got out.

Fourth and most importantly, a script consists of the specific actions likely to occur in the situation. These actions can be grouped into chunks called *scenes* (Cullingford, 1978). The script in

```
Header:  Going to a Movie

Props:  Theater, Tickets, Candycounter, Candy, Seats, Film

Roles:  Customer, Cashier, Refreshment Vendor, Usher, Owner

Pre-Conditions:  Goal of Seeing Movie, Money, Time

Outcome Conditions:  Less Money, Knowledge of Film

Actions:
```

Getting Tickets	Watching Film
Customer stands in line	Customer Enters Interior
| enables	| enables
Customer Gives Cashier Money	Customer Finds Seat
| result	| enables
Cashier Gives Customer Tickets	Customer Watches Film

Getting Refreshments	Leaving
Customer Orders Candy	Customer Leaves Interior
| result	| enables
Vendor Gives Customer Candy	Customer Exits Theater
| result	
Customer Gives Vendor Money	

FIGURE 9. A sample script for movie going.

Figure 9 contains four scenes—Getting Tickets, Getting Refreshments, Watching Film, and Leaving—and under each I have listed the actions that comprise it. Note that the props and roles mentioned in the actions are schema variables, (e.g., Customer or Cashier name variables that can be filled in by a person playing that role in the story). Also note that successive actions are connected by labeled relations: these are critical for comprehension and retrieval processes.

The script actions make up most of the plausible inferences one can draw when reading a story based on the script. To appreciate this, consider how our script can be used to understand and subsequently retrieve the following vignette. (1) Herb wanted to see a movie. (2) He got a ticket. (3) He found a seat up front.

When Sentence (1) is presented, it accesses the Movie-Going script because it mentions a precondition (i.e., Herb had a goal of seeing a film). Also, Herb will be bound to the role of Customer. Once the script is accessed, the reader is expecting something from the Getting-Tickets scene. This expectation is confirmed by Sentence (2), which matches the script action Cashier Gives Customer Tickets.[5] At this point our reader can infer some of the script actions in the first scene that were not explicitly mentioned. I will assume that only those actions needed to interrelate the explicitly mentioned facts are inferred. For example, our reader might infer that Herb gave the Cashier money, for this proposition interconnects the first two explictly mentioned ones (i.e., wanting to see a movie was the *reason for* Herb giving the Cashier money, and the latter *resulted* in Herb getting a ticket). Because Sentence (2) marks the end of the Getting-Tickets scene, our reader will now be expecting something from the Getting-Refreshments scene or, since the latter is optional, something from the Watching-Film scene. Sentence (3) matches an action in the Watching-Film Scene. Now our reader can infer some of the actions between the end of the first scene (explicitly mentioned in the preceding sentence) and the Find-a-Seat action of the third scene (explicitly mentioned in the current sentence). Again, she will presumably infer those actions needed to relate the explicitly mentioned sentences: for example, she might infer that Herb entered the interior of the theater because this proposition interconnects sentences (2) and (3).

In general, then, one matches each stated fact to a script action, and one infers nonstated script actions falling between stated ones that are needed to relate input facts. The resulting representation for our vignette looks like that in Figure 10. It contains the input facts, some inferred script actions, and relations between all propositions. It also contains a pointer from the node for Herb to the Movie-Going script itself.

Consider now two hypotheses about how information in this representation could be retrieved. In the *higher unit* hypothesis (Smith et al., 1978), our respondent would first follow the link from Herb to the script itself. If the task required recall, she could read the actions off the script. We further assume that those script actions corresponding to (a) stated facts and (b) inferences needed to connect such facts, are explicitly tagged as such, and that these tags are used as guides to recall. If the task was one of recognition, then after accessing the script, she would match each marked

5. More precisely, the proposition in Sentence (2) matches a simple inference drawn from the script action Cashier Gives Customer Tickets.

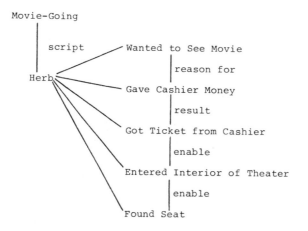

FIGURE 10. Example of representation for movie-going vignette after script processing (see text).

script action to the probe until she found a match. This process seems consistent with the experimental findings on recall and recognition accuracy. Thus for script-based facts, recall and recognition accuracy should be relatively high because only one new link need be examined and only one unit accessed in order to recover all presented facts. But good performance on the presented items would be purchased at the cost of an increase in memory confusions because all script actions corresponding to inferences drawn during comprehension are candidates for retrieval.

As for the results from the fan experiments, there should be little fan effect with integrated facts because the same higher unit, the script, is accessed regardless of how many facts relevant to the script have been learned. Related distractors should be difficult to reject because they often match tagged script actions that correspond to inferences drawn during comprehension. Lastly, there is the finding that latency increases with the number of themes learned about a character. If each theme corresponds to a script, an increase in the number of scripts means an increase in the number of script links off of the node for the main character (*Herb* in the above example), and this fanning will slow down the search for the relevant higher unit.

Unfortunately, the higher unit hypothesis has limited applicability. For one thing, the above process would seem useless to someone who had read two stories about two different people engaging in the same script, for it would confuse the facts about one person with those about the other. Another difficulty is that the hypothesis is limited to situations for which people presumably have scripts. This suggests that facts integrable by scripts will behave differently than those integrable by other kinds of schemas. The little data available on this point show no evidence for such a difference (Reder & Anderson, 1980).

The second hypothesis is the *interconnections* hypothesis. (It is somewhat similar to Anderson's [1976] notion of elaboration.) It ignores the script entirely at the time of retrieval and operates instead on the interconnected propositions in the representation. If asked to recall the story about Herb, our reader would start searching links from Herb. If she can retrieve any one of the input facts, she has a direct path to the others, since all were interconnected by inferences. If she can't retrieve any input fact, but can access an inference made during comprehension, this too will get her to the input, since all propositions are interconnected. Hence script-based facts should be well recalled because of their interconnectedness, but at the price of intrusions, since all inferences drawn during comprehension are candidates for recall. For a recognition task, the process operates slightly differently. If presented the probe *Herb found a seat up front*, our reader would first access a stored fact about Herb, compare it to the probe, and respond Old if there was a match. If no match was found, our reader would follow the connections from the accessed fact to see if any of them led to a proposition that matched the probe. Again, recognition of facts actually presented should be relatively accurate because they are all interconnected, but at the cost of false alarms to inferences that are also part of the connected network.

The interconnections hypothesis seems to have something of a problem, though, in accounting for the results from the fan experiments. Specifically, while inferences drawn during comprehension connect input facts, they do so at the expense of increasing the fanning off of predicate nodes (i.e., the interconnections are typically relations between predicates). This causes no difficulty in explaining how integration facilitates recall or recognition accuracy because every link from a predicate node *eventually* leads to another input fact, which could increase accuracy. But there is a difficulty in explaining how an increase in links off the predicate node can ever facilitate recognition *latency*. A possible solution to this problem is to note that a link between predicates essentially allows one to access an entire proposition without going through its terminal nodes. That is, given that the retrieval process has failed to match the probe to Proposition A, and given an inferential link leading from Predicate A to Predicate B, one can access Proposition B without going through the terminal nodes of the probe again. This facilitation of memory access may more than compensate for the increase in comparison or search time due to the extra link off the predicate node.[6] The other findings from the fan experiments cause no further problems for the interconnections hypothesis. Related distractors are difficult to reject because they often match inferences made during comprehension. And latency increases with the number of themes learned about a character because there are no inferential relations between the facts associated with one theme and those associated with the other.

Note that the interconnections hypothesis avoids the problems that plagued its predecessor. Since the script itself plays no role in retrieval, the hypothesis can handle the situation where one reads and retrieves multiple stories based on the same script. Getting the script out of the retrieval process also takes care of another problem: No longer need there be any major difference between integration via scripts and integration via other kinds of schemas. According to the present hypothesis, all that scripts do for memory is to interconnect propositions, and any kind of schema that can make comparable interconnections should lead to comparable results.[7]

3. A Comparison of the Two Kinds of Mechanisms

This has been a long section, and I had best summarize the major issues.

To account for integration effects, I considered two kinds of theoretical mechanisms. The first assumed that subdivided networks were a sufficient representation to handle the effects of integration. The critical processing ideas were that (1) since activation of a subnode is sufficient for recognition of a probe, the

6. The view of retrieval embodied in this solution makes a sharp distinction between gaining access to a memorized proposition (an *access* stage), and inspecting the contents of that proposition (a *comparison* or *search* stage). The proposed solution assumes that the speedup in the access stage is greater than the slowdown in the comparison stage.

7. In particular, schemas used to encode knowledge about goals and plans (e.g., Rumelhart, 1975; Schank & Abelson, 1977) should lead to the same kind of memory results as scripts do.

memorized fact corresponding to the probe need not be retrieved; and that (2) some of the subnode activation was due to concepts that were previously connected to the subnode and that occurred in the probe. The second kind of mechanism focused on a different kind of representation, namely, a network of interrelated propositions, some corresponding to input facts and others to inferences. This led to both the higher unit and interconnections hypotheses, but since the former was argued to be of limited applicability, I will consider only the interconnections hypothesis in what follows.

There are obviously many differences between the two kinds of mechanisms, but I think at a general level the critical difference is the following: The interconnections mechanism focuses on comprehension and assumes that memory effects are consequences of comprehension processes; subnode activation focuses on memory per se and assumes that memory for integrated facts can be accounted for without a thorough analysis of how the facts were initially comprehended. Given this general difference, specific differences fall into place. Thus in the interconnections hypothesis, I emphasized the role of world-knowledge inferences because no account of comprehension can do without them; in the subnode approach, little or nothing was said about inferences, not because Reder and Anderson (1980) don't believe inferences are needed in comprehension, but because their account of memory phenomena is not based on comprehension. Then there is the difference in parsimony. Subnode activation clearly seems the more parsimonious of the two when it comes to explaining memory data, but this may be the result of ignoring comprehension. That is, if Reder and Anderson had to stipulate what is involved in comprehending integrated facts, they might end up positing representational and processing aspects that look like those in the schema-based interconnections approach, and their edge in parsimony would be gone.

Though the key difference between the approaches is a general one, there may be a way of bringing some specific data to bear on a choice between mechanisms. In the subnode approach, it seems that activation from any concept connected to an operative subnode can contribute to recognition; in the interconnections approach, only inferences needed for comprehension can enter into the recognition process. I can illustrate this contrast by an experiment I recently performed.[8]

8. This study was done in collaboration with Mark Chambers and John Greeno.

Subjects first read four script-based stories, each consisting of seven propositions. For example, one story was:

> Jane went to a restaurant. She went to a table and sat down. Then she drank a glass of water and ate a sandwich. Later she paid the check with cash and went to get her coat.

Later, the subjects had to decide whether each of a series of probe sentences "followed" or "didn't follow" from one of the stories. According to the subnode idea, a subject's representation of the stories would consist of (1) four subnodes, one per story (e.g., Restaurants), with each being attached to the seven specific propositions in that story, and (2) connections between each subnode and all concepts previously known to be related to that subnode. Presumably subjects would decide whether or not a probe item follows from a story partly on the basis of whether or not the concepts mentioned in the probe activate the prior-knowledge concepts connected to any subnodes. This predicts that any probe mentioning a frequent script action should be judged to follow from that script-based story. And this simply was not the case. If a probe mentioned a script action that was in no way needed to understand the original story, subjects uniformly agreed it didn't follow from the story. To illustrate with the above restaurant story, the probe *Jane ordered desert* was judged by virtually all subjects not to follow from the story. Yet this probe corresponds to a very frequent action in the Restaurant script, more frequent than the script action corresponding to *Jane got up from the table* (as determined by the Bower et al., 1979, norms), where the latter probe was judged to follow from the story presumably because it was needed in understanding.

Having tried to make a case for favoring the comprehension approach, let me close this section on an evenhanded note by pointing out that even the interconnections hypothesis must give some role to subdivided networks. For script-based stories, if a character engages in activities from two or more unrelated scripts, the final representation would likely be in the form of a subdivided network: Each branch of the network would contain its own set of interrelated input facts and inferences, and the subnodes would be the relevant script headers.

IV. FACTS WITH CORRELATED PREDICATES

A. Empirical Evidence

As best I know, the organizational condition of present interest has been explictly studied only in a series of fan experiments that we recently conducted (Whitlow et al., 1980).

1. Fan Experiments

In our initial experiment, subjects learned either one, two, or three facts about a person designated by an occupation term. Half the subjects learned facts like those on the left side of Table 4, the other half facts like those on the right side. The only difference between the two sets of facts is that the predicates on the left are perfectly correlated whereas those on the right are not. For the sentences on the left, if someone *cleaned the wall*, they also *pushed the truck*, while if someone *moved the bucket*, that's all they did; not so for the sentences on the right, where if someone *cleaned the wall*, they might have *pushed the truck* or they might not have. Since all previously published studies of the fan effect used less than perfectly correlated predicates, we wanted to see if this effect held up when the predicates were perfectly correlated.

Learning was followed by the usual speeded recognition task. For correct responses to both Old and New items, we determined the fan effects separately for perfectly correlated predicates and for less than perfectly correlated ones. The results are in the first two rows of Table 5 (magnitude of the fan effect is estimated by subtracting the latency for the fan-1 condition from that for the fan-3 condition). There was a substantial fan effect when the predicates were less than perfectly correlated, but not when they were perfectly correlated.

Table 4
Example of Sentences Used in Whitlow, Medin, and Smith (1980)

Perfectly Correlated Predicates	Less Than Perfectly Correlated Predicates
The banker moved the bucket	The banker moved the bucket
The artist moved the bucket	The artist cleaned the wall
The lawyer cleaned the wall	The lawyer cleaned the wall
The lawyer pushed the truck	The lawyer pushed the truck
The farmer cleaned the wall	The farmer moved the bucket
The farmer pushed the truck	The farmer pushed the truck

Table 5

Magnitude of Fan Effects in Msec (Fan 3–Fan 1) for Whitlow, Medin, and Smith Studies

			Perfectly Correlated Predicates	Less Than Perfectly Correlated Predicates
Experiment 1		Old	150	250
		New	−100	200
Experiment 2	Concrete	Old	−140	650
		New	− 10	110
	Abstract	Old	80	225
		New	− 75	125
Experiment 3		Old	−130	540
		New	− 60	100
		Mean	− 70	275

At first we thought our results could be due to the following: With less than perfectly correlated predicates, a particular predicate (e.g., *pushed the truck*) sometimes occurs in the context of one predicate *(cleaned the wall)*, and sometimes in the context of another *(moved the bucket)*. (See Table 4). If context alters meaning, then the meanings of the less than perfectly correlated predicates were more variable than those of the perfectly correlated predicates, and this might have determined whether or not a fan effect occurred. A second experiment, however, convinced us that meaning variability was not the critical factor.

Again one group of subjects learned facts with perfectly correlated predicates, and another learned facts with less than perfectly correlated predicates. In addition, each group was split into two subgroups: One worked with concrete predicates (e.g., *lifted the bucket)* and was instructed to think of a particular predicate the same way when it occurred in different contexts (i.e., with different companion predicates); the other subgroup worked with abstract predicates (e.g., *moved the object)* and was instructed to think of a particular predicate in different ways when it occurred in different contexts. The former subgroup should have experienced less meaning variability. Though this variation affected recognition latencies, it did not determine whether or not there was a fan effect. We again found fan effects only when predicates were less than perfectly correlated (see the middle rows of Table 5).

A last experiment sought to rule out a possible artifact (personal communication from G. Bower, 1978). When subjects learn facts that always have perfectly correlated predicates, they can adopt a task-specific strategy. During learning they can tag each occupation term and each predicate with its fan level (1, 2, or 3), and then during recognition they can respond Old to any probe whose occupation term and predicate have the same fan level. A glance back at Table 4 should convince you that this strategy always yields correct recognitions only for sentences with perfectly correlated predicates. Thus in our previous experiments, this strategy was available only to subjects who worked with perfectly correlated predicates, and could be the reason they showed no fan effect.

To discourage this strategy, we had all subjects learn two sets of sentences, half having perfectly correlated predicates, and half less than perfectly correlated ones. With this design, subjects should be unlikely to use the above strategy, since it would frequently produce incorrect decisions on facts with less than perfectly correlated predicates. The results, presented in the bottom rows of Table 5, replicated our previous findings. Apparently the power of perfectly correlated predicates to offset the fan effect is not due to the use of a specific strategy.

2. Implications for Memory for Real-World Topics

In the above, I described the critical variable as *perfectly correlated* versus *less than perfectly correlated predicates*. While literally correct, this is probably misleading. Since each predicate occurred just twice in our studies, only a limited range of correlation was possible, and our subjects may have been able to detect a correlation only among perfectly correlated predicates. The less than perfectly correlated predicates may have been perceived as uncorrelated, and a better description of our variable may be *correlated* versus *uncorrelated predicates*. Following this line of argument, I suspect we could substantially reduce the fan effect with any set of predicates having a noticeable correlation.

If correct, the above conjecture has an important implication for fan effects. Since predicates about real-world entities or objects tend to be substantially correlated, one would expect little change in retrieval efficiency as more facts are learned about a real-world entity. To illustrate, consider classes of real-world objects, like various kinds of animals, plants, and human artifacts. As Rosch (e.g., 1978) has argued, the predicates associated with such classes tend to be highly correlated. Creatures with feathers, for example, also have wings and tend to fly; so if you already know that robins have feathers and wings, then learning that they also fly should not retard the efficiency of the retrieval process the way that learning an uncorrelated predicate would. More generally, to the extent that the world comes in packages of correlated predicates, there may be little retrieval interference engendered by learning multiple facts about the same topic.

B. Theoretical Mechanisms

In what follows, I briefly consider how well the theoretical mechanisms already discussed can be extended to account for the lack of a fan effect with perfectly correlated predicates.

We can start with the subnode-activation hypothesis. When our subjects came across a set of study sentences where everyone who *cleaned the wall* also *pushed the truck,* they may have assumed there was a category of people who clean walls and push trucks. Subjects might then use these categories as subnodes in a network like that in Figure 11. Here, the bottom nodes refer to the people who are members of each subnode or category. While the representation seems plausible, the subnode-activation hypothesis cannot account for the obtained lack of fan effects. Recall that this

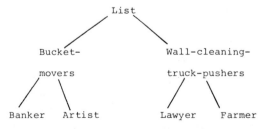

FIGURE 11. Segment of a possible subdivided network for correlated predicates (see text).

hypothesis explains the lack of fan effects as follows: A subnode can be activated before any stored fact because the subnode receives activation from concepts that have been previously linked to it and that also occur in the probe. In the present case, however, any subnode that corresponds to a set of predicates is novel. Therefore, there may not be any concepts previously linked to it, which means that there is no way for a subnode to be activated prior to activation of the learned facts.

As for the higher unit hypothesis, we again assume that subjects treat correlated predicates as defining a category of people. They would set up a higher unit for each category that contains the correlated predicates characterizing it. Information about an occupation term could be encoded by a single connection to the appropriate higher order unit. If later asked to recognize any proposition about a particular occupation terrm, subjects need consider only one link to access the higher unit, and could then unpack the unit. Therefore, the higher unit hypothesis is consistent with the lack of fan effects.

Finally, the interconnections hypothesis assumes that when presented correlated predicates, subjects infer a *co-occurrence* relation between them, thereby interconnecting the input facts. When later required to recognize a study sentence, subjects would use these interpredicate connections the way they presumably use interconnections established when reading integrable facts. That is, they would use the interpredicate connections as an aid in accessing a new proposition.

V. SUMMARY AND CONCLUSIONS

A. Recapitulation of Major Points

Of one thing there is no doubt. When learning multiple facts about the same topic, various factors induce us to organize the material, and this organizing leads to retrieval of the input facts that is substantially better than would be predicted by current models of sentence memory. This boost in retrieval shows up in three different memory indicators—recall accuracy, recognition accuracy, and recognition latency (i.e., reduced fan effects). More specifically, (1) facts that subdivide into distinct groups lead to reduced fan effects and to increased recall accuracy; (2) facts integrable by prior knowledge can result in reduced fan effects, as well as in increases in recall and recognition accuracy (though at the cost of thematically related intrusions in recall and poorer performance on related distractors in recognition); and (3) facts containing correlated predicates lead to reduced fan effects.

With regard to theoretical mechanisms, things are less clear. There is consensus on only one point—that a subdivided network can be used to organize facts from distinct groups. More precisely, (a) if people learn facts from distinct groups and (b) show a distinctive pattern on a speeded recognition task (increased latency with increases in the relevant fan but not with increases in the irrelevant fan), or show another distinctive pattern on a recall test (some-or-none recall clusters), then (c) they have represented the input facts in terms of a subdivided network.

When we move to our second organizational condition—facts integrable by prior knowledge—theoretical opinions diverge. The subnode-activation hypothesis holds that the facts are represented by a subdivided network with themes serving as the subnodes. As long as most distractors are unrelated to the themes, people can use activation of a subnode as a basis for recognition, part of this activation coming from concepts that were previously linked to the subnode and that now appear in the probe. Since specific facts need not be accessed, retrieval is rapid and independent of the number of facts learned about a topic. The alternative position focuses on the comprehension of integrable facts. It holds that comprehension involves using schemas to draw inferences about the input, as well as possibly establishing a link between some component of the input and the schema itself. Some inferences interconnect the input facts, thereby providing alternate access routes during recall or recognition, which boost memory in both kinds of tasks. If a connection between the input and the schema itself has been established, retrieval can be accomplished by simply accessing the schema and reading the input facts off of it. As only one link need be accessed, retrieval should be rapid and independent of the number of schema-based facts that were learned.

When we tried to extend these hypotheses to explain the lack of fan effects with correlated predicates, the clearest result was that the subnode-activation hypothesis failed. Specifically, while it seemed plausible that each set of correlated predicates was dominated by a single subnode in a subdivided network, such a subnode was likely a novel concept and hence unlikely to have concepts previously linked to it that could contribute to its activation.

While the above hardly provides firm answers to the theoretical questions raised in the introduction, it does suggest that no one mechanism is going to cover all organizational conditions. Thus, subdivided networks seem our best contender for describing what goes on with facts from distinct groups, but an unlikely alternative for explaining the results for facts containing correlated predicates. Similarly, our interconnections hypothesis works best in explaining variations in memory accuracy with integrable facts, and seems beside the point when it comes to accounting for results with facts from distinct groups. So we may need all three mechanisms—subdivided networks, higher units, and interconnections.

B. The Status of the Fan Effect

One strategy I have followed throughout is to take the fan effect as a kind of landmark, and to use reductions of this effect as indicators of organizational factors. While the theoretical importance of the fan effect seems to justify this strategy, I would be remiss if I did not point out some limitations on the generality of this effect.

We have seen that any one of three different factors can reduce the fan effect. Hence a substantial fan effect occurs only when the facts to be learned conform to the following conjunction of negative conditions: (1) The facts are not from distinct groups; (2) they are not readily integrable by prior knowledge, and (3) they do not contain correlated predicates. The work of Hayes-Roth (1977) supplies still another negative factor: (4) the facts are not well practiced. So a fan effect is obtainable in the laboratory only under a choice of parameters that captures a fourfold conjunction of negative conditions. And this means that the effect is not among our most robust laboratory phenomena. Furthermore, the above conjunction may rarely obtain in real life. The vast majority of real-life learning situations involve facts that are integrable by prior knowledge and/or have correlated predicates. Most times that we read text (or listen to utterances), we are exposed to multiple facts about a topic that are integrable by prior knowledge; if this was not the case, we would probably judge the text incoherent. And when I think of real-life cases where the facts presented are not integrable by prior knowledge, the situations that come most readily to mind are those in which we learn a novel concept.

And in these situations the predicates of the facts are often highly correlated.

The weak point in the preceding is that I am using laboratory experiments with a very restricted variation of fanning (generally from 1 to 3) to draw implications about real-life situations that may have a far greater variation of fanning. Thus many real-life situations may have a fanning variation of 1 to 100 (e.g., how much do you know about the mayor of San Francisco compared to what you know about the president of the United States?), and this huge variation may result in a substantial fan effect even in situations where our conjunction of negative conditions does not hold. The only way to check this is to perform laboratory experiments with conditions known to reduce the fan effect, but with huge variations in fanning. Without such experiments, we run the risk of studying a phenomenon that rarely occurs outside the laboratory.

Even if such experiments are performed and do yield substantial fan effects, there is still a problem in focusing so much effort on laboratory situations defined by the above conjunction of negative conditions, for the representations and processes operative in situations that do not meet the conjunction of negative conditions may be qualitatively different from those operative in situations that do meet our conjunction. We saw a good example of this in the fan experiments dealing with integrable facts (at least in those using unrelated distractors). Even Reder and Anderson's (1980) account of these results introduced some new representational aspects—namely, the subnodes—and new processing assumptions—namely, that activation of a subnode could trigger a recognition decision. These new aspects are qualitatively different from the entities in Anderson's (1976, chap. 8) ACT theory of sentence memory (though readily interfaceable with that theory), and they probably would not have been thought of unless people had done research on paradigms that were not specifically configured to yield fan effects.

C. A Comprehension Approach to Memory Phenomena

In discussing organizational mechanisms for integrated facts, I argued that comprehension processes, like inferencing, may lie behind memory effects. Essentially, I singled out facts integrable by prior knowledge as the one condition where we need to consider comprehension in order to understand memory. I would like to revise that stance and try a stronger argument. Namely, whenever we deal with memory for facts about the same topic, we first need to understand what goes on in the comprehension of these facts.

Let me go back to the beginning. I started by considering facts from distinct groups. No mention was made there of comprehension. Instead, I noted that the memory representation for such facts often consists of a subdivided network, and traced the implications of this for retrieval. But why is such a representation constructed? One possibility is that it facilitates retrieval. Another is that a subdivided network is the natural consequence of our comprehension processes operating on an input where the most salient relations between the facts are that some belong to one group, while others belong to different groups. That is, if the business of comprehension processes is to find relations between input facts, and the only salient relation is that some facts are members of the class of statements about countries, while others are members of the class of statements about animals, then all the comprehension processes can do is to construct a representation that depicts these class-membership relations. In short, subdivided networks are a kind of representation you get out of comprehension processes when your input is sparse on relations.

As for the studies involving facts with correlated predicates, we again have a case where the input is sparse on relations. The only relation the comprehension processes can pick up on here is that some predicates co-occur with others.

To sum up, we may have underestimated the extent to which memory phenomena are dependent on comprehension, by consistently using materials that lack the stuff that makes comprehension go—relations. Research concerned with memory for integrable facts may be the only way to redress this imbalance.

REFERENCES

Adams, M. J., & Collins, A. M. A schema-theoretic view of reading. In R. O. Freedle (Ed.), *New directions in discourse processing.* Norwood, N.J.: Ablex, 1979.

Anderson, J. R. Retrieval of propositional information from long-term memory. *Cognitive Psychology,* 1974, *5,* 451–474.

Anderson, J. R. Item-specific and relation-specific interference in sentence memory. *Journal of Experimental Psychology: Human Learning and Memory*, 1975, *104*, 249–260.

Anderson, J. R. *Language, memory, and thought.* Hillsdale, N.J.: Erlbaum, 1976.

Anderson, J. R., & Bower, G. H. *Human associative memory.* Washington, D.C.: Winston, 1973.

Anderson, J. R., & Paulson, R. Interference in memory for pictorial information. *Cognitive Psychology*, 1978, *10*, 178–202.

Black, J. B., & Bower, G. H. Episodes as chunks in narrative memory. *Journal of Verbal Learning and Verbal Behavior*, 1979, *18*, 309–318.

Bousfield, W. A. The occurrence of clustering in the recall of randomly arranged associates. *Journal of General Psychology*, 1953, *36*, 67–81.

Bousfield, W. A., & Cohen, B. H. The effects of reinforcement on the occurrence of clustering in the recall of randomly arranged associates. *Journal of Psychology*, 1953, *36*, 67–81.

Bower, G. H., Black, J. B., & Turner, T. J. Scripts in memory for text. *Cognitive Psychology*, 1979, *11*, 177–220.

Bower, G. H., Clark, M., Lesgold, A. & Winzenz, D. Hierarchical retrieval schemes in recall of categorized word lists. *Journal of Verbal Learning and Verbal Behavior*, 1969, *8*, 323–343.

Bransford, J. D., & Johnson, M. K. Considerations of some problems of comprehension. In W. G. Chase (Ed.), *Visual information processing.* New York: Academic Press, 1973.

Bransford, J. D., & McCarrell, N. S. A sketch of a cognitive approach to comprehension: Some thoughts about what it means to comprehend. In W. B. Weimer & D. S. Pelermo (Eds.), *Cognition and symbolic processes.* New York: Winston & Sons, 1974.

Cofer, C. N., Bruce, D. R., & Reicher, G. M. Clustering in free recall as a function of certain methodological variations. *Journal of Experimental Psychology*, 1966, *71*, 858–866.

Cohen, B. H. Recall of categorized word lists. *Journal of Experimental Psychology*, 1963, *66*, 227–234.

Cullingford, R. E. *Script application: Computer understanding of newspaper stories.* Yale University Department of Computer Science Research Report No. 116, 1978.

Dooling, D. J., & Lachman, R. Effects of comprehension on retention of prose. *Journal of Experimental Psychology*, 1971, *88*, 216–222.

Hayes-Roth, B. Evolution of cognitive structure and processes. *Psychological Review*, 1977, *84*, 260–278.

Hayes-Roth, B., & Hayes-Roth, F. The prominence of lexical information in memory representations of meaning. *Journal of Verbal Learning and Verbal Behavior*, 1977, *16*, 119–136.

King, D. R., & Anderson, J. R. Long-term memory search: An intersecting activation process. *Journal of Verbal Learning and Verbal Behavior*, 1976, *15*, 587–606.

Kolodner, J. L. *Memory organization for natural language data-base inquiry.*

Yale University Department of Computer Science Research Report No. 142, 1978.

Lewis, C. H., & Anderson, J. R. Interference with real world knowledge. *Cognitive Psychology*, 1976, *8*, 311–335.

Mandler, G. Organization and memory. In K. W. Spence & J. T. Spence (Eds.), *The psychology of learning and motivation* (Vol. 1). New York: Academic Press, 1967.

McCloskey, M. *Search and comparisons processes in fact retrieval and question answering.* Unpublished manuscript, The Johns Hopkins University, 1979.

Minsky, M. A framework for representing knowledge. In P. H. Winston (Ed.), *The psychology of computer vision.* New York: McGraw-Hill, 1975.

Moesher, S. D. The role of experimental design in investigation of the fan effect. *Journal of Experimental Psychology: Human Learning and Memory*, 1979, *5*, 125–134.

Nelson, T. O., & Smith, E. E. Acquisition and forgetting of hierarchically organized information in long-term memory. *Journal of Experimental Psychology*, 1972, *95*, 388–396.

Norman, D. A., & Bobrow, D. G. On the role of active memory processes in perception and cognition. In C. N. Cofer (Ed.), *The structure of human memory.* San Francisco: Freeman, 1976.

Norman, D. A., & Rumelhart, D. E. *Explorations in cognition.* San Francisco: Freeman, 1975.

Puff, C. R. Role of clustering in free recall. *Journal of Experimental Psychology*, 1970, *86*, 384–386.

Reder, L. M., & Anderson, J. R. A partial resolution of the paradox of interference: The role of integrating knowledge. *Cognitive Psychology*, 1980, *12*, 447–472.

Rosch, E. Principles of categorization. In E. Rosch & B. B. Lloyd (Eds.), *Cognition and categorization.* Potomac, Md.: Erlbaum, 1978.

Rumelhart, D. Notes on a schema for stories. In D. Bobrow & A. M. Collins (Eds.), *Representations and understanding: Studies in cognitive sciences.* New York: Academic Press, 1975.

Rumelhart, D. E., Lindsay, P. H., & Norman, D. A. A process model for long-term memory. In E. Tulving & W. Donaldson (Eds.), *Organization and memory.* New York: Academic press, 1972.

Rumelhart, D. E., & Ortony, A. The representation of knowledge in memory. In R. C. Anderson, R. J. Spiro, & W. E. Montague (Eds.), *Schooling and the acquisition of knowledge.* Hillsdale, N.J.: Erlbaum, 1977.

Rundus, D. Negative effects of using list items as recall cues. *Journal of Verbal Learning and Verbal Behavior*, 173, *12*, 43–50.

Schank, R. C., & Abelson, R. P. *Scripts, plans, goals, and understanding.* Hillsdale, N.J.: Erlbaum, 1977.

Shiffrin, R. M. Memory search. In D. A. Norman (Ed.), *Models of human memory.* New York: Academic Press, 1970.

Shoben, E. J., Wescourt, K., & Smith, E. E. Differential performance in sentence-verification and sentence-recognition: Implications for the distinction between episodic and semantic memory. *Journal of Experimental Psychology: Human Learning and Memory*, 1978, *4*, 304–317.

Smith, E. E., Adams, N., & Schorr, D. Fact retrieval and the paradox of interference. *Cognitive Psychology*, 1978, *10*, 438–464.

Thorndyke, P., & Bower, G. H. Storage and retrieval processes in sentence memory. *Cognitive Psychology*, 1974, *5*, 515–543.

Tulving, E. Cue-dependent forgetting. *American Scientist*, 1974, *62*, 74–82.

Tulving, E., & Pearlstone, Z. Availability versus accessibility of information in memory for words. *Journal of Verbal Learning and Verbal Behavior*, 1966, *5*, 381–391.

Whitlow, W. J., Medin, D. L., & Smith, E. E. *Retrieval of correlated predicates*. Unpublished manuscript, 1980.

Winograd, T. Understanding natural language. *Cognitive Psychology*, 1972, *3*, 1–191.

Can We Have a Fruitful Cognitive Psychology?[1]

James J. Jenkins
University of Minnesota

CAN we have a fruitful cognitive psychology? Perhaps the first question must be, Fruitful for whom? At present, cognitive psychology is obviously fruitful for the cognitive psychologists. Laboratories are bustling with activity; journals are bursting with articles; cognitive conferences are ubiquitous; and cognitive models are plentiful. Clearly, cognitive psychologists are managing to keep themselves busy and, perhaps even more important, employed. But that is not the kind of fruitfulness that I had in mind when I posed this question. I meant to address two other kinds of fruitfulness: First, is the field advancing as we feel sciences are supposed to advance? Are scientists making contributions that cumulate in some fashion and lead on to a more adequate and more coherent cognitive psychology? Second, is the field developing and deepening our understanding of cognitive principles, processes, or facts that can contribute to the solution of real problems and generate answers to relevant questions? While it is not easy to appraise either of these criteria in a precise fashion, those are the questions with which I am concerned.

In this paper I will try to explain why I think this question needs to be raised. There is ample reason to believe that cognitive psychology is not particularly fruitful and that many psychologists are only slightly aware of this situation. My first effort will be to convince you that there is some cause for alarm. Next, I will suggest a diagnosis of the sources of this difficulty. I believe there are important reasons for our failure so far in developing a fruitful cognitive psychology. These reasons argue that we must change

1. The preparation of this paper was facilitated by the Center for Research in Human Learning, University of Minnesota, Minneapolis, Minnesota. The Center is supported by grants from the National Science Foundation (BNS 77–22057) and the National Institute of Child Health and Human Development (HD–01136).

our goals and activities if we are to change the state of affairs. Then I will point to current activities in the field which I see as signs of progress. I think there is a spreading awareness that we must change the way we practice our science. Finally, I would like to discuss several lines of research that illustrate the kind of change that I hope is going on and comment on the different findings one sees when one changes one's orientation toward the field. At the end, of course, I will try to give you a summary or overall evaluation (as I see things at the first meeting of this symposium) and hazard an answer to the question asked in the title.

Is Anything Wrong with Cognitive Psychology?

One might suppose that there is no reason for concern. Given that it is very difficult to define progress or assess the state of a science, is it not sufficient that scientists are busy? Doesn't all the activity in the laboratories give ample evidence that the field is advancing and prospering? Not necessarily. Anyone who reflects on the vast waste of time and energy in pursuit of the great learning theories of the 1930s, 40s, and 50s cannot be sanguine about the use of mere activity as an index of progress. Indeed, I suspect that an unbiased observer studying the history of psychology from some distant point in time would have more reason to see progress and cumulative knowledge in the theories of learning in that period than in the activities of cognitive psychologists over the last two decades.

However the judgment of history turns out, there are current observers of the scene who "view with alarm" the activity of the field. One such example is Allen Newell, certainly a sympathetic observer and himself a participant in the area, who took the field to task in his fascinating and much cited little paper "You Can't Play 20 Questions with Nature and Win" (Newell, 1973). The burden of Newell's argument is simple. First, he says, cognitive psychology in its current mode of operation deals with phenomena. Every time we find a new phenomenon in our laboratories, we produce a flurry of experiments to investigate it. He gives a list of some 59 phenomena that we have treated in this fashion. These include such items as Posner's finding of the difference between physical matches and name matches, Shepard's studies of mental rotation, Sternberg's work on exhaustive search in short-term memory, and so on.

The phenomena are not merely studied for their own sake. Newell points out that investigators "conceptualize" their research by representing it as testing fundamental binary oppositions. The choice between polar opposites is, supposedly, what the research is about at an abstract level. He gives a list of some 24 oppositions (some recent in origin and some ancient) such as nature versus nurture, peripheral versus central, continuous versus all or none, serial versus parallel, analogue versus digital, and so on. We act as if our research efforts were going to make decisive choices between these alternatives and lead us to "the truth" about operations of the mind. (Hence, the parallelism with the game of Twenty Questions.) Unfortunately, this never seems to happen. Newell concludes regretfully,

> It seems to me that clarity is never achieved. Matters simply become muddier and muddier as we go down through time. Thus, far from providing the rungs of a ladder by which psychology gradually climbs to clarity, this form of conceptual structure leads rather to an ever-increasing pile of issues, which we weary of or become diverted from but never really settle. (Newell, 1973, p. 289)

Newell's diagnosis as to the responsibility for this state of affairs is that we do not put enough constraint on our theories or our research. We cannot predict a subject's behavior without knowing his or her goals, the structure of the task environment, and, most importantly, the invariant structure of his or her process mechanisms. But instead of trying to discover fixed and invariant structures, we present flow diagrams as models. Flow diagrams are unsatisfactory, however. Almost no one models the necessary control structures, and as long as the control structures are missing, it is possible to suggest "an infinite sequence of alternative possibilities for how a given task was performed, hence, to keep theoretical issues from becoming settled." Newell goes on to discuss a number of ways of increasing the constraints in a given psychological endeavor to limit the number of possible solutions, but at this point we need only recognize that we can have activity without accomplishment and publication without progress.

One reason for the difficult straits of cognitive psychology, of course, is that psychology in general is just plain hard to do. Our discipline faces unique problems for which it cannot turn to the older sciences for solutions. Meehl (1978), protesting the feeble nature of research in clinical psychology, reels off 20 reasons why psychology of the "soft" variety is difficult. These reasons range from the problems of defining response classes and classifying situations, through problems concerning the sheer number of relevant variables and the role of cultural factors, to the problems involved in trying to cope with intentionality, purpose, and meaning and the ethical constraints on permissible psychological research. (Given that Meehl says he came up with 20 problems in "10 minutes of superficial thought," it is reasonable to suppose that a complete, detailed list would be absolutely overwhelming.) To the point of this paper, the important aspect of his account is that although Meehl is concerned with a different part of the science, his description of the state of the field sounds virtually identical to Newell's:

> In the developed sciences, theories tend either to become widely accepted and built into the larger edifice of well-tested human knowledge or else they suffer destruction in the face of recalcitrant facts and are abandoned, perhaps regretfully as a "nice try." But in fields like personology and social psychology, this seems not to happen. There is a period of enthusiasm about a new theory, a period of attempted application to several fact domains, a period of disillusionment as the negative data come in, a growing bafflement about inconsistent and unreplicable empirical results, multiple resort to ad hoc excuses and then finally people just sort of lose interest in the thing and pursue other endeavors. (Meehl, 1978, p. 807)

Nor are Meehl and Newell alone in their critical appraisal of aspects of psychology. Other examples include Gergen (1973), McGuire (1973), Mischel (1977), Harré and Secord (1973), to name but a few. Finkelman (1978), confronts the entire field head-on and wonders whether a science of psychology is even possible. There can be no question but that "soft" psychology, whether in the clinic or the laboratory, is in conceptual and methodological trouble.

Sources of the Difficulty in Cognitive Psychology

Each critic finds specific aspects of his chosen area to bewail, and each such selection leads to a different set of prescriptions and therapies. I am no exception to this general rule. I have a long list of specific criticisms to offer, and indeed I spend much of my time trying to convince my graduate students that many practices in the field are injurious to our branch of the science. In the last decade, however, I have become aware of two considerations that seem to me to lie at the root of our troubles. A proper appreciation of these may make the specific criticisms superfluous. It is my hope that my readers will be willing to pursue the thoughts to their consequences.

I suggest that there are two fundamental reasons for the unsatisfactory state of cognitive psychology: One has to do with the nature of the organism, and the other has to do with the nature of our experiments. Let us consider first the nature of the organism. Why is it that we never come down decisively on one pole or the other of Newell's binary oppositions? The commonsense answer, of course, is that neither pole of the opposition is right; but why is that?

Walter Reitman (who was a visiting professor at our Center for Research in Human Learning one summer) pointed out to me that I had a curiously restricted view of the human being. Far from being a simple device with only limited computing power, the human with a paper and pencil has the formal power of a universal Turing machine (until death intervenes). In all respects except unlimited time, the human being *is* a universal computing device; that is, in principle, he or she can compute *anything* that is computable. This view led Reitman to be quite sceptical of our ability to describe the limits of subjects' behavior unless we understood in detail what strategies each subject was pursuing. (This point is very similar to Newell's above.)

The second consideration is due to Robert Shaw with whom I had the privilege of working during the formative years of our center. Shaw introduced me to the notion of "mimicking automata," that is, machines that behave like other machines. An interesting exercise in computer science is the determination of the power and class of a given machine. There are some algorithms for doing this in some cases. By analogy we were tempted to devise tests for human beings to try to find out what class of machines they were. Shaw pointed out that even with real machines it is sometimes difficult to discover what kind of machine one is dealing with because machines can simulate the behavior of other machines.

As an elementary example, it is commonplace on most of our campuses to program a more powerful computer to behave like a less powerful one. We usually do this whenever we buy a new central processing unit. Because everyone has programs written in a form that was acceptable to the old computer, we find it necessary to develop routines that enable the new computer to run like the old one. This usually reduces the advantages of the new machine in time and power, but it is an enormous convenience. Indeed, it is an economic necessity in that the users are not immediately required to rewrite all their programs. It also avoids a long period of inactivity of our computing center. Thus, it is common to trade power and operating speed for scheduling convenience, human time, and programming economy.

(There is a parallel with which clinicians are acquainted. Clinical psychologists sometimes say of a patient that he is "running old tapes." By this they mean that he is responding to a current situation in the fashion in which he earlier learned to respond to such situations. Thus, adults may respond to authority as they learned to respond to parental authority when they were little children, in spite of the fact that such behavior may be inappropriate to their current age and status. In a sense such patients run old programs of a simpler sort, although they are now more powerful and complex machines.)

It is perhaps less well known that one can make a smaller machine mimic a more powerful one. If there is a complex computation that a small machine cannot perform or can perform only with great cost, we can put the results of such computations into the machine in the form of special memory. Thus, we can store answers to problems that the machine cannot compute or cannot compute rapidly.

Now, if one puts these two notions together—first, that human beings are universal machines and, second, that machines can simulate other machines of different degrees of power—one may be pessimistic concerning the very idea of modeling the mind. When one looks at the models that psychologists build, one discovers, in fact, that they are not models of the mind, but rather models of the task being performed by the subjects in (we trust) particular ways. This is Newell's point again. These are not models of the mind in a general sense; they are only models of a particular exercise of the machine behaving its way through a particular program. In most cases when the psychologist turns his attention to a new experimental task or employs new kinds of materials, it is necessary to expand the model with a patchwork of new memories, new stages, new functions, and the like until it becomes so cumbersome that it is finally abandoned. Unfortunately, of this kind of proliferation, there seems to be no end.

I am ready to embrace the position that the task of building a general model of the mind is a task beyond the possibilities of science. It is surely not a reasonable goal for psychology. If human beings are universal machines of great power, and if they can become a specialized machine for any given task, we are wasting our time trying to get to a general model by building little special models for particular (and arbitrary) laboratory exercises.

Now, this is not to say that there are not interesting questions to ask. I am not pessimistic for one moment concerning the ability of my colleagues to find things to do. One question of appreciable importance is, What determines the kind of machine that a person becomes in a particular environmental context? I suppose that it would be reasonable to start with some version of a "fitness" hypothesis; that is, the organism becomes the kind of machine that is "best adapted" to the environment (or the experimental task) that faces it. However, "best adapted" is an undefined term. If the organism already has a program for handling a particular class of problem, it may simply apply it, even though the particular version of the problem facing it does not require so elaborate a procedure. The old program minimizes costs associated with thinking and developing new programs or going through the trouble of finding out just how difficult the environment is. In such a case we would suppose that gains are made in planning and preparation time by using an old routine. The *functional fixedness* problems and the Luchins "water jar" problems are of this general variety. They depend on the subject acting in traditional or previously reinforced fashion rather than thinking through each instance of the problem anew without the earlier assumptions.

It may be that there is some kind of conservation of, say, psychic resources. There may be a bias against using procedures that involve sustained attention, concentration, computing power, or overall energy. If the task can be seen to require less of these resources, the subject may change strategies (or programs) so as to minimize such expenditures. That is, the subject may become a simpler machine that is only concerned with getting the task accomplished at minimal cost.

Alternatively, we might suppose that the organism conserves on time or relative costs of particular operations or, most likely, that the organism conserves on different dimensions at different points in time and under different circumstances. A very complex but interesting question is, What are the criteria that the organism uses as it moves from one situation to another and chooses (so to speak) what kind of machine it will be?

This way of viewing the organism leads to some serious questions about the nature of experiments in cognitive psychology. If the organism is a universal machine, and if it can become the kind of machine it needs to be in any given environment, what is it that our experiments tell us about psychological theories for which they are supposed to provide evidence? If the psychologist sets up an experiment with a particular theory in mind, he or she will construct the environment in terms of the variables that accord with the theory. If the organism then adapts to the conditions of the situation (as we are supposing it does), then it is highly likely that the organism will behave in congruence with the theory. That is, the organism will behave in the situation in the way the experimenter has arranged for him to behave. The better the experimenter understands the environmental constraints of the theory, the better he or she will be in selecting the right variables and the right degree of complexity to induce the subject to become the particular kind of machine that responds to those. Thus, to the extent that the experiment is theory dominated, the organism may well demonstrate the veridicality of the theory by becoming the kind of machine that the theory presupposes. This is to say that if the experimenter really believes that the subject is a particular kind of machine and designs experiments for that kind of machine, the subject may well *become* that kind of machine.

In exactly this case we have the problem that all the experiments tend to be confirmatory. One consequence of this is that as long as we run the well-structured experiments that our rudimentary theories speak to, we may achieve endless confirmation of those theories, not because they are true in any deep sense, but just because the subjects can become the kind of machine that the theory requires them to be. Endless confirmation does not indicate that a theory is true about human beings in general; it may only indicate that in this kind of constrained situation, subjects will tend to become this kind of machine. In other words, we may have a theory of the experiment and experiments about the experiment rather than a theory of the subject, except in the most limited sense.

There is a fragment of a study that Robert Shaw performed at our center some years ago in which he tried to manipulate the kind of machine that the subject became. He employed some very simple tasks. One task, for example, required a subject to predict whether a red light or a green light would be flashed on during the next trial. Every series consisted of some number of red lights followed by the same number of green lights. The subject saw series after series in which this rule held. In the beginning, after discovering the general rule, subjects tended to count the number of red lights so they could predict the number of green lights. But counting is a highly sophisticated activity, and a counting machine is a more powerful machine than the subject needs to be. In this experiment, the subject can be successful as a simple "push down store"; that is, the subject needs only to put markers in correspondence with the number of red lights, then he puts out green predicators until he runs out of markers. He doesn't need to know *how many* markers there are, only that they are there. Shaw ran his subjects in this task for a long time until they were all doing very well. At this point, for the first time in the experiment, Shaw interrupted the subject after a string of red lights and asked him how many red lights he had seen. The typical subject had to "run out" a series of taps with his finger and count them before he could say how many red lights he had seen. That is, the subjects were indeed storing the lights as "markers" of some sort rather than as ordinal numbers. Until the subjects had tapped them out, they did not know how many there were. In this case, then, it looks as if there is some evidence that the subject has "geared down" to the level of the experiment.

A cynical way to look at this is to conclude that if we run stupid experiments, we can have stupid theories. The stupid theories will appear correct because the subjects can become as stupid as we require them to be. (If they don't, we can just practice them some more until we get the desired effect.)

I think these specific experiment effects are more common than we ordinarily suppose. While not many people remember the enormous rash of studies of "probability learning," even a cursory historical search will remind you that this problem occupied a number of significant researchers for quite some time. Mathematical models were built and tested in a variety of ingenious ways to explore probability learning. But this work has, in the main, faded away. W. K. Estes, one of the leading workers in the field of mathematical psychology, appraised the field (1975) as making many brilliant and interesting contributions, but pointed out that there was very little cumulative knowledge built up from these

efforts. Too many experiments were concerned with highly unusual situations occurring only in the laboratory. They had no
relevance for any setting other than those particular experiments.
In such extreme cases, the experimental results tell us nothing of
any importance about the everyday world and the behavior of
people in that world. Obviously, experiments can be so constrained by our assumptions, our theories, and their own artifi-
ciality that we do not learn anything of general significance from
them.

I do not claim that this insight is strikingly new. In some sense all
of us have known this for years. Thorndike's cats could not be
anything but "trial and error" learners; there was simply nothing
else they could do in that experimental situation. Kohler's apes, on
the other hand, showed insightful problem solving because that
was all that the setting and the experimenter would permit.
Paired-associate learning produces smooth, incremental learning
curves because the "standard" time intervals for the experiment
were chosen by Melton on the basis of a theory that said that
learning curves should look that way. Tolman's rats learned cognitive maps; Hull's rats learned responses. And so on.

I do not want to suggest that experiments are "untrue" or "invalid" or worthless. Obviously they *do* tell us that subjects can
behave in certain ways *under certain circumstances*. This will be of
interest to us if the circumstances are interesting, or important, or
highly frequent. But if these circumstances occur only in the laboratory, the experimenter must take on a considerable burden of
justification if he or she desires our interest.

Successful experiments usually demonstrate that the experimenter has an intuitive grasp of the boundary conditions under
which subjects will behave in the specified way. (It is unfortunate
that such intuitions are almost never captured in the experimenter's theory.) Seasoned experimenters who have worked in a
particular paradigm for some time are rarely surprised by the outcomes of experiments; they know how to structure conditions so
that the "right" outcomes may be observed. On the other hand,
when they move to a new experimental paradigm, even when it is
supposed to be about the same psychological function or process,
their intuitions are frequently in error. For example, most psychologists who studied memory in traditional fashions were surprised by the results of the Bransford-Frank experiments (1971).
They failed to predict the outcomes largely because the experiments made use of verbal materials which were interrelated (in-

stead of independent) and the criterion measures were based on false-positive recognitions rather than number correct. Most of my friends in the memory field mispredicted the outcomes, although their predictions did fit the data from a later experiment by Peterson and McIntyre (1973), who repeated the experiment with unrelated materials. Such instances demonstrate how limited is our ability to generalize our scientific knowledge over situations and how dependent our experiments are on our intuitions built up over long experience with particular experimental paradigms.

A further aside on psychological experiments may not be amiss here. It is apparent to me that for the most part we do not try to disconfirm theories as philosophers of science like Popper argue that we should. In a sense it is simply too easy to disconfirm a psychological theory. Rather than trying to disconfirm a theory, we usually try to meet the theory "on its own ground," or on grounds that are reasonable from the point of view of the theory, and attempt to show that it applies or does not apply to the situation that we have in mind. We may try to put a dent in the theory, or show that it can be extended to cover a slightly different class of instances, but we do not simply set out on any ground whatsoever to show that the theory will not predict behavior in some arbitrary situation. We all know that it will not!

A difficulty arises in that we forget our self-imposed limitations. Because these limits are part of the professional code that is not taught in an explicit fashion, they escape notice. You will not find these limits in the text books. They exist as a "gentleman's agreement." The student is slowly shaped to believe that some particular kinds of experimentation are the "proper ground" on which to study learning, or memory, or perception, or what-have-you. The art of the kind of experimentation "that counts," is assimilated in the classroom, from the examples that the student sees, and from the things that the professor regards seriously. The student also learns about the kinds of artifacts that affect this kind of research, the errors to which it is prone (that is, the circumstances that one must not include), the appropriate dependent variables and their analysis, and so on. Thus, as students become professionalized, they come to know *what counts* as a good experiment in their special field. Then they train others, do research in this mode, referee journal articles, pass on and criticize others' grant proposals, and so on, on the basis of that knowledge.

There is, unfortunately, no requirement that the knowledge built up in this fashion relate in any reasonable way to anything else. And, indeed, as I pointed out above, it may not. Some of what is learned may be relevant to some problem; some may not be; but the important thing is, *there is no obligation to find out.* Perhaps that is as it should be. After all, one can only do so much. But the complaints about our field, both from within and from without, suggest that we had better inquire and we had better show some concern.

The most dramatic example that I know of the power of academic constraints is the utter lack of impact of Thorndike's research on human learning in the early 1930s. In two books he stressed a new learning principle that he had encountered, which he called *belongingness* (Thorndike, 1931, 1932). He said that it was a more important and more powerful principle than all the variables studied previously by learning psychologists. You must also recall that Thorndike stood at the peak of his field; surely he was a man of enormous influence and prestige. But, in spite of that, because such a concept did not fit into the traditional theories and schemes that learning psychologists were accustomed to, his work on belongingness vanished with scarcely a trace. Where it can still be found today in the accounts of the history of learning and memory, belongingness has been carefully rewritten into a harmless phenomena, largely restricted to associative grouping.

Bartlett (1932), another pioneer who departed from the traditional associative approach, received better treatment. Perhaps this was because he was an Englishman and therefore entitled to hold unorthodox views, or perhaps it was because he had some "catchy" examples like the "War of the Ghosts" (which seems to be quoted in every introductory psychology book). At any rate, students at least heard that Bartlett believed in "schemes" and was concerned with something called an "effort toward meaning" (a theme that my colleagues have already addressed here today). Nevertheless, Bartlett had little effect on American studies of learning and memory. His work did not fit the prevailing experimental paradigms.

The long historical view shows us now that Thorndike and Bartlett (and Katona, 1940, as well) were concerned with organization, structure, and relations in the material, with the structure of the experiment and with structure available in the subject's experience. In short, they were trying to draw attention to what we see as the key issues in cognitive psychology today! From our position, almost 50 years removed from Thorndike's effort, we should be keenly aware that narrowing and trivializing these problems to make them fit into a favorite laboratory paradigm may again let these topics of vital importance escape from us.

My personal prediction is that this time we are going to lay hold of and wrestle with these real problems. Many researchers are showing increasing concern with meaningful questions. Instead of studying nonsense syllables, or lists of words, or even lists of sentences, they are moving to higher and higher levels of meaningful units. As both Thorndike and Bartlett saw, as we change levels, it appears that the phenomena change and that they change in systematic ways.

What this means, I think, is that the working assumptions in the field are slowly changing; most particularly, researchers are easing away from the assumption that psychology must be built "from the bottom up." It used to be commonly supposed that our task was to find "the basic elements" and then combine them. I have heard many distinguished psychologists assert that this was the only possible route for psychological science. "If you can't understand simple list learning, how can you expect to understand anything more complicated? First things first." One of the great theorists of American psychology is said to have put it even more radically, "If you don't understand the behavior of the rat in the Y-maze, of course you cannot understand the behavior of human beings."

But if relations, structures, and organizations are of crucial importance, then this elementaristic or atomistic approach cannot work. That is, if it is *relations* among elements that count rather than just the elements alone, then simple research on simple elements *cannot* tell us what we need to know. If for "relations," we begin to read "scripts, schemata, scenarios, frames, stage settings, knowledge structures, etc.," you can see that current cognitive psychology is trying to approach real problems again.

In this symposium we have seen some illustrations of the fact that the theories that we developed to coordinate the results of experiments on simple elements may be misleading because of the impoverished stimuli that we use. I have pointed out elsewhere (Jenkins, 1974a, 1974b) that memory research has suffered from this mistake from its very inception. When Ebbinghaus began studying the learning and memory of students in the school system, he discovered that the differences between learners in terms of what they already knew were so great that he could not see systematic changes as a function of the variables that he was manipulating. Ebbinghaus then made a fundamental mistake; he invented the nonsense syllable on the very reasonable grounds that he wanted to study memory independent of the learner's prior knowledge. This choice was well motivated; it is easy to see how and why it was done, but it was an almost fatal mistake with respect to the field of study. Any human-factors psychologist or systems psychologist can tell you that if you are concerned with improving the output of some complex system, you must study the component that produces the largest variance first. Adjusting or correcting smaller sources of variance has no appreciable effect on the output of the system as long as the major source of variance is uncontrolled. It was Ebbinghaus's fate to have selected the largest source of variance and set it aside for the time being. Unfortunately, American psychologists followed his lead and, as they took up nonsense syllables, lost touch with the effects of organization, of structure of materials, and of effects of prior knowledge and understanding.

While a large number of phenomena associated with the learning of nonsense syllables have been established and investigated over three-quarters of this century, it is not apparent what relationship, if any, these phenomena have to the events of learning and forgetting in everyday life or in the classroom.

A similar phenomenon in a very different field is found in the relation of auditory psychophysics to the study of speech perception. I have heard it argued that the way to study speech perception is to build "from the ground up," that is, through the study of auditory psychophysics. To some people this is so apparent as to be axiomatic. However, auditory psychophysics still concerns itself largely with questions that deal with elementary stimuli. Thus, we find experiments with relatively simple stimuli such as clicks, sine waves, and bursts of noise, in the investigation of a number of properties, particularly those that relate to the way the mechanisms of the sensory system operate. On the other hand, current speech-perception research has evolved from a set of studies in the 1940s which concentrated on speech qua speech. These studies began by working on the analysis and synthesis of complex signals rather than elementary signals. The research rested on the invention of two rather elaborate kinds of machines, the speech spectrograph and the speech synthesizer. The spectrograph gave a display of the speech signal as a spectrum over time, which seems to be especially compatible to the eye. The synthesizer allowed investigators to manipulate spectral values over time and observe their perceptual consequences. In this fashion, through analysis and synthesis of speech itself, our understanding of speech perception has advanced dramatically over the last 35 years. Of course, this is not to say that psychophysics is irrelevant to speech perception, but rather that speech perception profited from being studied in its own right, at its own level, as the kind of thing it was. Conversely, it has profited very little from efforts to "build it up" out of the hypothetical elements drawn from the general domain of auditory psychophysics.

One is reminded of the classic case of Pavlov when he was debating whether to devote himself to studies of "psychic secretion" (as salivary conditioning was first called). His fellow physiologists urged him not to do it on the grounds that it was not a good problem in physiology. They argued that if the phenomenon was real, they would eventually discover it as they worked up from simple levels, and if it wasn't real, he would be wasting his time. Fortunately for us, Pavlov ignored their advice.

I think that there is an important lesson for us in all of these examples, even though they are from radically different fields. That is, what is apparently the simplest way to study a phenomenon may not in fact capture the relationships, the structures, and the complexity which are necessary to the understanding of events at higher levels. There are obviously emergent properties: To study complex relations one must be dealing with enough elements to form the relations. No study of single tones will inform one as to melody, no study of simultaneous effects is informative about sequences, and so on.

These considerations suggest a safeguard, namely, to have evaluation criteria of some sort which are independent of the particular experiments that we are conducting. These criteria need not necessarily be "applied" criteria, although such are extremely valuable. One example that I am very fond of is found in the work of von Békésy, in his experiments on the nature of the cochlea. Reading through his researches as recorded in his collected work *(Experiments in Hearing)*, one finds cycles of research on the cochlea itself, followed by model building and experiments on the models of the cochlea, followed by a reexamination of the cochlea and new experiments on the cochlea, followed by more model building, and so on. Through cycle after cycle of such work both with nature (the cochlea) and with the abstraction from nature (the model), what he learned in each activity contributed to the full picture. His knowledge became progressively more precise and accurate with better understanding of both nature and models. In speech perception we see a similar cycle between analysis and synthesis, new analyses, new syntheses, and so on.

I don't think it is possible to say in advance what kind of criterion will be productive for a given field, but that there should be some kind of criterion other than the laboratory experiment itself is, I fear, amply illustrated for us by the history of many of the subfields of psychology.

Illustrations

My colleagues, Anderson and Smith, have stayed within an area which is in the mainstream of modern cognitive psychology: the memory for and comprehension of sentences and paragraphs (in essence, verbal propositions assembled into larger structures). I would like to give you illustrations from a couple of other areas both to emphasize the diversity of cognitive psychology and to show a glimpse of the promise that I think is inherent in the field. I do not want to claim that these illustrations are fundamentally different from the examples that you already have before you; they just show different aspects of the phenomena of the field and may help alert you to the degree of abstraction that is going to be required to characterize cognitive psychology.

The perception of visual events. The first area that I want to talk about is the perception of visual events and the memory for what is perceived. The second area is that of expert knowledge, in this particular case in a medical speciality.

Looking first at the domain of visual events, we can see immediately the same kind of difference between unrelated and related (meaningful) stimuli that I have complained about in the verbal area. In a number of studies (Shepard, 1967; Haber, 1970; Standing, Conezio, & Haber, 1970; Standing, 1973) memory for individual pictures has been studied. In the usual paradigm large numbers of pictures are shown to subjects. Then they are shown a series of pairs of pictures and asked to indicate which member of the pair they have seen before. By and large, even for staggering numbers of pictures (Standing has worked with as many as 10,000 pictures), subjects are surprisingly accurate in picking out a picture they have seen before versus one that they have not. Some investigators have leaped from these studies to the conclusion that memory for pictures is a highly specialized, unlimited kind of memory, that pictures are "copied directly" into long-term memory, and that the picture image sits there in some kind of un-changed state.

When experimenters change the nature of the entire set of pic-tures so that the pictures are related to each other in some way, it turns out that this "amazing picture memory" is in fact quite fallible. If the pictures are all from the same category (e.g., all inkblots, all snowflakes, or all faces), Goldstein and Chance (1970) have shown that there is great opportunity for confusion. A con-siderable error rate is observed in picture recognition. In our studies we have arranged that the pictures are related to each other by being pictures of the same event. The Minnesota studies (Jen-kins, Wald, & Pittenger, 1978) take a series of slide pictures of a person performing a simple act such as making a cup of tea or answering the telephone. We show the viewers some subset of these pictures as an acquisition task. The subjects are told that they are going to be asked to recognize the slides later. On the test they are shown the original slides, *"Belonging" slides* (that is, slides of the event taken at the same time as the originals but not previ-ously shown to the subjects in acquisition), and *Control slides* which do not fit the event in some fashion (contain extraneous objects, are taken from a different station point, violate some rela-tional aspect of the event, etc.). Under these circumstances we get high rates of false recognition of the Belonging slides, although the subjects have not seen those slides previously. At the same time Control slides are rejected at a high level of accuracy. (This is a demonstration similar in kind to some of those Thorndike per-formed back in the 1930s in the verbal domain. It was for this reason, of course, that we labeled the slides that "fit" the event as Belonging slides.)

Let me go through the procedure that we used in the visual-event studies to give a more adequate picture of what is going on, because the paradigm is not familiar to most readers. First, a series of pictures are taken at regular or at haphazard intervals. (We have used rates as fast as two per second and as slow as one every five seconds depending on the detail of the event and its own natural rate.) In our usual procedure the camera is in a fixed position and simply follows the action if the characters in the action move about.

The series of pictures of the event is divided into consecutive sets of three pictures each. From each of these sets of three, one picture is randomly chosen to be held out as a Belonging slide. (This procedure is used to prevent a rhythmic or cyclical gap from appearing in the flow of action.) This means that the event is incompletely *represented* in the set of remaining slides that we show to the subjects. It should be noted, however, that the event may be very completely *specified* by the slides.

In the acquisition presentation, the subjects are usually shown the slide series in the proper order (minus the withheld slides, of course). Subjects are usually given about five seconds to study each slide, and the slide series is shown twice to make sure that the subjects get an opportunity to study any aspect of the event that they wish.

In the test series the subject is shown (in random order) original slides shown in the acquisition set (Old slides), Belonging slides, and Control slides in equal numbers. The subjects are asked to perform one of several possible tasks. In the early studies we simply asked subjects to indicate which slides they had seen before, that is, which slides had been in the initial acquisition series. This is the most difficult task; the subject attempts to make an absolute judgment as to whether the test slide is old or new. In general, when we have used this procedure, the subjects recognize the Old slides with a high degree of success; about 80–90% of the Old slides are identified as having been seen before. The Belonging slides are falsely recognized as being "old" from 50% to 70% of the time. The Control slides are recognized as being new; they are called "old" less than 10% of the time. We take this as evidence that the subjects have in fact apprehended the event rather than merely "copying" a series of pictures into memory. Given that they "know" the event, they have difficulty rejecting the Belonging slides because those slides are fully in accord with their general knowledge.

A different criterial task, of course, will produce rather different data, but data which lead to the same kind of conclusion. For example, the subjects may be told, "The pictures you have seen are like parts of a jigsaw puzzle. We are now going to present you with another set of pictures, some of which you have seen before and some of which you have not. We want you to tell us which pictures would fit into the jigsaw puzzle and which ones would not." In essence, the subject is asked for a judgment of compatibility with the event sequence that he has just witnessed. The Belonging slides and the Old slides are now treated equivalently; both subsets of slides are judged to "fit" close to 100% of the time. In contrast, the Control slides, which violate some aspect of the event, are still rejected; they are judged as not fitting the jigsaw puzzle.

The above data suggest that the subjects have two kinds of information as a result of seeing the acquisition series of slides. One kind of information is about specific pictures seen. This is somewhat fallible information, but there is enough specific memory that some of the Belonging slides are detected as "new." The other information is as to the nature of the event depicted. This information seems to be highly robust. It is easy for the subjects to make judgments about whether something fits into the overall event; the judgments are highly polarized, and they are usually correct.

At a somewhat different level, it is also clear that the subjects have a good deal of information about their particular experiencing of the event itself. For example, if on the test we show the subjects a Control slide which is correct in all aspects with respect to the event but which was taken from a different station point, the subjects all recognize that this is a new slide. They are highly sensitive to the point of observation of the original series. This is an aspect, not of the event, but of their experience of the event, which apparently is faithfully recorded.

In a similar fashion the subjects are sensitive to the source of lighting of the original event (and probably to a host of other aspects that we have not yet investigated). One remarkable fact about this knowledge is that no subject ever thinks to tell us of such information when they tell us about the slides. Yet if we show a slide taken with a different lighting source, the subjects immediately recognize that the slide is new. In the case of the change in viewpoint, the subjects can usually tell us in what respect the slide is incorrect. The change in lighting, however, is more subtle; the subjects may not be able to identify why they know the slide is new and, even after they discover that the lighting is "incorrect," may not be able to tell us about the original source of light or the placement of the shadows. Yet they still know that this is an unfamiliar picture, even though it is a picture of a familiar event. We believe that this kind of experiment is a powerful method for investigating what it is that a subject acquires from an experience. The chief limitation on it is the limitation of the ingenuity of the experimenter in devising new Control slides.

In general, we would be prepared to argue that any invariant of the visual experience or any invariant of the event has a high probability of being picked up by the subjects and made one of the constituents of the event, as demonstrated by recognition criteria. It appears to us that events generate their own significant criteria.

"What counts" in the event will determine to some extent what the subjects will remember. Consider a very simple case. If in the acquisition phase of the experiment subjects are shown a series of human profiles, half facing left and half facing right, they will have great difficulty in identifying left-right reversals in test slides. However, if they are shown an event in which there is meaningful action and the action flows to the left and then to the right, subjects are highly accurate in recognizing lateral reversals of the slides (Kraft & Jenkins, 1977). In a similar way, we suppose that almost any aspect of an event series can become salient if it is important in defining the nature or the quality of event that is involved. We do not think that events come with a universal set of features, but rather that the experience of the event generates its own criteria for what counts as being "similar" and what counts as being "important."

John Pittenger and I (Pittenger & Jenkins, 1979) investigated the case of the moving observer in the still environment by taking photographs straight ahead as one took a walk across a campus. We showed a selection of these slides in the same event-acquisition paradigm. Roughly the same phenomena are obtained. Subjects falsely recognize slides which could have been part of the original sequence (Belonging slides) and reject slides that do not belong even though they represent other possible walks across the campus. This study also showed a gain in the ratings of the Belonging slides as a function of familiarity with the campus on which the walk took place.

We have speculated about events in which both the event and the observer are changing simultaneously. We wonder to what extent the subjects would detect the degree to which the motion of the camera and the motion of the event were in or out of phase. We suspect that for some kinds of events subjects will be highly accurate in saying what the observation point was at any particular stage of the event, while for other kinds of events they will not have this information. However, we have not yet conducted any such study; perhaps our readers will do so for us.

Our general point of view is that *events*, like propositions and schemata, are candidates for consideration as cognitive units. When an event is apprehended, it is not merely a copy of the particular slides seen or even the particular experiences that the subject had, but an apprehension of the total event, parts of which may have been unseen. While there may be specific memory for the sources of information, it is obviously not necessary that this be the case. Memory for the event may be complete and for that matter veridical, while the subject may have a great deal of difficulty in saying what he did or did not see. (Studies of the errors of eyewitnesses are, of course, extensions of this line of work.)

What counts as a unit and what the subjects see obviously depends on a host of variables. A very important variable is the orienting task or, more generally, what the subject is trying to do. We have developed a picture event in the laboratory which shows a small object (a salt shaker) rotating around a large object (a jam jar) which sits in the middle of an octagonal tray. When we show selected slides from this series to naive subjects, we get a very pronounced Belonging effect. Of the Belonging slides, 70–80% are falsely recognized as being in the acquisition set, and *none* of the Controls are falsely recognized. When this event is shown to experienced subjects who are trying to achieve specific memory and who are knowledgeable concerning mnemonics (say, graduate students in cognitive psychology), almost no generalization to Belonging slides is found. There are a variety of ways of coding these pictures, such as labeling the rotation positions verbally by clock positions, which lead to highly specific memory and the ability to discriminate the particular slides seen from the event slides in general. Thus, what the subject is trying to do interacts with and overcomes the structure of the event.

On the other hand, the event sequence which shows a woman making a cup of tea shows almost no effect of experience in determining its outcome. In fact, repeated study of the original acquisition series and repeated testing show almost no change in the proportion of responses made to Old, Belonging, and Control slides. Here, the particular event overrides the subjects' efforts toward achieving specific memory.

This example also makes clear that what the cognitive units are and what is retained by the subjects depend on what structures are afforded by the materials. From the outset we have seen that if the materials lend themselves to a story or to a sequence of actions, what gets apprehended is quite different from the cases where the materials do not afford such interpretations. In the Shepard, Haber, and Standing research cited earlier the phenomena of recognition are markedly different from the phenomena we see in our experiments. The materials afford structures which interact with what the subjects are trying to do, and it is this interaction which determines the structures and units that we see in operation in the experiments.

It is also clear that what we see as cognitive units and structures depends on what it is that we choose to measure and use as our inference base. In our early studies of events, our measures were absolute judgments of "old" or "new." This gives us one base for inferences about subjects' memory. If we collect confidence ratings along with the judgments, we find, however, that even when both Belonging slides and Old slides are called "old," there is ordinarily an advantage for the Old slides in terms of confidence ratings. In this case the confidence ratings presumably give us some measure of the specific memory effect which is still present in spite of the classification. If we do the "jigsaw puzzle instructions," the Belonging slides and the Old slides are treated indistinguishably and we are likely to stress the apprehension of the event as a whole and ignore the role of specific memory. What we infer about the detail of subjects' memories is in part determined by our cleverness in constructing Control slides. If we do not test for particular variations, we cannot know whether the subjects' representations do or do not contain the relevant information. Thus, our inferences concerning cognitive units and structures cannot be much better than our skills in building and interpreting a variety of criterial tasks.

Finally (and this will lead us into the next illustration), what kinds of cognitive units are employed and what kinds of structures are formed will depend on the knowledge or expertise in the subject matter that the subjects bring to the experiment. We have some pilot work on short movies which offers convincing support that what subjects see and remember depends on what they already know. For example, Robin Ridley Johnson and I did a little study with a film of the compulsory floor exercises from the 1972 Olympics gymnastic competition. We showed this film to gymnasts and nongymnasts and then questioned the viewers about gymnastic and nongymnastic information contained in the film. As the reader might suppose, the gymnasts were vastly superior in their knowledge about the performance of the gymnast in the picture and could report in great detail on the particular stunts. Even when the stunts were described and depicted as recall cues, nongymnasts had more difficulty than gymnasts in saying whether such a stunt had been present or not. Just having one's eyes open and facing the screen does not guarantee that the information on the screen will be transferred to the viewer; one apparently needs higher order structures to perceive and assimilate the information.

I find that most readers are acquainted with this phenomenon as spectators of sports events on television. My favorite anecdotes come from Olympic diving. The contestant flashes through the air, goes through some incredible set of maneuvers, and enters the water. The TV commentator turns to his guest expert for an opinion and the expert says something like, "It wasn't a very clean dive. He didn't get his hand fully behind his head like he should have." Then the slow-motion instant replay comes on and we all see in very slow motion that the diver indeed did not get his hand positioned fully behind his head as he spun through the air. Did the expert actually see that hand position in real time? Or does the expert know the consequences of the failure, so that he automatically deduces that the defect occurred? Or does the expert have a template or a Gestalt against which the total performance is judged and against which the defect stands out? We do not know. It is clear, however, that what is available to the expert is not available to us under the same time constraints. We are quite interested in studying this as an instance of perception and memory being governed by the knowledge that one possesses.

To remind myself of these variables, I represent them in a tetrahedron. This calls attention to the *orienting task*—what it is that the subject is trying to do. It reminds one of the role of *materials*—what kinds of structures do the materials afford? It directs us to think about the criterial tasks that we employ—what are the bases for our inferences? Finally, it emphasizes the subject variable itself—what is the effect of the degree of expertise that the subject brings to the task?

The Study of Expertise

As a final example I would like to call attention to the study of expertise and specifically to the work of one of my colleagues, Paul Johnson. Some years ago Johnson decided to try to understand and to model the expertise that is involved in pediatric cardiology. He selected the problem because of its obvious importance, because there are clear, final criteria (inspection of the heart), and because cooperative experts were available to him in the University of Minnesota medical school. In addition, it was clear that among physicians there was a tremendous range of skill and knowledge concerning this somewhat esoteric area. Following essentially the Carnegie-Mellon style of attack, he has been inter-

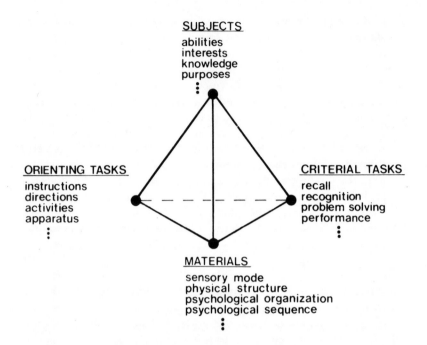

viewing cardiologists and studying what it is that they know and what it is that they do as they work through cases attempting to achieve a diagnosis. In studying these cases, Johnson and his collaborators have had to learn a great deal about pediatric cardiology, and cardiology and medicine in general. (One reason I think that psychologists rarely undertake these tasks is that they have to learn too much in order to understand the knowledge structures. It is like undertaking the acquisition of a whole new specialty itself.)

Johnson and his colleagues have made considerable progress in modeling the knowledge of pediatric cardiologists and have "paid their way," so to speak, by developing training techniques and exercises along the way as they pursued the research. They have, for example, developed a computerized set of cases which the cardiologist in training can work through from intake to final disposition. The neophyte is given a case and allowed to make choices of seeking further information, trying particular treatments, conducting maintenance routines, and so forth. If the student follows a poorly structured routine and neglects maintenance, the physician may well lose the patient; the virtue, of course, being that patients in the computer are readily resurrected, whereas flesh and blood patients are not.

The degree of sophistication achieved in this area is shown by the recent development of synthetic cases. Johnson and his colleagues can now build a plausible case, having a given diagnosis with appropriate symptomatology. They can further complicate matters by giving the case a salient symptom that often accompanies another disorder, presenting a "catch trial," so to speak. Such a case presents a problem in that if one is only attending to salient symptoms, one can readily misclassify the case in a "rush to diagnosis." Such cases have been tested on novices (senior medical students), on appropriate apprentices (appropriate residents in the hospital), and on experts in pediatric cardiology. The novices fail to get the correct diagnosis, even though they are not misled by the salient symptom. They just don't know enough to know what the symptoms mean. The residents are sometimes taken in by the misleading symptom. They know enough to "go for" the diagnosis, but not enough to see that the pattern of symptoms is not appropriate. The expert cardiologists tend to look at the entire pattern of symptoms and detect that the appropriate pattern for the false diagnosis is not present.

When Johnson's computer program of knowledge was run on these cases, it behaved very much like the residents. It tended to go for the false diagnosis; that is, it overweighted the salient symptom. He is now modifying the program to make it utilize more systematic support before it decides on a diagnosis.

As a further test of the adequacy of his computer program for diagnosis, Johnson generated 16 cases in which he systematically removed or changed symptoms from a standard case in order to see which changes influenced the probability of particular diagnoses. Then he gave this set of cases with changed symptoms to his experts, residents, and medical students and asked them to assign probabilities of diagnosis to each case. While the results are highly complex (ratings of 8 diagnoses for each of 16 cases for the simulation, experts, residents, and students), the simulation generated very high correlations with the experts, frequently higher than the correlations between the experts and the trainees.

My purpose here is merely to indicate that there are many ways to evaluate the adequacy of the representation of diagnostic knowledge. Against several kinds of criteria, Johnson's program seems impressively adequate. Furthermore, the program makes possible new experimentation, which in turn makes it possible to upgrade the program and to draw attention to neglected aspects of diagnosis in the training of new pediatric cardiologists. (For more information on this project, see Feltovich, Johnson, Moller, & Swanson, 1980; Johnson, Feltovich, Moller & Swanson, 1979; Johnson, Severance, & Feltovich, 1979; Swanson, 1978.)

Final Remarks

It should be clear that I am in agreement with my colleagues Anderson and Smith. There is consensus that cognitive units are of a variety of sorts and kinds. Anderson, who has done as much work as anyone in the field on representations, impressively did not try to argue for "representational imperialism"; rather, he offered us candidates for some classes of cognitive units. Smith, in turn, made the same arguments. No one here thinks there is just one kind of cognitive unit and insists that everything is coded in the same way. We all seem to be firmly on the side of "representational populism," holding that cognitive units may be of different kinds and sizes depending on what is being cognized.

Smith's appeal that we not get lost in memory as a "thing apart" struck a very responsive chord in me. Not very long ago I reread William James on memory and found that, quite unlike his treatment of habit (which is so often cited), he held that memory was a cognitive process, but not a separable function. James argued that the only thing that separates memory from the collection of other cognitive processes is our *belief* that it is something that occurred in the past. Other than that it is indistinguishable from the other higher mental processes.

I think the emphasis that we have seen here on what I could call "true functionalism" is an important emphasis to be restored to American psychology. It seems to be coming back with vigor.

Returning now to my main theme, I repeat that I think there is a malaise in cognitive psychology, a concern with trivia, a lack of direction. One of the questions that I am asked most frequently when I go on speaking trips is, "Where is the field going?" Significantly, it is the staff members rather than the students who are asking this question.

I think we are finding some directions for cognitive psychology by concerning ourselves with meaningful problems. Real problems rather than presupposed theories seem to provide real guidance. The problem orientation appears to be a healthy one for us because real problems provide extralaboratory criteria by which we may judge the success (or lack of it) of our laboratory work. We are in need of such criteria to ensure that we are not just doing "experiments about experiments."

To reiterate the argument: If we believe that human beings are universal machines, and if we believe that they can become any kind of machine that they need to be in a given situation, then the only work that we can do is to model their behavior in particular situations and particular environments, facing particular kinds of problems. Whether those models will be interesting depends on whether those situations, environments, and problems are interesting. We need to remember to consider what our subjects are trying to do, what kinds of materials they are working with, what kind of expertise they bring to the task, and what kinds of output criteria are important. If we can keep this orientation, I think that cognitive psychology can have a fruitful future. If we forget this orientation, I think we will find ourselves playing Twenty Questions for the rest of our days.

REFERENCES

Bartlett, F. C. *Remembering*. Cambridge: Cambridge University Press, 1932.

Békésy, G. von. *Experiments in hearing*. New York: McGraw-Hill, 1960.

Bransford, J. D., & Franks, J. J. The abstraction of linguistic ideas. *Cognitive Psychology*, 1971, 2, 331–350.

Estes, W. K. Some targets for mathematical psychology. *Journal of Mathematical Psychology*, 1975, 12, 263–282.

Feltovich, P. J., Johnson, P. E., Moller, J. H., & Swanson, D. B. *The role and development of medical knowledge in diagnostic expertise*. Paper presented at the 1980 annual meeting of the American Educational Research Association, April 1980.

Finkelman, D. G. Science and psychology. *American Journal of Psychology*, 1978, 91, 179–199.

Gergen, K. J. Social psychology as history. *Journal of Personality and Social Psychology*, 1973, 26, 309–320.

Goldstein, A. G., & Chance, J. E. Visual recognition memory for complex configurations. *Perception & Psychophysics*, 1970, 9, 237–240.

Haber, N. R. How we remember what we see. *Scientific American*, 1970, 222(5), 104–112.

Harré, R., & Secord, P. F. *The explanation of social behavior*. Totowa, N.J.: Littlefield, Adams & Co., 1973.

Jenkins, J. J. Can we have a theory of meaningful memory? In R. E. Solso (Ed.), *Memory and cognition: The second Loyola symposium*. Potomac, Md.: Erlbaum, 1974. (a)

Jenkins, J. J. Remember that old theory of memory? Well, forget it! *American Psychologist*, 1974, *29*, 785–795. (b)

Jenkins, J. J., Wald, J., & Pittenger, J. B. Apprehending pictorial events: An instance of psychological cohesion. In C. W. Savage (Ed.), *Minnesota studies in the philosophy of science* (Vol. 9). Minneapolis: University of Minnesota Press, 1978.

Johnson, P. E., Feltovich, P. J., Moller, J. H., & Swanson, D. B. *Clinical expertise: Theory and data from the diagnosis of congenital heart disease.* Paper presented at the meeting of the American Educational Research Association, 1979.

Johnson, P. E., Severance, D. G., & Feltovich, P. J. Design of decision support systems in medicine: Rationale and principles from the analysis of physician expertise. In *Proceedings of the Twelfth Hawaii International Conference on System Sciences*, Hawaii, 1979.

Katona, G. *Organizing and memorizing.* New York: Columbia University Press, 1940.

Kraft, R. N., & Jenkins, J. J. Memory for lateral orientation of slides in picture stories. *Memory & Cognition*, 1977, *5*, 397–403.

McGuire, W. J. The yin and yang of progress in social psychology: Seven koans. *Journal of Personality and Social Psychology*, 1973, *26*, 446–456.

Meehl, P. E. Theoretical risks and tabular asterisks: Sir Karl, Sir Ronald, and the slow progress of soft psychology. *Journal of Consulting and Clinical Psychology*, 1978, *46*, 806–834.

Mischel, W. On the future of personality measurement. *American Psychologist*, 1977, *32*, 246–254.

Newell, A. You can't play 20 questions with nature and win. In W. G. Chase (Ed.), *Visual information processing.* New York: Academic Press, 1973.

Peterson, R. G., & McIntyre, C. W. The influence of semantic 'relatedness' on linguistic integration and retention. *American Journal of Psychology*, 1973, *86*, 697–706.

Pittenger, J. B., & Jenkins, J. J. Apprehension of pictorial events: The case of a moving observer in a static environment. *Bulletin of the Psychonomic Society*, 1979, *13*, 117–120.

Shepard, R. N. Recognition memory for words, sentences and pictures. *Journal of Verbal Learning and Verbal Behavior*, 1967, *6*, 156–163.

Standing, L. Learning 10,000 pictures. *Quarterly Journal of Experimental Psychology*, 1973, *25*, 207–222.

Standing, L., Conezio, J., & Haber, R. N. Perception and memory for pictures: Single-trial learning of 2500 visual stimuli. *Psychonomic Science*, 1970, *19*, 73–74.

Swanson, D. B. *Computer simulation of expert problem solving in medical diagnosis.* Ph.D. thesis, University of Minnesota, 1978.

Thorndike, E. L. *Human learning.* New York: Century, 1931.

Thorndike, E. L. *The fundamentals of learning.* New York: Teachers College, Columbia University, 1932.

Subject Index

Acoustic Pathways, 24
ACT, 125–26, 128–29, 130, 131, 134, 145, 166–68, 205
Activation, 141, 144, 150, 159
Active memory, 124–25, 126. *See also* Working memory
Alerting, 4, 40, 44
    effects, 20–21
    mechanisms, 20
    pathways, 25, 26, 35
    phasic, 5, 37
    systems, 26, 39
Alertness, 5, 19–20, 21, 24–25, 33, 35, 42, 44
Alertness, tonic, 37
All-or-none
    encoding, 127, 134, 135, 136, 146, 148–49, 150
    learning, 125, 126
    recall, 132, 135, 136, 157, 158
    retrieval, 125, 126, 127, 131, 134, 135, 136–37, 146, 156
Anagram task, 96
Analogies, 153–54, 155
Approximate knowledge, 78–79
Archival memory, 73–75, 79, 83, 115
Arousal effects, 22
Associative interference, 167
Associative strength, 167
Attention, 2, 3, 4, 5, 6, 13, 19, 20, 21–22, 24, 26, 28–29, 32–33, 36, 37, 39, 40, 41, 43, 44
Attention, obligatory, 17, 18
Attentional mechanisms, 3–13, 18, 23, 31, 33, 41, 42–43, 44

Automatic alerting, 20
Awareness, 4, 5, 7, 20, 30

Belongingness
    as learning principle, 222
    in visual event memory, 227–29, 230, 231, 232
Bilateral conflict, 22
Binary oppositions, in cognitive theory, 213, 215

Capture, visual, 24
Caretaker scales, 36–37
Categorization tasks, 56–60, 61, 65, 66, 68
Chronometric techniques, 10–11
Clustering, 117, 176, 178, 203
Codes, 55, 61, 69
Cognitive
    naturalness, 122, 123, 132, 145, 147, 158
    organization, 29
    structure, 29
    styles, 33, 34, 42. *See also* Individual differences
    units, 230–32, 236
Cognitive psychology
    criteria for fruitfulness of, 211–12
    criticisms of, 211–26
Comprehension, 186, 188–90, 191, 193, 194, 195, 196–97, 203, 205–6
Concepts, 123–24, 142–43, 147–48, 156–58
Constant Rate and Exhaustive

Scanning (CRES) model, 88–93, 96, 103, 117. *See also* Random-sampling-with-replacement model
Constraints, 122–23
Constricted vs. flexible control, *see* Individual differences
Correlated predicates, 198–202, 203–5, 206. *See also* Perfectly correlated predicates
Correspondence, 145, 147–48, 149, 150–58, 159
Cortical centers, 15
Cortical visual systems, 20–21
Covert attention
  capacity, 33
  movements of, 10–11
  orienting of, 12, 33
  visual, 12, 43
Criterial tasks, 232, 233

Detecting, 4, 6–8, 37, 39, 40, 42
Developmental level, 69
Directed search, 180
Discrimination nets, 179
Distress, 39
Diurnal cycle, 5

Efficiency, 123, 132, 145, 158
Elaboration, 157, 158, 163, 164, 171, 185, 194
ELINOR, 165–66, 167
Emotion, 29
Estimates, of quantities, 77–79
Events
    as cognitive units, 230–31
    nature of, 229
Exogenous stimuli, 21, 30, 39, 43
Experiments
    boundary conditions of, 220
    confirmatory, 218
    nature of, 218
Expertise
    degree of, 233, 237
    in subject matter, 232

study of, 233–36
Eye movements, 8, 9, 10, 12, 14, 15, 16–17, 18, 21, 24, 30, 42, 43
Eye movement system, relationship to attentional system, 11–12, 13, 21–22, 43–44

Factuality scores, 77
False alarms, 184, 186, 194
False positives, 109–11, 117, 118
Fan effects, 140, 142, 168–69, 172–75, 182–84, 186, 187, 188, 193, 198–203, 204–5
Fan experiments, 180, 193, 194–95, 198–200, 205
Fanning, 171, 178, 181
Feature codes, *see* Perceptual codes
Feature detectors, 61, 69
Feature grouping, 67–68
Feature selection, 67
Field-dependent, *see* Individual differences
Field-independent, *see* Individual differences
Flanker effects, 63–67. *See also* Good readers vs. poor readers
Flexibility, 33
Flow diagrams, as models, 213
Fovea, 8–9, 10, 11, 12
Frames, 124, 156
FRAN model, 156
Free recall, 177–78, 180, 181
Free recall, of categorized lists, 175–77, 179
Functional fixedness problems, 217

Generic memory, 26–29
Good readers vs. poor readers, 66–67

Habituation, 22, 23–26, 27, 30, 34
Habituation of pathways, 24, 25, 26, 44
HAM, 129, 130, 166–68
HAM-ACT, 167, 170, 171

Heart rate deceleration, 5, 38
Hierarchical representations, 179
Hierarchies, 142, 149–50, 151, 156,
    159, 180
Hierarchy theory, 61
Higher unit hypothesis, 192–94,
    196, 202
Higher units, 190, 193, 204

Identifiability, 121–22
Individual differences, 3, 4, 31–43,
    44, 69–70
    constricted vs. flexible control,
        33
    field dependents, 34
    field independents, 34
    introversion-extroversion, 34
    leveling-sharpening, 33
Inefficiency, 123, 131
Inferences, 77, 78, 186, 188–95, 196,
    197, 203
Inferencing, 205
Integrable facts, 182–84, 188, 194,
    202, 203, 204–5, 206
Integrated facts, 182–84, 188, 193,
    196, 205
Integration, 171, 184–86, 195
    by prior knowledge, 171, 172,
        182–84, 202–3, 204–6
    effects, 195
    of input facts, 163, 184
Intelligence, 31–32, 34
Interconnections, 189, 192, 194, 195,
    203, 204
Interconnections hypothesis,
    194–95, 196–97, 202, 204
Interference, 139, 140, 142, 148, 157,
    158
Interference and cognitive units,
    140–44
Interitem associations, 109
Internal control mechanisms, 10,
    22–43
Internal mechanisms, 2, 3, 4, 6, 25,
    26, 30, 31, 34–35, 42, 43, 44

Intersensory facilitation, 19
Introspection, 79–81, 111, 113
Introversion-extroversion, *see* Individual differences
Intrusions, 184–85, 203
Invariants, 229

Knowledge base, 69

Letter codes, *see* Perceptual codes
Leveling-sharpening, *see* Individual differences
Lexical decision tasks, 59
Lexical memory, 73, 81
Lexicon, 104, 117
Lifespan approach, 8, 35, 44
Limited capacity central attentional
    mechanisms, 4, 7
Limited capacity effect, 40
List generation, 81–87, 94, 103,
    108–9, 115, 117, 118
List generation, strategies in,
    111–13
Localization, auditory, 21
Locus coeruleus, 5
Long-term memory, 7, 73
Luchins "water jar" problems, 217

Matching tasks, 59, 60, 67
Materials
    role of, 233, 237
    structures afforded by, 231, 233
Meaning variability, 199
Memory, inferential use of, 78
Memory representations, accuracy
    of, 76
Mental abilities testing, 31
Metacognition, 29, 30, 31
Midbrain, 5, 8, 9, 14, 15
Midbrain vs. cortical control, 14–15,
    16
"Mimicking automata," 215–16
Models of mind, 216–17
Models of task, 216
Model systems, 2–3, 8, 13, 26

Motivated remembering, 79, 81, 115
Motivated retrieval, 73–75
Motivation, 93, 97–98

Nonsense syllables, 223
Norepinephrine pathways, 5

Occipital lesions, 7
Oculomotor orienting, 24
Oculomotor system, 9, 18, 21
Old-New recognition test, 174
Organization, 202, 204
    devices, 180–81
    in recall, 104
    of input facts, 163, 164
    of new information, 164
Organizational effects, 187, 188
Organizational mechanisms, 164,
    169, 205
Orienting, 3, 4, 6–8, 13, 23, 28–29,
    37, 38, 39, 40, 42, 44
    covert, 6, 7, 13, 33, 35
    effects of lesions on, 7
    external control of, 13–22
    overt, 6, 7, 11, 12, 38, 39, 40
    reflex, 6, 26
    speed of, 34, 41
    sustained, 18, 38
    tasks, 231, 233
Orienting Reaction, 5, 38
Orthographic redundancy, 102–3
Outcome conditions, 190

Palindromes, 81, 110, 112–13, 114
Parallel processing, 57–58
Parallel vs. serial models, 122
Parallel vs. serial search, 122
Parietal lobe injury, 7, 16
Partial matching, 146, 155, 157
Partial recall, 127–28, 131, 132
Passive vs. active retrieval, 74
Pathway activation, 4, 5–6, 25–26,
    28, 35, 37, 40, 41
    automatic, 42
    in reading, 41–42

Pathway processes, 33
Pathways, 4, 10, 24, 25, 28, 35, 40, 42
Pattern matching, 147
Patterns, 145–46
Pediatric cardiology, 233–36
Perceptual boundaries, 54–55
Perceptual codes, 61
Perceptual learning, 67–69
Perfectly correlated predicates,
    171–73, 198–202. See also Corre-
    lated predicates
Phonemic similarity, 80
Phonetic codes, 32, 41–42
Phonetic pathways, 24
Preconditions, 190, 191–92
Prefamiliarization, 35
Preferences, 13–19, 24, 28, 43
Primary visual system, 9–10, 16
Priming, 5–6, 108, 130, 136–39, 144
Priming stimulus, 5
Production systems, 125, 155
Propositions, 123–24, 125–32, 134,
    139, 142–48, 149, 150, 156, 157,
    158, 159
Props, 190, 191
Prototypes, 27–28, 31
Psychoanalytic perspective, 29, 33
Psychometric tradition, 31–32

Radical behaviorism, 121
Random-sampling-with-replace-
    ment model, 88, 92, 93–94, 98–99,
    103, 117. See also Constant Rate of
    Exhaustive Scanning (CRES)
    model
Random search, 86, 98
Reaction time, 11, 16, 25, 33
Reactivity, 36, 39, 40, 43
Recall, 169, 176–77, 178, 184–85, 188,
    192, 194
    accuracy, 184–85, 193, 194,
        202–3
    intrusions in, 184–85, 203
    tests, 185, 203
Recognition, 167, 168–69, 179–81,

185, 187–88, 192, 195, 196, 198, 200, 203, 205
  accuracy, 184, 188, 193, 194, 202–3
  latency, 169, 173–75, 182–84, 186, 187–88, 194, 199, 202
  memory, 75
  pathways, 26
  tests, 175, 184, 186
Responsivity, 37, 40
Reticular activating system, 5
Retinal-collicular pathways, 8, 14, 15, 16
Retrieval, 74–75, 79–80, 81, 108, 109–10
  direct, 109–10
  indirect, 109–10
Retrieval process, dual–mode, 117
Roles, 190, 191, 192

Sampling rate, 93–94, 104
Scanning, 9, 28, 33
Scanning patterns, 17
Scanning patterns, infant, 21, 22, 23
Scenes, 190–91, 192
Schemata, 30, 123–24, 132–40, 142–48, 149, 151, 152–53, 156, 158, 159, 188–95, 196, 203
Schema variables, 191
Script actions, 191–93, 196
Scripts, 124, 135, 136–39, 140–41, 144, 149, 152, 155, 156, 190–94, 195, 197
Scripts, headers, 190, 197
Search, 79–80, 85–86, 93, 104, 105, 115, 118
  constraints, 101–2, 110, 117
  strategy, 111–13, 117
Search process, dual–mode, 118
Selective search, 180–81, 187
Self-awareness, 29, 31
Self-recognition, 29–31
Self-regulation, 36, 39, 40, 43
Semantic
  categories, 175, 176, 180

concepts, 7
memory, 28, 73
networks, 123–24, 125, 145
nodes, 7
pathways, 41–42
Semantic memory models, *see* ACT, ELINOR, HAM, HAM-ACT
Signal detection, 41
Some-or-none recall, 135–36
Spatial attention, 8, 10–13, 26
Spatial attention, orienting of covert mechanisms of, 21
Spatial behavior, 8
Speech perception, relation to psychophysics, 224–25
Spelling pattern codes, *see* Perceptual codes
Spreading activation, 140, 144, 150, 167, 168, 180
Stroop test, 62, 66
Structural similarity, 80–81
Subdivided networks, 171, 179, 181–82, 186–88, 195–97, 203–4, 206
Subdivision, 175, 176, 179, 180, 181
Subject strategies, 215–218
Subnode activation, 178, 187, 195–97, 202, 203–4, 205
Subnode-activation hypothesis, 186–88, 201–2, 203–4
Subnodes, 142, 171, 176, 177–78, 179–80, 181, 186–88, 196–97, 201, 203–4, 205

Tagging, 156
Temporal
  bias, 15–16
  organization, 39
  stimuli, 8
  visual field, 12, 21
Temporal-nasal bias, 12
Tetrahedron, 233
Thalamus, 5
Thematic relatedness, 138–40, 154–55
Themes, 155

Threshold detection, 11
Time-sharing, 33

Unilateral versus bilateral stimulation, 16
Universal computing device, human as, 215–19, 237

Variables, 145–46, 151, 152, 153, 155, 157
Visual
    code, 41–42
    event perception, 226
    images, 41, 111

scanning, 21, 24, 28
Voluntary control, of gaze, 43

Word frequency, 105
Word production rate, 82–87, 88–92, 94, 116
Word strings, 131
Working memory, 124–25, 126, 137, 141, 147, 148, 149, 150, 151–52, 156, 157, 158, 159
World knowledge, 182–84, 185, 188–90, 196
Written language, 53

Author Index

Abelson, R. P., 124, 133, 135, 149, 152, 155, 164, 190
Adams, M. J., 75, 164, 190, 192
Adams, N., 140–42, 145, 150, 168–69, 182–83
Allen, J., 115
Anderson, B. J., 36
Anderson, J. R., 121, 124, 125, 126–27, 128–29, 131, 141–45, 148, 150, 153–54, 155, 156, 157, 158, 163, 164, 166–67, 168–69, 175, 180, 183–84, 186–88, 194, 196, 205
Anderson, R. C., 128, 129
Arbib, M. A., 9
Aston-Jones, G., 5

Baron, J., 41
Barten, S., 37
Bartlett, F. C., 30, 222
Bates, J. E., 36, 37
Békésy, G. von., 225
Bennett, C. A., 36, 37
Ben-Shalom, H., 35
Bertelson, P., 21
Birch, H. G., 36
Birns, B., 37
Bjork, E. L., 65
Black, J. B., 135, 164, 176, 185, 197
Blakemore, C., 24
Bloom, F. E., 5
Bobrow, D. G., 124, 147, 150, 164
Boles, D., 16
Bornstein, M. H., 28
Bousfield, W. A., 87, 176

Bower, G. H., 124, 125, 126–27, 128–29, 131, 135, 140, 156, 163, 164, 166, 168–69, 176, 179, 185, 197, 200
Bransford, J. D., 184–85, 220–21
Brazelton, T. B., 37
Bremer, C. D., 58, 60
Bridger, W., 37
Broadbent, D. E., 7, 34, 149
Bronson, G., 14, 16, 40
Brooks-Gunn, J., 30
Brown, A. L., 40
Bruce, D. R., 176
Bruder, G. A., 59
Bruner, J. S., 18, 40–41
Bushnel, M. C., 11

Cain, R. L., Jr., 36
Campbell, F. W., 24
Campos, J. J., 14, 15
Carey, W. B., 36
Carroll, J. B., 32
Carvellas, T., 87, 88, 94–102, 105
Cerella, J., 27
Chance, J. E., 227
Chess, S., 36
Clark, M. C., 156, 179
Cofer, C. N., 176
Cohen, B. H., 135, 176, 177
Cohen, L. B., 18, 40
Cohen, Y., 9, 12, 15, 16, 19
Colavita, F. B., 20
Collins, A. M., 164, 190
Conezio, J., 226

Conway, J. C., 9
Cooper, L. A., 6
Corbit, J. P., 24
Coren, S., 15
Cornel, E. H., 25
Cowey, A., 10
Cullingford, R. E., 190

de Lemos, S. M., 32–33, 41
Deloache, J. S., 40
Derryberry, D., 36–37
Diamond, S., 36
Dooling, D. J., 185–86
Dyk, R. B., 33

Egeth, H. E., 20
Eichelman, W. H., 59
Eimas, P. D., 24
Emde, R. N., 18, 22–23, 38
Engen, T., 23
Eriksen, B. A., 63, 65
Eriksen, C. W., 63, 65
Ernest, C. H., 41
Escalona, S. K., 35, 37
Estes, W. K., 61, 69, 219
Eysenck, H. J., 34
Eysenck, M., 34

Fantz, R. L., 14, 24
Faterson, H. F., 33
Feltovich, P. J., 236
Finkelman, D. G., 214
Flowers, J. H., 63
Fodor, J. A., 124
Foote, S. L., 5
Forgy, C. L., 152
Francis, W. N., 102, 105
Franks, J. J., 220–221
Friedman, S., 17, 23–24
Frost, N., 32
Furby, L., 36

Gaensbauer, T. J., 23
Gallup, G. G., 29, 30
Gardner, H. E., 69

Gardner, R., 33
Gassel, M. M., 7
Gergen, K. J., 214
Gibson, E. J., 60, 67
Gilliland, K., 34
Goetz, E. T., 129
Goldberg, M. E., 10, 11
Goldstein, A. G., 227
Goodenough, D. R., 33–34
Gray, J. A., 34
Greenwald, A. G., 63

Haber, N. R., 226, 231
Haith, M. M., 14, 15, 16, 21, 28
Hamilton, J., 36
Handley, A., 87
Harmon, R. J., 23
Harré, R., 214
Hasher, L., 36
Hawkins, H. L., 33
Hayes-Roth, B., 140, 157, 168–69, 204
Hayes-Roth, F., 168–69
Heilman, K. M., 16
Hendrix, G. G., 145
Hertzig, M. E., 36
Hines, T., 42
Hintzman, D. L., 25
Holzman, P. S., 33
Hubel, D. H., 10, 15
Humphreys, M.S., 34
Hunt, E., 32

Indow, T., 81, 87, 88, 103, 108–9

James, W., 236
Jeannerod, M., 7
Jenkins, J. J., 223, 227, 230
Johnson, D. M., 87
Johnson, M. K., 184–85
Johnson, N., 69
Johnson, N. S., 135
Johnson, P. E., 233–236
Johnson, R. C., 87
Johnson, R. R., 232

Jordan, T. C., 20
Jusczyk, P. W., 24

Kahneman, D., 12
Kandel, E. R., 23
Kaplan, C. P., 15
Kaplan, I. T., 87, 88, 94–102, 105
Karp, S. A., 33
Katona, G., 222
Katz, J. J., 124
Kaye, H., 23
Keele, S. W., 27, 32–33, 41
Kelly, S. R., 36
King, D. R., 168–69, 180
Kinsbourne, M., 42
Kintsch, W., 129
Kisley, A., 18, 38
Klein, G. S., 33
Klein, R. M., 19, 20
Kolodner, J. L., 177
Korn, S., 36
Kraft, R. N., 230
Kraut, A. G., 25, 35
Kucera, H. G., 102, 105

LaBerge, D., 3, 56, 58, 60, 61, 65–66,
    67, 68, 69
Lachman, R., 185–86
Landauer, T. K., 123
Latz, E., 17
Lawry, J. A., 59, 68, 69
Lesgold, A. M., 156, 179
Lewis, C. H., 168–69
Lewis, J., 32
Lewis, M., 30
Lewis, T. L., 15–16
Lindsay, P. H., 165
Link, S. W., 155
Linton, H., 33
Lipsitt, L. P., 23
Lloyd, B. B., 27
Lounsbury, M. L., 36, 37
Lubow, R. E., 35
Lunneborg, C., 31

MacKinnon, G. E., 66–67

Mackworth, J. F., 24–25
Mandler, G., 179
Mandler, J. M., 135, 156
Mark, A. L., 87
Marshall, J., 7
Mates, J. W. B., 9
Maurer, D., 15–16
McCarrell, N. S., 184–85
McClelland, J. L., 61, 69
McClosky, M., 173–75, 180
McDevitt, S. C., 36
McGuire, W. J., 214
McIntyre, C. W., 221
McKoon, G., 129–30, 136
McLean, J. P., 6
Medin, D. L., 172–73
Meehl, P. E., 213–14
Mendelson, M. J., 15, 21
Metcalf, D., 18, 38
Metlay, W., 87, 88, 94–102, 105
Milewski, A. E., 15–16
Miller, G. A., 150
Minsky, M., 124, 164
Mischel, W., 214
Moesher, S. D., 168–69, 183–84
Mohler, C. W., 11
Moller, J. H., 236
Morais, J., 21
Mountcastle, V. B., 10
Murphy, L. B., 13
Murray, J. T., 65

Nebylitsyn, V. D., 34
Neely, J. H., 6
Neill, W. T., 32–33, 41
Neisser, V., 1–2
Nelson, T. O., 179
Newell, A., 125, 212–13, 214, 215,
    216
Nickerson, R. S., 19, 74, 75
Nissen, M. J., 19, 20
Norman, D. A., 124, 163, 164, 165

Oldfield, R. C., 28
Ortony, A., 124, 150, 164, 190

Owens, J., 135

Paivio, A., 41
Papousek, H., 3, 35
Paulson, R., 131, 168–69, 175, 180
Pavlov, I. P., 34, 225
Pearlstone, Z., 177
Pederson, F. A., 36
Perenin, M. T., 7
Petersen, R. J., 60
Peterson, R. G., 221
Pittenger, J. B., 227
Polansky, M. L., 63
Posnansky, C., 66
Posner, M. I., 3, 4, 5, 7, 8, 10, 11, 12, 15, 16, 19, 20, 24, 26, 27, 29, 35, 42, 212
Puff, C. R., 176
Pylyshyn, A. W., 122

Rao, S. L., 41
Ratcliff, R., 129–30, 136, 155
Rayner, K., 66
Reder, L. M., 133, 141–45, 148, 150, 155, 157, 158, 168–69, 183–84, 186–88, 194, 196, 205
Reicher, G. M., 33, 176
Reitman, W., 215
Remington, R. W., 11
Resnick, L. B., 32
Revelle, W., 34
Robinson, D. L., 11
Robinson, J., 22
Rodriguez, E., 33
Roediger, H. L., 83
Rosch, E., 27, 201
Rosen, L., 14
Rothbart, M. K., 36–37
Rumelhart, D. E., 124, 135, 150, 163, 164, 165, 190
Rundus, D., 83, 169, 178
Russo, J., 14
Rychener, M. D., 125

Sager, L. C., 20

Salapatek, P., 15
Samuels, J., 3
Samuels, S. J., 56, 58, 60, 61, 69
Sanders, M. D., 7
Sawusch, J. R., 24
Schaffer, W. O., 65–66
Schallert, D. L., 129
Schank, R. C., 124, 135, 149, 152, 155, 164, 190
Schiller, P. H., 9
Schnur, P., 35
Schorr, D., 140–42, 145, 150, 168–69, 182–83, 192
Schustack, M., 153–54
Secord, P. F., 214
Sedgewick, C. H., 87
Sekuler, R., 24
Severance, D. G., 236
Shaw, R., 215, 218–19
Shepard, R. N., 212, 226, 231
Shiffrin, R. M., 83, 169, 178
Shoben, E. J., 168–69
Shulman, G. L., 6, 12, 15, 16
Simmons, R. F., 124
Simon, H. A., 150
Simon, L., 34
Smith, E. E., 140–42, 145, 150, 168–69, 172–73, 179, 182–83, 192
Smith, H. T., 13
Snyder, C. R. R., 29
Sokolov, E. N., 5, 6
Spence, D. P., 33
Spencer, W. O., 23
Standing, L., 226, 231
Stechler, G., 17
Sternberg, R. J., 32
Stone, L. J., 13
Strauss, M. S., 27
Strawson, C., 41
Stroop, J. R., 62, 66
Studdert-Kennedy, M., 55
Swanson, D. B., 236

Tennes, K., 18, 38
Teplov, B. M., 34

Terry, P., 56, 58, 60
Thomas, A., 36
Thompson, R. F., 23
Thorndike, E. L., 220, 222, 227
Thorndyke, P., 135, 140, 168–69
Thorpe, L. A., 83
Togano, K., 87, 88, 103, 108–9
Townsend, J. T., 122
Trevarthen, C., 21
True, S. D., 9
Tulving, E., 156, 177, 180
Tunstall, O. A., 34
Turner, T. J., 135, 185, 197
Tyler, L. E., 31, 32

Underwood, B. J., 6

Wald, J., 227
Warner, J. L., 63

Warren, N. T., 6
Warren, R. E., 6
Warrington, E. K., 7
Watson, R. T., 16
Weisberg, D., 20
Weiskrantz, L., 7
Wescourt, K., 168–69
Whitlow, W. J., 172–73
Williams, D., 7
Willows, D. M., 66–67
Wilson, G. O., 34
Wilson, W. R., 29
Winograd, T., 124, 147, 150, 164
Winzenz, D., 156, 179
Witkin, H. A., 33–34
Wurtz, R. H., 10, 11

Zacks, R. T., 36
Zajonc, R., 29